615.8554 LEE

City University
Library Information Services
Northampton Square

WITH

AF742197

THE ARCHITECTURE OF AESTHETIC MUSIC THERAPY

CITY UNIVERSITY LIBRARY
Northampton Square, London EC1V 0HB
Tel: 020 7040 8191
Web: http://library.city.ac.uk

This book must be returned or renewed on or before the last date stamped below

HEAVY FINES ARE CHARGED ON OVERDUE BOOKS

SEVEN DAY LOAN

- 2 APR 2004
26/04/04
16 FEB 2005

THE ARCHITECTURE OF AESTHETIC MUSIC THERAPY

Colin Andrew Lee

Barcelona Publishers

Copyright © 2003 by Barcelona Publishers

All rights reserved. No part of this book may be reproduced in any form whatsoever, including by photocopying, on audio- or videotape, by any electronic means, or in information storage and retrieval systems. For permission to reproduce, contact Barcelona Publishers.

ISBN 1-891278-17-7

2 4 6 8 9 7 5 3 1

Distributed throughout the world by:
Barcelona Publishers
4 White Brook Road
Gilsum NH 03448
Tel: 603-357-0236 Fax: 603-357-2073
Website: www.barcelonapublishers.com
SAN 298-6299

Cover illustration and design:
© 2003 Frank McShane

To my parents,

Kathleen and Basil Lee

CONTENTS

FOREWORD

Although I have lived through several decades of music therapy history, I am continually overwhelmed by the wealth of new publications available to us. However, I sincerely believe that within the ever burgeoning literature, *The Architecture of Aesthetic Music Therapy* will stand out as a significant and far-reaching contribution to the future of our profession. It is a personal book about a personal journey and I am deeply honored to write the foreword.

The Architecture of Aesthetic Music Therapy is not a "how-to" book nor is it intended to make us feel good about the work that we do. Quite the contrary, this book may challenge you, shake you up, and to some it may even be seen as controversial. But, even if you do not agree with all the ideas presented by Dr. Colin Lee, this landmark book is certain to provide rich material for discussion and debate. A careful and "never-to-be-forgotten" reading will be rewarded by pulling back the curtain of complacency and self-imposed limitations to reveal fresh insights and creative potential for the 21st century.

Much of what we do is borrowed from other professions and grounded in theories extrinsic to music, particularly psychology, medicine, and education. This is not wrong. But the fact remains that we are not primarily physicians, psychoanalysists, or teachers. First and foremost, we are musicians. Music is our primary tool and we offer a music-centered therapy. In no way does this negate the need for scientific rigor and accountability but, as stated by Dr. Lee, "in our understandable efforts for recognition with these other professions we are forgetting to make links with the theories and practices of music."

Above all else, this book takes an uncompromising position for the integrity of music. It is almost as if Dr. Lee is reaching back into time to the original source, Paul Nordoff, the composer, pianist, and therapist and moving directly forward from that same source as a composer, pianist, and therapist. As was the work of Paul Nordoff and Clive Robbins, Dr. Lee's Aesthetic Music Therapy (AeMT) is rooted in the notion that musical dialogue through improvisation is at the core of the music therapy process. The purpose of the book is to promote the development of clinical musicianship, to the level which will allow this musical dialogue to flourish.

Far from being a dry theoretical discourse, this book is lively, articulate, and highly original. It is also totally authentic and devoid of academic arrogance or jargon. Dr. Lee's passion for the work and his deep respect for his clients, as well as his humanity, is evident throughout and is further revealed and enlivened by many clinical examples of his own work.

For example, Dr. Lee's discussion of three significant works of Bach, Beethoven, and Cage were particularly illuminating. They have given me a new way to think. Is it possible that the counterpoint in the Credo from Bach's Mass in B minor can be related to the complexities of a musical relationship with a client? Can a consideration of the music Beethoven wrote after he became deaf shed light on a client's creativity when faced with illness? Does the music of John Cage and other experimental composers speak to us as therapists about the possibility of strengthening clinical relationships through experimental music-making? Are there clinical implications in the "Tristan" chord? Can clinical improvisation with a professional string quartet work in the same way as with a music therapy group? These questions are just a few examples of the highly creative thinking put forward in this book.

Many of us, including myself, will never reach this level but I think of it as something for which to strive. Knowing that we may never reach the heights is not a reason not to try. The excitement is in knowing that the possibilities exist.

I personally came into the field from the perspective of a chamber music pianist and accompanist for my husband who was a violinist. After turning to music therapy at a relatively late age, I always kept a separation between my musical self and my music therapist self. Although I was aware that my music therapist self operated best when my musical self was at its best I never made a direct connection between the two.

Working with Dr. Lee over the past several years as his "oldest ever" student, his colleague, and his friend has changed the way I view my work. I am discovering my musical music therapist self and have exchanged the confidence of security for the excitement (and vulnerability) of a new journey. Dr. Lee exhorts us all to renew our passion and to set our sails toward the future even though the final destination may never be attainable. The challenge is in the journey and I have "set my sails". . .

Rosemary G. Fischer
Professor Emeritus of Music Therapy
Wilfrid Laurier University
Waterloo, Ontario
Canada

ACKNOWLEDGMENTS

The writing of this book has been an extraordinary experience. Many people have been influential in its evolution from abstract thought to concrete final product.

Two people in particular acted as key figures during its writing. Dr. Rosemary Fischer, my music therapy mentor, was my daily companion. She listened to my insecurities, read every sentence as it appeared, and gave me the courage to continue. As my colleague she challenged me and as my friend she was always there to lend a sympathetic ear. Rosemary's faith in my ideas was unflinching and without her this book would simply not exist. David Olson played an equally important role. As editor, attorney, and colleague he questioned every sentence and asked me constantly to clarify my ideas. It was his recommendation to abbreviate Aesthetic Music Therapy to AeMT. David also encouraged me to laugh and not take myself too seriously. I am indebted to his belief in my work, his attention to detail, and the remarkable friendship we shared.

Key music therapists have been influential during my career and inspired my writing on many levels. Kenneth Bruscia first planted the seed of giving my ideas a name. It took many years before I found the confidence to take this step and many years more before I conceived the plan for this book. On a turbulent plane journey from Boston to Berlin with Michele Forinash I proposed the term Aesthetic Music Therapy. Her excitement then and since has been crucial as the work has developed. Kimberly Khare listened tirelessly to my constant stream of consciousness and helped formulate the beginning concepts of AeMT. Clive Robbins' continued encouragement of my career and ideas has been, and continues to be, an inspiration. Special thanks must go to Rachel Verney, my teacher and supervisor during my work at Sir Michael Sobell House Hospice. The writings on clinical listening and levels of listening was strongly influenced by her ideas. The challenges set through our work continue to this day.

Since teaching and directing the music therapy programs at Wilfrid Laurier University, Canada, I have been surrounded by a community who has supported and encouraged me daily. To my fellow faculty Carolyn Arnason and Heidi Ahonen-Eerikainen and all the supervisors and part-time faculty who have listened and tolerated me during the "highs" and "lows" of the writing process. Thank you Heidi for your invaluable contribution to my work with the Penderecki String Quartet. Your insights were crucial in the writing of chapter 13. To the students for allowing me to bring into class those moments of revelation as the book developed. Thank you Dr. Charles Morrison, Dean of Music, for supporting my work and Debra Martz Melanson, my administrator, for guiding me during my regular bouts of irrational administration. Special thanks to the Penderecki String Quartet for daring to partake in the music therapy process and for their continued enthusiasm in continuing our professional alliance.

Thanks to Trevor Wagler for the typesetting of music examples and Jascha Narveson for the final typesetting of the text and mastering of the CD. Most clinical examples used to illustrate the arguments of the book come from my work at London Lighthouse and Sir Michael Sobell House Hospice, Oxford. Remembering clients who have died continues to add richness to my work as clinician, teacher, and human being. I keep each spirit present and allow their dignity to affect me as I struggle to make sense of my living.

Thank you Paul and Crystal Jardin for allowing me to stay at your beautiful cottage on Conestoga Lake, where I planned the initial writings of the book. To my new friends in Toronto who have embraced me and allowed me to keep my British humor. To my close friends in England and Boston. To my parents and family for being grounded and consistent when I was not! Special final thanks must go to my partner Robin whose unfailing presence in my life makes all my work possible. Your strength and fortitude continues to inspire me to this day.

The author would like to thank the following for permission to reproduce material published elsewhere: on p.190 an extract from *Integrated Cancer Care*, edited by Jennifer Barraclough and published by Oxford University Press, and, on p.183, the second movement from John Cage's *Sonatas and Interludes For Prepared Piano*, published by the C.F. Petters Corporation. Every effort has been made to obtain permission to reproduce copyright material throughout this book. If any proper acknowledgement has not been made the copyright holder should contact the publishers.

FIGURES

CD EXTRACTS

PREFACE

Music is an enigma. Its power to influence human existence is concrete yet transient. We know so little about the qualities of music and how it has the capacity to affect change. Would a physician contemplate surgery if he did not know the intricate biological workings of the body? And yet music therapists use music with little knowledge of its structural makeup. We use music and yet seem ignorant of its complexities. We interpret through extra-musical theories in the hope that its intangibility may somehow become tangible. Yet, until we examine the qualities of music itself, its biological structure, its outcome will remain a mystery. Gary Ansdell (2001) writes:

> As a practicing music therapist I experience the phenomenon of the "music itself" working in my clinical everyday work. Why then do I find so few examples in the current music therapy literature of serious attention being given to the nature and function of music itself within music therapy? (p. 2)

This question is perhaps the most pertinent for music therapy entering the 21st century. We can measure the outcome of music and speculate on how sound affects the body, but if we do not understand the organization of music, then the results will reveal only one part of the whole. Before theorizing about the outcome of music therapy we must first understand the science of its process.

Music therapy should be influenced by present-day trends in music. Contemporary music has entered a period of creative renaissance. Barriers of style and genre have become less prevalent. The restrictions of such strait jacket terms as classical, jazz, pop, and world are fast dissolving in favor of a universal musical expression. The plaintive and overtly simplistic tonal landscape of composers such as Gorecki have now been balanced with the realistic and strident expression of a younger generation of composers such as Ades, Martland, and the more established work of Carter and Boulez. Music is now open to all possibilities. Music therapy should reflect these recent innovations. It is not enough to base our musical expression within the narrow spectrum of popular tonal music; we need to understand, be inspired by and directly influenced in our clinical work by the whole spectrum of contemporary music.

One of the dilemmas music therapy faces is that of musical accessibility. To be influenced by present-day music in clinical practice is often to abandon music that is directly accessible for the client. The balance between preferred and abstract music is a corporeal yet fragile choice for therapist and client. What does it mean to surrender musical accessibility in favor of a potentially less clear dialogue and relationship? On what emotional and clinical level do we base our musical choices with clients, and does accessibility mean a less potent process? In an interview for his 75th birthday, Pierre Boulez, the composer and conductor, expresses his view that:

> The notion of accessibility strikes me as superficial, and produces the least interesting results. Accessibility can have an immediate resonance, but it does not survive the period which saw it come into. (Gervasoni: Guardian Weekly, April 13–19, 2000)

What does this statement have to say to music therapy?

If music therapy is to gain further credibility in the next millennium we must set our sights beyond our individual lifetime's work. The polarities of music-centered practice and music medicine both have roles to play in validating the potency of outcome. Each has expanded the bounds of contemporary clinical practice. It is my belief that a possible interface between the two could produce fascinating results. Music therapy is a complex phenomenon and as such we must look ever deeper at the musical and therapeutic criteria that go into making the whole.

It is my intent to make the musical scope of this book as broad as possible. While it is impossible to adequately cover all areas of music and their impact on music therapy, I will suggest possibilities for future writing and research. Music therapists should not be limited in the music they use. While musical preference is important we must also have the potential to provide other musical avenues that will balance and make the therapeutic process more directed, potent and aesthetically powerful. This means we need to explore and be aware of musical parameters that are potentially outside our experience. If we do not attempt to make accessible all styles of music, then are we not failing our client's needs? While this may seem an impossible task if we do not constantly challenge our musical contributions, then we may be in danger of taking the music out of music therapy.

I am a music therapist and composer. For the last ten years I have developed an approach to music therapy that is music centered and humanistic. On one level Aesthetic Music Therapy (AeMT) is a personal narrative of my ideas, experiences, and philosophies on music and the human condition. It is both the culmination of a fleeting moment of inspiration and a lifetime's work. It speaks to my reverence of music and my determination that music therapy should be looking forward and breaking new ground.

Music therapy needs both innovation and consolidation. This book attempts to understand the relationship between music and human expression, to find a blueprint for a new approach to music therapy. Notwithstanding the dangers of articulating one's beliefs, AeMT is a testament to the musical flow of the clients I have worked alongside. Without their presence this work would not exist. Music allows vulnerability that is the essence of human frailty and liberation. In these chapters theory and practice are placed side by side to form a dialogue that is practical, philosophical, and emotional. The ideas proposed in AeMT are new and still in transition. The questions raised will continue as the work develops; one view can never hold the absolute truth. This work speaks to the challenges that have been integral in my growth as a music therapist, composer, and musician. The definitions raised do not attempt to provide a new theory of music therapy. Rather this is a collection of philosophical ruminations and case studies that address topics necessary for defining a music-centered approach to clinical practice.

Chapter 1

BEGINNINGS: ON MUSIC

> How can music ever be a mere intellectual speculation or a series of curious combinations of sound that can be classified like the articles of a grocer's shop? Music is an outburst of the soul.
>
> – Frederick Delius,
> Fenby, *Delius as I Knew Him* (1936) , quoted in Watson (1994)

The beginning of a piece of music is filled with expectancy and potential as themes and counterthemes present the foundation for its developing structure. A clinical improvisation is like the unfolding of a precomposed piece of music. The structure is balanced with the intent of the client. As themes are presented, the dialogue between client and therapist reflects both the relationship and aims of the therapy. Just as a symphony reveals its form, so clinical improvisation integrates the freedom of the client with the musical responses of the therapist. As the improvisation unfolds, the nature of the musical relationship is revealed and integrated with the therapeutic intent. Thus a clinical symphony emerges.

DEFINING AESTHETIC MUSIC THERAPY

Aesthetic Music Therapy (AeMT) considers music therapy from a musicological and compositional point of view. Looking at theories of music to inform theories of therapy, it proposes a new way of exploring clinical practice. AeMT is in part a natural continuation from Paul Nordoff's philosophy of music, aesthetics, and music therapy. AeMT is also a reflection of my own personal philosophy and life experiences and the writings of other theorists.

AeMT can be defined as an improvisational approach that views musical dialogue as its core. Interpretation of this process comes from an understanding of musical structure and how that structure is balanced with the clinical relationship between client and therapist. The therapist must therefore be a clinical musician. Clinical musicianship includes:

- clinical listening
- clinical applications of aesthetics, music analysis, and musicology
- clinical form and music form
- clinical understanding of seminal works
- clinical relationship and aesthetics
- clinical analysis from a composer's perspective.

In music therapy we should always think both as a musician and as a clinician. If we balance one above the other, or ignore one over the other, then we are in danger of providing either a nonmusical dryness or a musical experience with no therapeutic content or direction. The purpose of this book, then, is to promote the development of clinical musicianship. All topics addressed relate to this central theme.

During the 1980s John Cage challenged 20th century music to re-define perceptions of sound, music, and notation and it is only now that his contribution to music is being accurately gauged. He offered new landscapes of sound, improvisation, and "chance" that had been missing in music for centuries. Cage's music is unbounded and fresh–a revelation of creative thinking and expression. Does music therapy need a similar sense of renewed freedom? Do we need contemporary and contentious ideas rather than the safety of aligning clinical practice to extramusical theories?

Background

In his book *Defining Music Therapy* (Bruscia, 1998), Bruscia states that "every definition of music therapy sets boundaries for the field" (p. 3). He further articulates his belief that new definitions help to define and expand it; without new and controversial ideologies the profession would stagnate. Music therapy should never be "set in stone" and new definitions should never be introduced to the exclusion of others. The relationship between music and people raises too many questions and is too broad to be confined to specific beliefs. The ideas expressed in this book set new perspectives for music therapy and raise more questions than can ever be answered within the confines of a single publication.

Do definitions once defined become invalid? Can one definition be authoritative? Are differing definitions mutually exclusive? Interpretation is a never-ending process of balancing that which we think we know against that which we surely don't. AeMT celebrates and critiques the field of music therapy and offers alternatives for contemporary thought. Clinical practice should always acknowledge a sense of the experimental, but never at the expense of theoretical knowledge and progress. Clinical musicianship utilizes the innovative AeMT archetype to understand new meanings, boundaries, and definitions of clinical practice.

Looking at aesthetics as "beyond the beautiful" provided reflections that strongly influenced the beginnings of AeMT. Gfeller (Davis, Gfeller, & Thaut, 1999) places aesthetic experience and entertainment side by side. On one hand this suggests that the aesthetic is peripheral and on the other hand the authors go on to describe Schoenberg's *A Survivor from Warsaw*, suggesting that this piece carries a disturbing message about the human condition and yet is also aesthetic in nature. The power of the aesthetic experience is that it can appear either from a spontaneous moment (Ansdell 1995) or as a carefully graded part of a process. Beauty takes many forms and to deny elements of dissonance in therapy is to deny the essence of the work itself. By expanding our views on the aesthetic, so we will broaden our views on therapy itself.

In the concluding passages of *Music for Life* (1995) Ansdell states that Bateson (1980)

> . . . tried to show how the aesthetic gives an intuition of the unity and fundamental connections between things: whether a Mozart symphony, the structure of a leaf or the complexities of human communication. He repeatedly came back to the concept of the aesthetic (in which he included pattern, metaphor and symbol, creativity, dream, myth) as the link between the natural and the human world, between thinking and feeling, creating and knowing. It is absolutely not a doctrine of "prettiness," but an understanding of shared meaning and value in the world. (pp. 216–217)

Rilke's discourse on "terrible beauty" further elucidates this concept. Prettiness shows only a limited understanding of aesthetics. The power of "terrible beauty," is as essential to the therapeutic process as that of "attractive beauty."

Francis, the client in *Music at the Edge* (Lee, 1996), attempted to express the possible link between beauty and pain within his music.

> I'm expressing the way that I would rarefy or objectify the world. It's the song that emerges from the different elements that have played on my soul. I think it's partly a striving to express one's inner sense of harmony and beauty. This expression also reflects the knocks, destruction and pain that distort the very basic life-giving feeling of

> expansion, the ability to feel what's going on around one. Is there an inner harmony which one strives for? Can one get into harmony with outer reality? Is that sometimes part of the struggle? That we [sic] . . . the gap between the outer and inner is so great. The difference between the imposed world of inherited values is so distant from the life-giving force, that wells up within you. This leads to jarring, destruction and violence. I think that when one is in touch with the creative flow, the life-flow within art . . . creation isn't a form of compensation or waking up . . . I think you can latch on to an inner message, almost like a genetic meaning that interprets the environment within the available language of tools. It's not just compensating form, it's something that hasn't been worked and wasn't there (pp. 115–116).

This expresses the idea that aesthetic musical creativity contains a myriad of emotional levels. Francis's struggled to find an avenue of expression that would portray an authentic parallel with his physical and emotional deterioration was caught in complex musical representations. That all were aesthetic in content there is no doubt. What remains an enigma, however, is the balance between his dissonant and harmonious expressions, and how they were placed within the clinical setting.

Aigen (1995a, 1995b, 1998) explains that the reason music therapy has not been more interested in researching or examining the aesthetic is because it is beyond empirical analysis. With the emergence of qualitative design as an accepted form of research, however, the aesthetic of music therapy is now gaining recognition. Aigen relates the philosophy of John Dewey (1934, 1958) to music therapy. Dewey maintains that the aesthetic permeates all levels of human existence and adds meaning to life, and that it is the process and not only the outcome that holds aesthetic fulfilment. Aigen (1995a) explains how resistance to discharge becomes the means to aesthetic expression:

> Unrestrained discharge is only therapeutic in the extent to which it serves as precursor of further expressive capacities and thereby does not facilitate self-awareness. Aesthetic considerations transforms discharge into expression. Their manipulation provides the only possible rationale for music therapy treatment. Why else would we employ an artistic medium unless those factors that define it as such are integral in its application? (p. 247)

With respect to "art," Aigen (1995b) asks the following questions:

> What is the essence of art? Are aesthetic judgments objective? Are these judgments universal or culturally relative? What is beauty and what is its relationship to art? (p. 468)

and regarding music therapy:

> Are aesthetic considerations relevant in determining either clinical interventions or client outcome? How and when do they come into play? Which conceptions of aesthetics are consonant with clinical practice or clinical theory? What are the healing properties of aesthetic experiences? Are they essential or incidental to the clinical music therapy process? (p. 468)

These questions highlight the complexities of trying to understand the balance and connection between "clinical" and "aesthetic." If we objectify the creative essence of music therapy then we are in danger of misunderstanding the nature of the phenomenon itself. This dilemma is at the heart of future research. Aigen (1998) embraces these polarities in his illuminating research on the role of music in Nordoff and Robbins music therapy. He examines the need for the empirical nature of music to influence outcome, as well as the notion that both are contained within the potential for creativity, freedom, and aesthetic content.

A justification of the development of a theory which considers the role of music in therapy is the basis of Ruud's work (1998) on aesthetic theory.

> An aesthetic experience produced by music implies the possibility of creating a new category of experience, of experiencing the world in a new way. (p. 79)

Verbal reflections and interpretations can only provide us with a finite amount of information about the musical relationship. It is only through the musical structures themselves that we can truly understand the process. Is it possible to accurately state that any musical expression has any one specific meaning? The transient nature of music means that no single interpretation can be definitive. By placing human existence within the design of music we create new values that don't belong to the parameters of verbal specificity.

The Harvard Dictionary of Music describes musical aesthetics as being: "the study of the relationship of music to the human senses and intellect". This definition inspired me to look beyond the classic notion of aesthetics as being related only to the beautiful. I subsequently discovered words that described the aesthetic experience and began classifying them as they related to my clinical work:

- clinical clarity: finite-precise-empathetic-expressive-discriminating-refined
- consonance: delicate-beautiful-tender-exquisite
- dissonance: brutal-disturbing-intense-profound-powerful.

Aigen (1995a) supports these analyses when presenting his work on an evolving aesthetic foundation of clinical theory:

> I recognize that to infer that all music is generated from aesthetic considerations would render the term "aesthetic" meaningless, and this certainly is not the nature of my experience. Rather, I would say that through music therapy practice my capacity for aesthetic experience has been expanded to include that which I formerly considered to be monotonous, ugly, dissonant, clashing, disorganized, unrefined, and aggressive. It is not that I no longer perceive these qualities in music, but that they have acquired aesthetic value for me through bringing to life the truth of an individual's existence and the struggle to give meaning to this existence. (p. 255)

So what connections could there be between aesthetics and music therapy, and what would be the exact nature of aesthetics as related to clinical practice? The following words were crucial in these beginning links. The aesthetics of:

- Listening
- Playing
- Disability and Pathology
- Meeting
- Being
- Expression
- Insight
- Release
- Emotion
- Form
- Tone
- Consciousness
- Intuition
- Capacity
- Outcome
- Process

NORDOFF AND ROBBINS AND AESTHETIC MUSIC THERAPY

Using music as an aesthetic foundation for our understanding of music therapy is not a new concept. For therapists educated in the Nordoff and Robbins approach, music is both the essential core and an extension of the clinical process and therapeutic relationship. The inherent knowledge underlying AeMT is that music is intrinsically healing; what must be learned during training, then, is how to adapt one's musical skills to develop resources which are clinically, artistically, and aesthetically suitable for both the client and the process. Aigen (1998) describes how:

> The Nordoff and Robbins approach is perhaps unique in emphasizing the objectivity of music and the therapeutic value of this quality as it becomes aesthetically realized. (p. 249)

The aesthetic realization of music is what makes Nordoff and Robbins so potent and artistically dynamic, and separates it so clearly from other music therapy approaches. Nordoff and Robbins was heavily influenced by the musical qualities of Paul Nordoff's symphonic-like improvising and his extensive composing prior to entering music therapy. It was his previous experiences as a composer that strongly influenced his musical bias toward the work. The balance between composing, performing, and music therapy has always been the essence of my actualization as a music therapist. Nordoff's teachings most notably through Healing Heritage (Robbins & Robbins, 1998) motivated and gave me the impetus to establish further contemporary clinical connections with classical precomposed music. My history and experience of music was quite different from Nordoff's yet we shared a sense of compositional form that intensely influenced the structural content of clinical improvisation. It was this metamorphosis of musical form and clinical form that culminated in the inception of AeMT. AeMT is a continuation of the original Nordoff and Robbins approach and the individual experiences of the author as a composer/music therapist. It is not offered as an alternative to Nordoff and Robbins but rather is proposed as the consolidation of one music therapist's views and questions on music, therapy, and aesthetics.

Distinguishing features of AeMT discussed below, that have been influenced by Nordoff and Robbins, will help show the correlation and differences between both approaches.

The clinical application of seminal works

Paul Nordoff's study of precomposed music was at the cornerstone of his explorations on music and therapy. AeMT has continued and developed this philosophy to consider critical works of the Western classical repertoire and their influence on the development of clinical practice. By studying both specific works and overall genres AeMT hopes to formulate qualitative techniques that will balance the clinical and artistic in music therapy.

The clinical application of orchestral instruments

The original instrumental focus of Nordoff and Robbins was based on the therapist's work from the piano. Contemporary trends have extended to include the use of guitar and other orchestral instruments. AeMT embraces all instruments as essential clinical tools within the musical dialogue. The clinical application of musical resources to include all instruments is dependent on the technique, timbre, range, and tone quality of each instrument.

New contemporary components for the expansion of musical resources

The Nordoff and Robbins approach to clinical improvisation is to build, develop, and adapt musical resources for the clinical setting. AeMT proposes an expansion of resources to include present-day trends in classical, popular, jazz, dance, and world music.

Thinking architecturally

Considering the overall structure of music therapy architecturally was influenced by Paul Nordoff's compositional approach to improvisation. Taking this one step further, AeMT attempts to understand the music therapy process/session/improvisation in terms of its universal musical structure. Assessing structure, then analyzing each component in terms of its architectural whole, is an attempt to understand the many layers of the therapeutic relationship in improvisation.

Clinical improvisation as composition and composer

Paul Nordoff approached music therapy as a composer. Thinking compositionally and being a composer/music therapist influences one's thinking as a clinical improvisor. AeMT proposes that an understanding of compositional form will help influence the therapist's musical and therapeutic responses. Musical composition and clinical process therefore become natural allies.

Musical form and clinical form

Generally speaking in music therapy clinical form influences musical form. AeMT, however, is based on the philosophy that musical form influences clinical form. Nordoff and Robbins. Understanding of musical form is in concert with this view, the difference being that AeMT examines musical form from a music analytic and compositional foundation first and foremost. Looking further into the musical intricacies of clinical improvisation will inform our understanding of clinical balance.

Disability as creativity

The Nordoff and Robbins humanistic philosophy believes in the potential of every human being to be musically creative. AeMT extends this belief to regard disability as a potentially creative force. Disability–a negative word in itself–as imposed by a healthy society denies that human disorder can be positive. In AeMT disability and creativity are not mutually exclusive. Each is musically and humanistically influenced and neither is disregarded at the expense of the other.

Nordoff and Robbins and AeMT have many similarities. To consider AeMT, however, purely as an extension of Nordoff and Robbins is to belie its focus. Defining a new approach to music therapy, one is constantly reminded of the need for clinical clarity. Nordoff and Robbins and AeMT are inextricably linked. Understanding music therapy in terms of music itself is the main focus that differentiates the two philosophies. Looking to musical examples and rejoicing in the clinical impact of great musical works of the Western classical repertoire is at the core of AeMT. In AeMT composing and clinical improvisation are allies, each being influenced and affected by their artistic and analytic processes. Continuing the work initiated in Healing Heritage (Robbins & Robbins, 1998) and exploring the historical wealth of music opens up panoramas for the future of clinical practice that, in my opinion, may be unparalleled for the future influence and learning of music therapy.

DESIGNING A SESSION: SONATA FORM AS CLINICAL STRUCTURE

How does an AeMT session evolve? AeMT's structure is influenced by the organization of music. Fischer (date-unpublished) developed a method of teaching the groundwork of clinical improvisation by basing the building blocks of learning on sonata form. Considering the architecture of a session in terms of classical sonata form is a natural progression that, like the work of Fischer, links the ideologies and learning of music and therapy.

Exposition

The aim of the exposition is to introduce the main musical arguments. Two central themes, with contrasting emotional content, are introduced with a modulating bridge passage. The complexity of the exposition may be elaborated on and extended by adding more corresponding themes.

The opening of a music therapy session is crucial in setting the scene for the universal musical and clinical arguments. The client should be welcomed with music as they enter the room. Improvising random intervals, listening to the sounds, pitches, and timbres of the client as they enter the room can influence the harmonic and tonal center of a session. Finding the architectural tonic of a session can determine the clinical and musical infrastructure inherent in a client's initiation and response. The architectural tonic should never be predetermined but rather created as a direct response to the client as they begin the session. Discovering the architectural tonic is fundamental to a AeMT session. The therapist must be flexible in musically and structurally guiding the session from the evolving architectural tonic. Defined activities developed from previous sessions should be transposed accordingly as the architectural tonic finds its balance and influence. It colors the music, reflects the clients needs, defines the ongoing aims and objectives, and finds a balance between the general clinical direction of the session and the ongoing musical foci.

The greeting song, a formulaic principle in music therapy, should be used with care. If a greeting song has been used in previous sessions then its repetition may have clear clinical benefits. This does not mean, however, that in AeMT a repetition of a greeting song is imperative. An alternative is to use its theme as a developing motive. If the musical content of a greeting song is as important as its nonmusical aim then its potential becomes much broader and more inclusive within the opening of a session.

In the exposition the main musical arguments are introduced. It is essential that the client be provided with a clear musical structure that allows the flexibility to feel safe and yet is able to move forward within the creative potential of the session. The exposition is normally where more structured sections of the session are introduced. Working with children this may include a drum activity, or naming song. Working in a freer improvisational style the music will be simpler and more direct in content, setting the musical groundwork for the potentially more complex structures of the development. The exposition requires finite listening and response. It holds the key for critical clinical creation and demands committed intensity from both client and therapist.

Development

The development section is at the core of classical sonata from. It allows the composer the opportunity to develop musical ideas with total creative freedom. Taking themes, fragmenting them, inverting them, and then freely integrating them, adds to the essence that gives the development section its critical stance within the overall composition of the movement.

The development section of an AeMT session is crucial as it provides the opportunity for elaboration of aims and objectives as well as the overall compositional shape. Musically, once the architectural tonic has been ascertained the therapist can offer other ideas that are related to and influenced by the critical tone. In the development section the client and therapist develop ideas freely while always being aware of the content expressed in the opening exposition. Combining and interlinking activities and/or ideas from the exposition allows a freedom that can facilitate the true essence of the developing therapeutic relationship.

Recapitulation

The recapitulation repeats and adapts the material of the exposition. The movement ends with a return to the tonic. The recapitulation is important because it solidifies the main argument and growth of the therapeutic process. It gives the client a sense of completion. Returning to the themes and ideas of the exposition can mean either a reinstatement of an activity or the return to an opening theme. It is essential in AeMT that the conclusion includes a return to the opening key and/or the architectural tonic. This allows stability for the client, the therapeutic process, and the session itself.

The therapist should consider the closing section of a session as a means to embrace what has already occurred, providing an outlet that will allow the client to come full circle in the musical experience. The client must perceive in the recapitulation a sense of completeness–completeness in the clinical effectiveness of the session and completeness in the musical dialogue and their part within it. Returning to already established and understood musical inventions will give the client a sense of completion and will allow the potential for the continuing therapeutic process in sessions to come.

Coda

The coda can be either a small final supplement or be developed to be equal in stature to the previous sections. In AeMT the coda can include a good-bye song that then potentially leads to musical ideas as the client leaves the room. A good-bye song should be used only if deemed essential to the closing of a session and if appropriate to the individual needs of the client. The coda in essence provides a closing musical statement that invites the potential for future work.

Sonata form is only one way of considering the structure of a music therapy session. An AeMT session can take many directions and is as flexible as the process and the therapist's ability to contain and reflect the client's music. The core of AeMT is based on the moment-to-moment creation of im-provisation. Structure unfolds from creative spontaneity. A typical AeMT session may include greeting and good-bye songs, instrumental activities, and songwriting techniques. Their composition may be similar to other approaches in the inclusion of a beginning, middle, and end. What differentiates AeMT is that all musical techniques originate from improvisation and are not pre-determined. Improvisational motives thus move into themes and structures that can culminate in either songs and structured activities or simply remain as themes in the ongoing dialogue. It is the therapist's responsibility to understand, hear, and reflect the client's music in a way that provides clarity and focus for the ensuing aim(s) of the session(s). Songs, instrumental activities, and other structured forms originate from the relationship in the musical moment of contact. Therapeutic significance comes from a musical originality that is unique to every moment, session, and therapeutic process. It is not the compositional content that differentiates an AeMT session but rather its architectural musical makeup. The choice of key, harmony, melody, and texture for each improvisation and their relationship to others is paramount. Considering musical connections as improvisations develop defines the therapist's understanding of the process. Therefore each section/activity of a session should have a musical relevance to the other. In an AeMT session there is no such thing as an arbitrary musical choice.

ON BEING MUSIC CENTERED

What is it to be music centered in music therapy? How important should our understanding of music be? Does being music centered denote a need for an advanced level of musicianship? Should music therapists be first and foremost musicians or clinicians? What can an understanding of musical components tell us about the music therapy process? By being music centered is one in danger of becoming therapeutically naive and unbalanced? Should music be the essence of music therapy or a by-product?

To be music centered is to consider music as the core of therapy. That is not to deny extramusical inferences as critical in our understanding but rather to acknowledge music as the fundamental and inspirational essence. Historically music therapy has drawn its clinical theories from extramusical sources. It is my belief that there are flaws in this continued dialogue, especially if it is to the exclusion of other more musical philosophies and theories. In molding our investigations to fit other allied concepts, we cannot accommodate the subtle nature of music itself. Extramusical theories are flawed because they consider only the empirical nature of numbers and the interpretive assumptions of words. Just as the argument against music analytic research is its musicality so it could be suggested the argument against extramusical theories are their nonmusical emphases. Have we not missed one essential connection, the theory of music itself? As a profession we have discussed and debated the balance between the "art" and "science" of our practice, but rarely have we acknowledged theories of musicology or composition.

As more classifications and subdivisions appear so music therapy becomes stronger and richer. Whatever the nucleus of these current theories the significance of music should always, at some level, have a role. Even the simplest music is worthy of detailed investigation and interpretation. Music should never be subservient but integrated with respect and knowledge within the ever-shifting balance between music and therapy. Being inspired by music will keep that sense of creativity that is necessary for continuous innovative practice. There are no easy or direct answers in these pages but an overriding belief in music as a tool to influence human growth.

MUSIC THERAPY AND MUSICOLOGY

The 5th European Music Therapy Congress held in Napoli, Italy (2001), devoted one-third of its program to musicology. Even Ruud wrote on behalf of the scientific commission's rational for this decision:

> There seems to be a constant need to focus on the value of music in music therapy. As an interdisciplinary field of study, music therapy is often presented with good clinical studies, relevant treatment theories or discussions on methodological and practical aspects of doing music therapy. The role of music in therapy is often given only speculative and general comments, not reflecting the systematic knowledge dealt with in the field of musicology. We also know how music in contemporary society is taking upon itself new roles of mass entertainment, identity building, search for authenticity and so on. Lately, there has been an interesting development within the field of musicology itself. Evolving as a new interdisciplinary field, musicology has had to dialogue with new emerging knowledge from the field of feminist studies, anthropology of music, popular music and cultural studies, to name but a few important trends. As a result of this, whole new concept and understanding of music as "musicking," as a performed activity is brought out. In this picture, music therapy may itelf be an interesting producer of knowledge about music. It seems the right time to start dialoging with musicology.

Ansdell has made some of the most important contributions in initiating links between music therapy and musicology. In his first paper: "Musical Elaborations. What has the New Musicology to say to music therapy?" (1997), he poses the question why music therapy and the new musicology have had so little contact and states that potentially both disciplines could learn from each other's theoretical developments. He offers the following fundamental questions:

a) What is music? – its nature as a phenomenon
b) Where is music?–its location in the person and culture
c) How is music?–its ways of meaning and affecting us
d) Why is music?–its 'purposes' (social/therapeutic etc) (p. 38).

Ansdell chooses specific pieces of literature for his argument (Cook, 1990; Firth, 1990; Kramer, 1995; Nattiez, 1990; Said, 1991). All these texts speak directly to music therapy. In his conclusion (Ansdell, 1997) writes:

> To the music therapist I would say that we live in interesting times. Not only is the new musicological thinking beginning to give serious attention to many of our own areas of concern, but musicology's interest in our work is significant. Music therapy finds itself in many different clinical contexts, and it is clear that it must always keep abreast of the latest clinical thinking in order to develop and legitimate its practice. Is it not equally vital, however, that it also keeps in touch with the latest serious thinking about music, in order to keep this side of the discipline vibrant and contemporary? (p. 43)

In his keynote address at the 5th European Music Therapy Congress, Ansdell gives a more recent summation of his views and beliefs on the possible connections between music therapy and the new musicology. He raises the ongoing question as to why music therapy has taken so little interest in studying and researching the role of music. How do we facilitate practical and theoretical links that will add to our growing understanding of the music therapy process and be clinically and artistically important? In making links with traditional musicology Ansdell considers my own research as belonging to the problem of the "Music Therapist's Dilemma (Ansdell, 1999)."

> Lee's work seemingly points to the nub of the music therapist's dilemma. Because his analytical methodology remains fundamentally rooted in the "traditional" formalist musicology it creates the same dilemma as any structural analysis: how form translates into context–in Lee's case: how musical form translates into therapeutic content. (p. 12)

Ansdell looks to the new musicologists: De Nora (2000), and McClary (2000) and the music therapists: Ruud (1998), and Stige (1998), as providing the beginning links between musicology and music therapy:

> . . . musicology in its contemporary form is a key discourse music therapy cannot avoid engagement with in the future. Music therapists need to be aware of the ground of their thinking and assumptions in both therapeutic and musical dimensions. Fortunately the advent of the New Musicology holds potential for a far better fit between the phenomenon produced in music therapy practice and the available analytic methodologies to examine this. It provides exactly the right measure of both support and challenge to music therapy to foster intellectual growth (p. 23)

In his book *Music Therapy: Improvisation, Communication and Culture* (1998) Ruud critiques musicology, music and mass media studies, popular music and cultural studies, anthropology, and poststructural theory. In considering analysis and music therapy Ruud proposes that analysis should not be separated from the clinical context from which the players originate. The problem for him becomes:

> To what extent can we expect a correspondence between the music as heard and the experience as it occurred for the client? Is it possible to translate from the analysis to the experience? Even if it were, is it possible to generalize anything about the effects of music beyond the particular situation? (p. 9)

In defense of my contribution to musicology and the focus of this book, is my belief that if we are to evaluate the role of music in music therapy then we must be prepared to use analytic theories of music, even if these are deemed as "traditional musicology." The pretext for writing this book, and my lifetime commitment to research, is that music therapy needs to consider the "nuts and bolts" of musical content in relation to therapeutic outcome. This means looking in detail at musical notation and listening, acutely, for it is only through detailed analysis that we will begin to understand how music works. It is not the pretense of music analysis to make universal assumptions about the effects of music and therapy. Rather, it attempts to examine each musical interaction in the belief that by understanding the constructs of one, this will in turn illuminate our knowledge of the others. The union of music and therapy is complex and to study one or the other in isolation is a foolish notion. Music analysis, while placing its emphasis on the music, also balances its findings withing the dynamics of the whole. The musicology literature relating to music therapy that contains no essence of musical notation or audio recordings is, I believe, in danger of continuing the tradition of avoiding the core of our work. No amount of intellectual, verbal, or written discourse will compensate for the need to analyze, listen, and understand the musical composition of music therapy.

THE AESTHETICS OF MUSIC

It is not the intent here to cover the vast literature on the aesthetics of music. Rather, the focus will be on those writers who have influenced the making of specific theoretical and philosophical connections. The literature on aesthetics deals primarily with listening–the capacity through which the qualities of composition are conveyed to the recipient through precomposed music. While not directly applicable to the creative act of music therapy, the philosophical ideas raised in the literature are highly relevant to the development of clinical practice. Reading this literature and relating it to the music therapy relationship makes absolute sense. The ideas presented therein raise many questions about the connections between aesthetics and the clinical applications of music.

Perhaps the most important literary contribution, and the one that has the greatest implications for music therapy, is Scruton's comprehensive text *The Aesthetics of Music* (1997). His writings strongly influenced the philosophical underpinnings of AeMT. If we begin by examining some of Scruton's opening comments, we get a sense of what we might learn from this insightful literature. He states that:

> Aesthetic interest is an interest in appearances: its object is not the underlying structure of things, but the revealed presence of the world–the world as it is encountered in our experience. (p. 5)

The musical authenticity offered to clients–the pure reality of sound–is often a reflection of the world in which they live. If the therapist's sounds penetrate and affect the client's sense of his or her world, then Scruton's views are directly applicable to the intrinsic musical relationship between client and therapist. The "revealed presence of the world," as encountered through improvisation–the aesthetic possibilities of the personal/musical connection–shows that the creation of direct experience is fundamental to musical communication. Scruton also discusses:

- the language of criticism–that which determines aesthetic character;
- aesthetic value–that which "lifts human feeling free of everyday life, and endows it with artistic form";
- aesthetic judgment–that which is decided through personal experience;
- musical competence–success and failure as a result of objective musical content;
- judgment of taste–"do aesthetic values matter?"; and
- absolute music - music not directly connected to emotions.

These value-related issues are addressed in this book inasmuch as they have become integrated into the practical realities of AeMT.

Levinson (1990) explains that a piece of music's aesthetic character or content is dependent upon its structure–the large-scale relationships blended with the smaller individual components. The overall design of musical structure is reliant upon the parts and how each affects the whole, and it is this intriguing link–the manner in which both large and small structures are contained in the design of clinical improvisation–that is one of the foundations of AeMT. Levinson goes on to discuss aesthetic uniqueness, stating that:

> Works of art taken individually are often said to be unique. What does this amount to? Clearly it amounts to more than numerical uniqueness, a distinction that fails to distinguish works of art from anything else. Presumably, it is aesthetic uniqueness that is meant. Works of art differ from one another aesthetically, one might say, because of differences in structure, every difference in structure yielding an aesthetic difference. (p. 107)

There are many distinct aspects to music therapy: temporality, client, therapeutic relationship, process, session, and improvisation/activity, among others, and each of these should be informed by aesthetic uniqueness. The response of the therapist to the unique aesthetic content of the client's moment-to-moment music-making is indicative of the degree to which he or she understands the client's therapeutic process.

What makes a piece of music aesthetically valuable? What of aesthetic judgment and taste? Is musical competence important in creating the aesthetic? How do we assess the therapeutic value of the aesthetic experience? These questions speak to one's musical philosophies and values. Scruton (1997), shares his views that:

> Our aesthetic preferences become values just as soon as we find ourselves in them–just as soon, in other words, as they become part of the attempt to create a place for ourselves in the world, and to situate ourselves among our fellows. For many people, this process of value formation–the transition from subjective preference to the judgments of taste–exists only imperfectly and in truncated form. (p. 370)

Music therapists attempt to create a world which is balanced between aesthetic reality and clinical intent. Placing ourselves in the vulnerability of musical creativity, we are open emotionally and practically to the aesthetic values that condition good clinical practice. While this is in essence objective, our client's subjective musical tastes must also be taken into account. How we frame the client's musical preference speaks to our understanding of their music and their potential for therapeutic growth. Does this mean that taste becomes a part of the therapeutic relationship, and if so, how do we subjectively translate their aesthetic preferences into the process?

When we talk of the "beauty of music" in reference to music that is "exhilarating," "transcendent," or "jubilant," are we making value judgments based on our perceptions and boundaries of the aesthetic? Are these the same perceptions as those of our client? Music therapists, for the most part, overlook music that represents the "ugly" or "offensive." The values of the client, however, may include these musical representations as being "refreshing" or "joyous." Aesthetic value becomes ever more complex when we introduce the therapeutic relationship and the intended meaning of therapeutic growth. The aesthetic qualities of music therapy affect all levels of expression, relationship, and outcome. Contemplating the complex theories and philosophies of music aesthetics and applying them to music therapy is, on one level, a huge paradigm shift. On another level, it is the most natural of connections. If practitioners of music therapy can be as open to theories of music literature as they are to those of medicine, psychology, and psychotherapy, the profession at large can hope to promote equilibrium between the "art" and the "science" of clinical practice.

MUSIC THERAPY AND AESTHETICS IN CONTEXT

The value of the aesthetic has always been of interest to music therapy. The fact that clinical music can facilitate observable change alongside the less discernible dynamics of elegance and spirituality is a feature that makes our profession so unique. The debate between art and science, quantitative and qualitative research, etc., has given rise to a compelling clinical potential. From early music therapy literature (Gaston, 1968) to contemporary thinking (Lecourt, 1998), aesthetics is a subject that has intrigued theorists. The reason is clear: aesthetics and music cannot be separated, they are by nature and value as one. We cannot eliminate the aesthetic potency of the musical relationship. Even the most empirical and scientific music therapy research has intrinsic aesthetic content.

The classic definition of aesthetic relates to that which is beautiful and has meaning. Ansdell (1995) states that "The traditional yardstick of the beautiful in music involves a balance between form and feeling: the formal qualities of unity, integration and coherence balanced against expressive authenticity and taste" (p. 216). In The Field of Play, Kenny (1989) describes the aesthetic as relating to the human person and that "each therapist and client is a complete and whole aesthetic" (p. 75). She further proposes that "As one moves toward beauty, one moves toward wholeness, or the fullest potential of what one can be in the world" (p. 77). Aesthetic potential is not described in relation to the therapeutic musical process but rather as an innate human quality. The aesthetic as a primary element or field is in preparation for the musical space (Kenny, 1996):

> In the final analysis, the aesthetic represents a way of being which carries information and conditions. It stresses the importance of subtle, non-verbal cues communicated before the onset of concrete activity. It represents the sum total of who we are, and transmits information about who we are on a subtle level before the onset of relationship. (p. 69)

Separating musical from human-relational aesthetics is an interesting divide, and separating musical aesthetics from other experiences is equally so. Are aesthetics fundamental to the therapeutic process? Or as Bruscia (1998) suggests, are they something other than the directly clinical:

> . . . the dynamic motivation is experiencing music in and of itself, and for its own sake, rather than the sake of the therapy process or any of its other extrinsic values for the client. (p. 147)

Bruscia also suggests that the aesthetic is not dependent on expertise and therefore all clients have the ability to create beautiful music regardless of disability or illness. Experiencing oneness and inner growth through the aesthetic is a potentially powerful therapeutic force:

> ...we help our patients to articulate their inner realities as beautiful; this is the manifestation of the aesthetic. (Aldridge, 1996, p. 18)

> All humans seek ontological meaning and beauty in their lives and music is able to provide expressions of both. (Salas, 1990)

Lecourt (1998) describes the role of aesthetics in countertransference as ". . . that area of human experience concerned with beauty and artistic phenomena" (p. 137). Fundamental to her argument is the warning that a consideration of the aesthetic in music psychotherapy may potentially distort the client/therapist relationship, that the therapist's emphasis on the aesthetic can allow merging but also separation. Lecourt describes "aestheticization" as distancing that allows the aesthetic to mask the potential distress of the authentic and needed process. By transforming sounds of pain into music, it potentially bypasses the core of therapy itself. A further danger is that by concentrating on the quality and aesthetic content of the music, the therapist may move away from the direct connection with the client to a purely musical dialogue (Turry, 1998). That the content of aesthetic music must be good, and that to collude with this sense of artistry is to be untherapeutic, further adds to the debate between the aesthetic and the clinical.

Lecourt's evaluation of Nordoff-Robbin's case study of Edward, I believe, misinterprets the potential for aesthetic considerations and the use of clinical music in the musical/therapeutic struggle. Nordoff's music neither attempts to contain Edward nor to place his painful cries within a more consonant, harmonious context. Rather the music is a reflection of Edward's anguish; the austere improvisation allows Edward the emotional distance necessary for their developing relationship. The recent studies on Edward (Aigen, 1999; Ansdell, 2000; Bergstrom-Nielsen, 1999; Forinash, 2000; Neugebauer, 1999; Robarts, 1999; Rolvsjord, 1998) further highlight the complex nature of the process and show how musical clarity and clinical expression interrelate. Lecourt's interpretation of consonance equaling tonality and aggressiveness equaling atonality are musically naïve. To enter the aesthetic is not inevitably to enter the rounded and harmonic. Aggressive music can be aesthetic just as consonant music may not; music is far more complex than her argument would suggest.

Aesthetic in Lecourt's (1998) view denotes that which does not confront. The therapist therefore needs to be aware that:

> . . . the aesthetic aspects of music must not be used to fill the patient's narcissistic gaps or to meet the therapist's narcissistic needs. The idealization of music as providing such pleasurable gratifications is quite dangerous. (p. 157)

While imbuing music with aesthetic content within the clinical/musical relationship may indeed be a means for the client and/or therapist to fulfill their egotistical needs. Most music therapists, however, are aware of this trap.

The aesthetic content of music therapy has always been considered important although we have yet to fully understand the significance of its impact on the therapeutic alliance. The actualization of the client's aesthetic individuality through music is at the center of AeMT. Understanding and interpreting aesthetic content is complex because it attests to the many strands that go to make up individuality, process, and outcome. The therapist's perceptions of aesthetic content, relationship, pathology, and artistry span seemingly disproportionate principles. Finding a balance between being clinical and being artistic is an ongoing dilemma. As music therapy has matured so the need for a self-sufficient theory has, I believe, become essential–a theory not dependent on other theories, but that finds a nexus accommodating the precision of creative artistry and the pragmatic nature of being clinical. Until this genesis is found music therapy will always be in debt to other philosophies.

IMPROVISATION AND COMPOSITION

Composition and improvisation are allies. One even might say they are one and the same. Nettl (1974) suggests that improvisation and composition, rather than being viewed as separate processes, should be seen as two points on a continuum. Just as music therapy is located on a line between 'art' and 'science' so the continuum between improvisation and composition should be open to and influenced by the ongoing therapeutic direction. Composition is an ordered and specialized process. It is also a concrete and refined form of improvisation. Composition and improvisation are both crafted yet free from the potential of preordained form. The spontaneous creation of improvisation produces a sense of freedom that is acutely therapeutic. The foundations of improvisation and composition are the same. Themes are stated and repeated, they are developed and presented to make a coherent whole. It is interesting to see how the structures of improvising are defined in Javanese Gamelan music (Sutton, 1998). *Garap* is to develop musical ideas, *cengkok* is the embellishment of melody, and *wiletan* describes the intricacies and understanding of melody. These terms show the importance of improvisational devices in other cultures and emphasis placed on improvisation as a standard and accepted art form.

Form and structure balanced with freedom can be clinically captivating. Kartomi (1991) states that "since improvising and composing both involve workings and re-workings of creative ideas, they are essentially part of the same process" (p. 55). The sparks generated from the compositional character of improvisation and the improvisational character of composition makes clinical improvisation an exhilarating and compelling part of contemporary music. As our ability to improvise develops, so our sense of composition becomes ever more acute. Structure becomes embedded in the moment-to-moment expression of freedom.

Many great composers including Bach, Mozart, Beethoven, and Liszt were known as accomplished improvisors. Schubert's style of composition can be seen to be similar to the creative process of improvisation (Nettl, 1998, p. 9). It is interesting to think of Schubert as a composer influenced by improvisation and begs the question that if music therapy had been a profession in his day, perhaps he may also have been a clinician. That some of the great composers could have been music therapists is a fascinating notion and poses the further question as to why there are no influential composer/music therapists today. I believe the answer to this question lies in the fact that the clinical/musical and clinical/compositional processes of music therapy are misunderstood and disrespected by the field of music. If it is true that music therapists are exceptional musician and care deeply about the music they use with their clients, why then are our links to the theories and profession of music so tenuous?

Begbie (2000) in his discussion on composition and improvisation suggests that:

> . . . the customary picture of improvisation as a discrete and relatively frivolous activity on the fringes of music-making might need to be replaced by the one that accord it a more serious and central place. Instead of regarding throughly notated and planned music as the norm and improvisation as an unfortunate epiphenomenon or even aberration, it might be wiser to recall the pervasiveness of improvisation and ask whether it might be able to reveal fundamental aspects of musical creativity easily forgotten in traditions bound predominantly to extensive notation and rehearsal. (p. 182)

If improvisation is to gain more respect in Western music, then what implications will this have for music therapy? I would suggest that the issues for music therapy in this equation are both complex and fascinating. There is a balance among the acceptance of improvisation and the appreciation of clinical improvisation as an art form and the scientific foundation necessary for the substantiation of clinical practice. How do we bridge the gaps between the organizational requirements of composition, the creativity of the client's expression, and the need to quantify and validate? Further, how do we evaluate clinical practice that does not deny the complexities of musical structure, innovation, and the boundaries set by extra-musical theories? These are en-grossing questions because they challenge all music therapy theories which do not embrace music as essential to the process.

Berliner (1994) speaks of the division between jazz improvisation and composition as the eternal cycle. In jazz, composition and improvisation are allies. Improvisers learn and prepare "licks," patterns, and harmonic progressions that form the bases for the ensuing musical dialogue. In this regard jazz improvisation and clinical improvisation are similar. Clinical improvisors must have available a musical dictionary of ideas that can be used in the un-folding musical exchange. Jazz improvisors practice and rehearse models of practice that balance composition and improvisation dependent on their style. To be a competent jazz improvisor, and also a clinical improvisor, is to have a rich catalogue of formulas.

> As soloists are perpetually engaged in creative processes of generation, application, and renewal, the eternal cycle of improvisation and precomposition plays itself out at virtually every level of musical conception. (Berliner, p. 242)

When music theorists speak of the structure of improvisation they are of course speaking from an artistic viewpoint. It could be argued that this has nothing in common with the complex dynamics of music therapy. It is my counterargument however, that when comparing the building blocks of improvisation with composition, the musical and extra-musical elements combine to produce illuminating results for both areas. Developing musical ideas as a result of a therapeutic relationship or as a result of a musical relationship have similarities. Paul Nordoff (Robbins & Robbins, 1998), as a composer and music therapist, thought of improvisations as huge dynamic compositional structures. These architectural constructions manifested them-selves through his many styles of playing. He could be at once symphonic, emulate a sense of chamber music, or provide lieder with operatic or show-tune accompaniments. I believe that improvisation for Nordoff was a clear extension and influence of his own composed music. Clinical improvisation and clinical composition are partners. It is the balance between the two that leads to our understanding of the relationship between organization and freedom and the impact this has on the therapeutic process.

Improvisation as searching, rather than meandering, a term I recently described through my writings on composition and improvisation, is an illuminating phrase that speaks not only to the struggles of our clients but also to the therapist in finding clinically and artistically appropriate music. Clinical improvisation, improvisation as searching, and the music therapy relationship combine to produce an authoritative experience that reveals the potency of music therapy. As the client searches to find their place in the world and in the musical interchange, so improvisation is able to reflect this open, extemporaneous path. To enable the client the opportunity to freely explore, the music therapist must be both spontaneous and ordered. This is the paradox of the clinical/creative process. Improvisation as searching is the quintessential experience between composition and improvisation, freedom and structure in music.

AESTHETICS OF IMPROVISATION

Outside the clinical setting, the aesthetics of improvisation is a primary consideration for the performer. Perfecting the musical content is balanced alongside preserving the freedom that improvisation demands. The artist's aesthetic response to the unfolding musical dialogue is balanced with the moment-to-moment creation of the whole. The aesthetic response is at once finely graded and yet immersed in the complexities of the overall composition. How does an improvisor perceive that sense of freedom and balance it with a coherent aesthetic experience? This is the key to great improvisations; the player integrates expertise with intuition to form a sophisticated logical experience. Good clinical improvisation is based on this premise.

In differentiating precomposed music from free improvisation, Scruton (1997) notes that:

> When musicians improvise together, obeying no instructions other than those which they agree either explicitly beforehand, or tacitly in the course of playing, an extraordinary feat of coordination occurs. It is as though human movements were lifted free from the bodies in which they originate and released into tonal space, there to achieve a togetherness beyond anything that could qualify our bodily life. (p. 438-39)

This extraordinary quote is clearly relevant to music therapy. Allowing clients the opportunity to be free of their pathology and/or illness is the cornerstone of AeMT. I would suggest that this experience is clinically specific, spiritual, and defies human logic.

The quality of music is not considered by most approaches in music therapy to be the most important part of the process. It is expression in and of itself, not the artistic content, that makes music therapy effective. Thus the aesthetic is secondary to the client's articulation, be it "beautiful" or "ugly." Begbie (2000), in his exploration of improvisation and theology, throws new light on the subject. The intent of the improvisor–both clinical and artistic–and the coordination between freedom and constraint suggests that:

> . . . improvisation, by enabling a freedom in relation to a vast array of constraints, can enable a freedom with respect to a fundamental continuous constraint which permeates them all, namely the world's temporality, . . . the theological resonances of this are considerable. (p. 201)

While it is not within the purview of this book to discuss the theological implications of such a passage, the key concept is that the tension between freedom and constraint in improvisation mirrors that found in day-to-day living. As a music therapist I believe in the humanity of music, that it has the ability to transcend the bounds of our conscious existence. The "world's temporality" determines our clients' experiences, and so the question becomes: "Can music express that sense of temporality that speaks to illness, pathology, and human pain?" Begbie proposes that the reason improvisation has been such a powerful force in church music is because improvisation is ". . . not primarily a conceptuality but a rich and multi-faceted *practice* . . ." (p. 270). Clinical improvisation holds an essence of truth for all clients. The richness of its discipline as nonverbal communication, as artistic release, and as a compensatory tool bestows, as Begbie would suggest, a multifaceted experience. The aesthetics of improvisation in music therapy then empowers the process, regardless of the content and level of the expression.

IMPROVISATION AND MUSIC THERAPY

Music therapy has long tried to understand and quantify that which makes the interpersonal and intermusical dynamics of improvisation so compelling. The terms clinical, therapeutic, and creative all denote improvisation that is based on a relationship. The qualities examined in the music therapy literature are easily applicable to other aspects of improvisation and visa versa. Improvisation contains the essence of music-making. It has the ability to transcend the reality of music as a learned and practiced phenomenon. In Overduin's treatise (1998) on improvisation for organists he describes how

> Even the simplest and shortest improvisation–in spite of labels such as exercise or assignment–should be thought of as a piece of music, striving for something beautiful. (p. 4)

As such, improvisation is therapeutic no matter under what guise it appears.

Improvisation, while based on relationship and intuition, is not a random act of impulse. Good improvisation is a blend of free invention and premeditated thought. For the client in music therapy the unexpected is balanced alongside form and shape. Freedom can only make sense in improvisation if it is equated with structure. Parker (1999) writes:

> All the best improvised music balances processes of continuity (with the inherent dangers of formuliac repetition) and change: an oral tradition dies if it does not evolve. (liner notes)

The seemingly unpremeditated eloquence of improvisation is combined with clarity of foresight as the musical direction unfolds. The challenge to the music therapist is to consider various musical components as they impact and affect the musical and therapeutic process.

> Indeed, part of the challenge to the improvisor is to invent musically coherent melodic lines over changing harmonic structures which, in their specific realization, often cannot be anticipated; the similarly unpredictable rhythmic dimensions also enforce spontaneity.
> (Hagberg, 1995, p. 82)

Definitions of improvisation in musicology and music scholarship (Nettl, 1998) highlight different philosophical viewpoints. They focus on the comparison between organization and unpredictability, improvisation as composition, and its ephemeral qualities that are beyond analysis and rational explanation. A consideration which provides a bridge to music therapy is the belief that improvisation reflects human freedom and emotion (Nettl 1998). Improvisation exclusively as an act of performance (Bailey 1992) highlights the disparities in our developing theories, although if we substitute client for audience there can be possible philosophical connections and avenues for learning. These contradictions and similarities aside, clinical improvisation has a further challenge, that of making theoretical and practical links with musicology. Until the musical intricacies of music therapy are recognized and respected our work will always remain outside the remit of allied developing theories. Pressing (1998) gives an overview of improvisation in music therapy in Nettl's (1998) comprehensive overview of recent trends in improvisation:

> Musical improvisation continues to be used in therapeutic situations to facilitate arousal and engagement and enhance social interaction, and can succeed in drawing out patients, for example some autistic children, who are otherwise nearly unreachable. (pp. 57–58)

Clinical improvisation is far more complex and survives on deeper emotional levels than this summation suggests. How then do we explain to theorists the sophistication of clinical improvisation and the links that could be made between our two disciplines when such a definition as described here is so overtly simplistic?

PSYCHOLOGICAL IMPLICATIONS

A potential computational theory of improvisation has been developed mainly through the work of Pressing (1978, 1984, 1987, 1988, 1992, 1997, 1998). When discussing the psychological foundations of improvisational expertise (1998), he raises interesting suggestions that are relevant for music therapists. He explores the fact that information-processing and gesture for an improvisor is a learned and precise skill:

> For the improviser must affect real-time sensory and perceptual coding, optimal attention allocation, event interpretation, decision-making, prediction (of the action of others), memory storage and recall, error correction, and movement control, and further, must integrate these processes into an optimally seamless set of musical statements that reflect both a personal perspective on musical organization and a capacity to affect listeners. (p.51)

Pressing (1984) suggests that improvisers "use a referent set of cognitive, perceptual, or emotional structures (constraints) that guide and aid the production of musical materials." In music therapy the referent is taken from various sources: spontaneous themes developed in the moment, themes as a source of leitmotiv, activities developed from session to sessions, and song form. The music therapist's referent is an intricate balance of musical and therapeutic responses interwoven with the cognitive and emotional responses and relationship between client and therapist. A musical knowledge base is fundamental for the music therapist and should include:

> musical materials and excerpts, repertoire, subskills, perceptual strategies, problem-solving routines, hierarchical memory structures and schemas, generalized motor programs, and more. (Pressing, 1998, p. 53)

Without a toolbox of resources it is impossible to provide relevant clinically and aesthetically directed music.

The therapist's ability to remember music themes and motives is another required skill. Theorists recognize the complexities of music memory (Ericsson & Charness, 1994) and propose thinking in broader strokes rather than precise musical components (Smith, 1991). To accurately remember melodic phrases, rhythmic patterns, or chord progressions that have been spontaneously improvised takes many years of practice. This is a skill, however, all music therapists should attempt to attain.

Also relevant for music therapy, Wolpert (1990) found there were differences in recognition tasks between musicians and nonmusicians. Non-musicians responded mainly to instrumentation whereas musicians responded to melodic structure and harmonic accompaniment. The role of the therapist is to facilitate melodic, rhythmic, and harmonic creativity through which the client can articulate their abstract sense of their musical selves.

CLASSICAL MUSIC

Improvisation in classical western music from the 17th to 19th centuries was a peripheral activity. Even though many composers improvised and used spontaneous music-making as central to their compositions, this aspect of their musicianship has not often survived the passing of time.

> We know . . . both from anecdote and from fairly trivial inference, that a lot of the composer-performer's musical compositions must contain material that had its origins in improvisational performance... (Kivy, 1995, p. 164-165)

Improvisation often preceded composition and acted as a source of inspiration for developing themes and for the formation of refined compositional structures.

> In improvisation, the freedom of the performer is greater still–and here notation follows performance, rather than proceeding it. (Scruton, 1997, p. 111)

The historical analysis of improvisation in performance is now being explored as a way to understand specific forms of historical practice. Magrini (1998) unwittingly makes links with music therapy:

> . . . improvisation is one aspect of a complex of musical behavior which is meant to activate and bring forth meaningful social relations. (p. 194)

In Goertzen's (1998) study of Clara Schumann's improvised preludes we find connections between the power of improvisation and its ability to influence the growth of musicianship:

> Improvisation was a fundamental part of Clara's study of the piano throughout her years of training, as a means of developing both technical mastery of the instrument and understanding of the musical styles of her day. (p. 239)

In Paul Nordoff's (Robbins & Robbins 1998) illuminating study, Healing Heritage: Paul Nordoff Exploring the Tonal Language of Music, western classical music is analyzed and studied to facilitate the development of musical resources in music therapy. As a music therapist educated in the Nordoff and Robbins tradition my clearest recollections and moments of unadulterated inspiration came from what were than called Talks on Music. Listening to Paul Nordoff's teachings and beginning to make links between music and therapy I was constantly exhilarated by his lectures, at the potential music had when specifically geared toward therapy. The logic and clarity of Nordoff's ideas, investigating the structures of music alongside the structures of the therapeutic process, is a natural evolutionary process. That this kind of detailed examination of precomposed classical Western music in direct relation to improvisation did not continue, to the best of my knowledge, after his death in this form, bears witness to the potency of his ideas and musical foresight. The text has an improvisatory nature that gives a wonderful indication of what it might have felt to have been there. Nordoff's clarity and knowledge of musical repertoire leaves one truly breathless. Healing Heritage is not only an historical document, it is as alive and fresh now as when he delivered the lectures in 1974. I consider this book to be the single most important document in the music therapy literature. It is the only work that looks in-depth at the potential of Western classical music on music therapy. That Schumann, Brahms, and Mompou can teach us about the links and influence of clinical practice and aesthetics should be a source of inspiration for music therapists.

> When you get a melodic idea . . . remember the tune. Write it down, or play it over and over and over. Then find for it harmony that is alive, a harmony that supports it, enhances it, moves it forward. And we'll begin to get some lovely, lovely harmonies in our improvisation for the children. And they have just the same effect on them as that wonderful harmonic change in the Schumann had on us. You can be sure of that. (p. 87)

JAZZ

Improvisation and jazz are natural allies. Jazz originated as a response to the constraints of western classical music. Syncopation, harmonic sophistication, and freedom of musical thought have placed it as one of the most influential and innovative forms of 20th-century music. Writings on jazz improvisation have focused on the techniques and performances of specific musicians. Miles Davis (Smith, 1998) developed an improvisational vocabulary that was manifested through intricate musical communication and visual cues with players. The complex intermusical relationships resulted in some of the most inspiring improvisations ever recorded. George Russell (Monson, 1998) developed modal jazz, a tonal theory derived from the circle of fifths and the new harmonies of bebop. Modal jazz allowed for greater freedom of improvising and when used by Cecil Taylor and Ornette Coleman it evolved alongside western ideas of the avant-garde.

Keith Jarrett, a more recent figure in jazz improvisation, has influenced some music therapists, including the author, in the development of clinical music. His sense of improvisation is altogether different. Solo improvisations are built on broad thematic ideas that are emotional yet carefully controlled. Interestingly Jarrett's preparation for giving a concert is not dissimilar to the concentration needed before an improvised music therapy session:

> Before a concert, Jarrett would try to empty himself of all preconceived ideas, and then allow the music to flow through and out of him. He said that if he was not able to empty himself he would, almost invariably, have a concert that was not as good. (Carr, 1992, p.65)

Berliner's major contribution, Thinking in Jazz (1994), explores aspects of jazz improvisation with clarity and insight. Techniques, balancing structure and freedom, composing in the moment, and precomposition are all areas of study that can be directly related to the further understanding of clinical improvisation. This inspirational work explores what it means to improvise, how improvising is conceptualized, and the complex interpersonal and intermusical foundations that encompass the process of jazz improvisation.

The influence of jazz studies on improvisation and music therapy has been spearheaded by Even Ruud (1998). Ruud suggests improvising in music therapy has fewer rules than jazz, though for the clinical improvisor and jazz musician this is dependent on their musical and theoretical bias. Improvisation as a transitional ritual is compared to the rite of the novice jazz musician and that of the student music therapist in training. The experience of "flow"–unconscious presence–and "void"–empty space–further emphasizes the subliminal connection between music-making in jazz and music therapy. Both jazz and clinical improvisation rely on spontaneity and can facilitate a state not unlike a "stream of consciousness" and transcendence. In music therapy this sense of being "beyond" often heralds an explosion in the therapeutic relationship and the developing direction of the work. In jazz these moments of passage are the most spiritual and intoxicating a listener can experience.

Free jazz has historically been discussed under the broad banner of jazz though it cannot be easily classified and has equal connections with contemporary classical music. Free jazz is usually improvised and is devoid of rules and theoretical musical devices. It is in essence a form of musical liberation that on first hearing can sound arbitrary. If one looks beyond the immediate, however, subtle formations often appear. These less direct formations give it its musical potency. Free jazz has potentially clear connections with clinical improvisation and similarities can be found in the respective processes of music-making. The freedom of musical dialogue and relationship in free jazz and music therapy often produce similar musical and therapeutic results. That is not to say that a group playing free jazz would want to emulate a music therapy scenario or that a clinical improvisation would in any way be like a free-jazz performance. Rather, the argument rests on the focus of musical interrelations and the freedom engendered from each. There are occasions when music as "art" and music as "therapy" can indeed find a natural merger that is informed and explored from both disciplines. Derek Bailey and Evan Parker, two key figures in free jazz, have developed a school of music that is beyond classification and theoretical rationalization.

ETHNOMUSICOLOGY

The ethnomusicological implications for music therapy have been recognized as important mainly through the work of Joseph Moreno (Moreno 1988, 1995, Moreno, et al., 1990). Moreno (1988) observed that American music therapists use music from a relatively small western musical pallette. He has urged music therapists to look to the potential influence of world music on clinical practice, and to broaden the music used in music therapy to include multicultural influences. Bradt (1997) also recommends that music therapists know and understand the meaning of music in different cultures. Music therapists should be knowledgeable about multicultural styles, and recognize the organization of modes/scales and general theoretical makeup of different music from around the world. Estrella (2001) in her impassioned chapter on multicultural music therapy supervision raises some pertinent questions:

> Music therapists have a unique responsibility to examine and research the questions of culture's influence on music. How does culture impact the experience of mutual music making within music therapy sessions? How does culture impact the experience of music, and the definition of aesthetics? How does culture specifically impact the music therapy supervision relationship? Are there special cultural considerations to which the music therapy supervisor must attend? (p. 62)

Therefore, what of the studies on improvisation and ethnomusicology, and what can music therapy learn from this work? Improvisation in the West has taken second place to the ability to play precomposed music. The hallmark of a musician in Western music is someone who has learned and practiced the art of performing composers' music. In the Middle East, however, improvisation is revered because of musicians' learned ability to be musically free and unpredictable (Nettl, 1998). These different emphases of musicianship have affected the development of music in each of these cultures. It is interesting therefore to speculate how music therapy may have developed if it had begun in the Middle East.

For a music therapist delving into the chapters on ethnomusicology in Nettle's edited book on improvisation (1998) there is a treasure trove of ideas, philosophies, and analyses pertinent to all aspects of clinical improvisation. In Arabic music the modern tarab style of the East Mediterranean world and Egypt is a "style that emphasizes live musical performance, gives prominence to instantaneous modal creations, and treats music as an ecstatic experience" (Racy,

1998, p. 97). The improvisor must be able to communicate emotions, the "soul" or "feeling" of the improvisors' music, enabling the listener to become ecstatic. It could be argued that a tarab music therapist should provide a musical/emotional environment for the client to express their sense of ecstatic creation in creative music-making. This is the essence of what we hope to offer our clients; an experience that is intrinsically healthy. The aesthetic of improvisation in Latin music (Manuel, 1998) demands specific learned techniques and "control and economy of style (p. 143)"–this resonated clearly with the demands placed on the clinical improvisor. The raga (Viswanathan & Cormack, 1998), a complex musical form, is fundamentally defined by its scale. Further:

> . . . every raga has certain pitches that have specific functions. At the svara level, these functional tones are a raga's second most fundamental identifying feature. (p. 224)

The sophistication and development of musical scales, ideas, and ornamentation and the music's cultural background could be of enormous significance in the future development of clinical improvisation. Improvisation in North Indian music (Slawek, 1998), as in Arab music, is based on the assumption that the improvisor is able to play freely and has the ability to facilitate heightened emotions for the performer and listener. The ritual of playing can lead to levels of catharsis and altered states of consciousness. Improvisation in North India is a complex combination of precomposed pieces, rehearsed patterns, and creative improvised material:

> Every performance is a new exploration of a particular musical experience that will lead both the performers and audience into unchartered territory. (Slawek, 1998, p. 363)

The analyses of music material used by Middle East improvisors is engrossing (Nettl & Riddle, 1998) and has connections with similar work achieved in music therapy. Exploring the use of tetrachords, pentachords, and octave scales can provide music therapists with a new range of musical ideas and flavors. Analyzing the use of melodic devices and sequences, ornamentation, and rhythms can only enhance the evolution of clinical improvisation.

MUSIC AND EMOTIONS

The writings on music and emotions are theoretically and philosophically complex. The literature is based on the supposition that music translates emotions–the extent of which is determined by the receptivity and willingness of the listener (Meyer, 1956). That music contains emotions would seem an obvious notion for music therapists. What is complex, however, is the nature of emotion and the emotional sophistication that music has with which to communicate the human condition. If music can translate emotions, then the question becomes, How does one evaluate that translation? Taking into account that emotions conveyed through music are complex (Levinson, 1990), Scruton (1977) states that by communicating an emotion, it becomes an actuality of experience. Walton (1997, in Robinson, Meaning and Music) describes how music can influence the reality of feelings and sensations and Sharpe (2000) concludes that "emotions are the starting point for our expressive description of music" (p. 59). Structural complexities allow musical emotion to be communicated not only as a total experience, but also through the smaller parts that make up the whole (Levinson, 1997).

These contemplations give a sense of the complex phenomena that music therapists deal with on a daily basis. The questions become how and why does music convey emotional states, and how do we interpret and make sense of music as an emotional force. In his analysis of experiencing music as a cognitive skill Sloboda (1985) writes:

> . . . music is capable of arousing in us deep and significant emotions. These emotions can range from the "pure" aesthetic delight in sound construction, through emotions like joy or sorrow which music sometimes evokes or enhances, to the simple relief from monotony, boredom or depression which everyday musical experiences can provide. (p. 1)

We offer our clients a time to be free from the bounds of their illness and/or pathology through the expression of emotions. It follows that if music can allow emotions to be clearly and specifically expressed, then the potency of the music therapy relationship is assured.

MUSIC AND LANGUAGE

Does music mirror verbal language and, if so, what are the implications for music therapy? Music is a language of emotions. What does this suggest for the creative processes in clinical improvisation? The spoken (or written) word is a way in which two human beings communicate, but in order to do so, both must understand the logic of sentence construction and the subtleties of the language in which they are conversing (Sharpe, 2000). For many clients these forms of communication are not available. However, we do not need these prerequisites to achieve discourse through music. Could it therefore be argued that communicating musically requires less intellectual ability than communicating on a verbal level? On what intellectual level do we require musical language to be significant? Scruton (1997) says that "language is unique to rational beings." Taking that approach, and given the "nonrational" nature of many clients, music therapy could then be described as a noncommunicative process. Of course this is a ridiculous suggestion. Rationality is not required in order for music to be perceived as a form of language. The paradox of music is that it can be both rational and nonrational within an instant, and that is why clients find it such a powerful form of explicit and implicit communication.

Language is not as subtle as music (Treitler, 1997) and we should be careful when comparing the two (Begbie, 2000). While Addis (1999) holds that music and language are analogous in that each has a variety of forms, the specifics of which must be understood in order to achieve communication. This is in direct contradiction to the underpinnings of AeMT. The power of the musical dialogue is precisely that–participants can share language at an intricate and refined level without understanding the complexities of style, grammar or syntax. It is interesting to note that the words "style," "grammar," and "syntax" are applied to music, though all have their origins in language (Agawu, 1991). Historically, the nonverbal nature of music has precluded the use of a verbal model to describe it; Nattiez (1990) had problems in articulating the intricacies of his work because music is fundamentally nonverbal. The most controversial answer to this divide was prepared by Keller (1994), who devised a theory of functional analysis where music was analyzed not through language but by music itself. It is the nonverbal essence of music that places it beyond the specifics-oriented nature of verbal language.

IS MUSIC REPRESENTATIONAL?

It would seem natural that music is representational–that it transmits ideas and concepts. But not all theorists would agree (Kivy, 1991). How does our imagination respond to music. (Walton, 1997, in Robinson)? Unlike paintings, music cannot depict the symbols necessary for specific representational images:

> . . . when I step outside my game with music and consider the music itself, all I see is music, not a fictional world to go with it. There is just the notes, and they themselves don't call for imagining anything. (Walton, 1997, p. 82)

Addis (1999) proposes three kinds of representations:

- conventional–the representation "depends on neither the inherent nature of the representation nor on that of the one who uses that representation";
- natural–the representation which "by its inherent nature, determines both that and what it represents"; and
- quasi-natural–a three-term relation involving the representing object, that which is represented and the representer.

When attempting to understand music as representation, most theorists parallel their discussions with the visual arts (Scruton, 1997; Walton, 1997). Scruton concludes that while it is his view that music is not representational, there may be other open questions:

> . . . music is not representational, since thoughts about a subject are never essential to the understanding of music. But, it might be said, I have done nothing to show that we must understand music as we presently understand it, nothing to show that there could not be a new way of understanding music which yet had the character of an aesthetic interest, and which accorded to music the status of narrative. (p. 138)

Music therapy requires a new way of looking at music as communication and representation. The narrative of the therapeutic relationship in creative music-making presupposes that musical representation is significant. Whether we look to the specific representations during the unraveling of the therapeutic process, or the more fluid experiences of free-flowing nonrepresentational expression, the music in music therapy must include a representation of the relationship. One must then ask oneself how to translate the complex forms of therapeutic representation necessary for further understanding. In music therapy, then, representation may be conventional–that the client and/or situation does not require representational specifics, natural–that the therapeutic situation dictates a specific and finite representation, and quasi-natural–involving the therapeutic representation, that which is being represented and the client/therapist relationship.

CLOSING THOUGHTS

How do we describe what happens in a piece of music, how do we describe the musical relationship and musical events that happen in clinical improvisation, and how is each related to the other? What makes Beethoven's music so distinct from Ravel's (Blacking, 1974), and what makes one client's improvising so distinct from another's? If indeed a client characterizes their persona through music then how could our understanding of these structures color our responses and the potential musical worlds we make available? There are many forms of analysis both musical and extramusical. If analysis is the key to understanding, then the theoretical reasoning we adhere to will reflect both our questions and the enigmas we are trying to unravel. Because music therapy balances itself between two beliefs, that of "art" and "science," then we must address the potential of each separately and also the connections between the two.

These questions point to the heart of AeMT. Without asking these essential questions our understanding of clinical music will be limited. The essence of a client's playing and the musical relationship with the therapist is based on music that is perceived, instantly analyzed, and responded to. Our understanding of musical textures, interactive themes, and improvisational inventions between client and therapist transpires to form the intensity of the musical and clinical dialogue. By understanding music itself, its role in the therapeutic alliance, and the interface between the knowing of music and relationship, we can begin to understand the true nature of improvising in music therapy.

Interlude

THREE MAJOR WORKS OF THE WESTERN CLASSICAL REPERTOIRE: INTRODUCTION TO CHAPTERS 2, 7, and 11

> Music, being identical with heaven, isn't a thing of momentary thrills. … It's a condition of eternity.
> – Gustav Holst
> Letter to W.G. Whittaker, 1914

In analyzing Debussy's Prelude, Book 1, no. 4, "Les Sons et les Parfums Tournent dans L'Air du Soir," Paul Nordoff extracts the use of the perfect cadence and six-four chords as providing a grounding for Debussy's rich and unexpected harmonies. Relating this to the potential of AeMT invites the music therapist into the richness of Debussy's musical landscape and thus the richness of our heightened therapeutic encounters:

> It's from this kind of freedom that a real music therapy–a clinical improvisational therapy–could come into being. Because if this hadn't taken place, we just wouldn't be here today. This has paved the way musically for all the things we do, for our deliberate, conscious use of each harmonic element, each musical component. We owe Debussy a tremendous amount, as therapists, just for this very reason. (Robbins & Robbins, 1998, p. 79)

Studying Healing Heritage (Robbins & Robbins, 1998), the clarity of Paul's ideas as he analyzes the structures of music alongside the structures of the therapeutic process seems an effortless process. The question becomes why music therapy did not continue the detailed examination of precomposed music in relation to clinical improvisation after his death. His inspirational connections between music and therapy bear witness to the potency of his insights. The text has an improvisational nature that gives an indication of the inspirational nature of the lectures. Nordoff's knowledge of the repertoire leaves one breathless.

What then does AeMT owe composers such as Debussy and what can we learn from each composer's approach? Music, social context, and the individuality of the composer combine to present a scenario between music, the creator, and the time in which they lived. Wagner's *Ring Cycle* is a prime example. The magnitude of his creative imagination and musical inventiveness, the social climate in which the operas were written, the structure of each opera, and its relation to the whole cycle can be compared with a single music therapy session and its relation to the overall therapeutic process. Consider how Wagner carries forward dramatic ideas and develops them within each plot and subplot. The interweaving of musical themes and leitmotives, their development within the narrative, and the overall musical structure could, if we are open, present an innovative view of music therapy. If this is the case, then what of the magnitude of Western music and its potential to define the future of clinical practice?

The three seminal works presented and discussed in Chapters 2, 7, and 11 are intended as musical backbones to the arguments of this book. Their historical significance and personal influence on my maturation as a musician have significantly influenced the evolution of AeMT. I consider them to be critical because of their impact on the course of music and because each contains a revelation of compositional form.

How then do we withdraw and find that which is significant from the investigating of seminal works? What connects the compositional and therapeutic process and how do we extract the essence of music and relationship that speaks to our evolving knowledge of music and people? The three chapters presented are beginnings and intended to reflect this book's main philosophical argument. These chapters discuss structural musical features and offer suggestions for connections with music therapy. To some, these leaps may seem farfetched; for others, as for me, they are logical and revealing. As questions and answers emerged during the writing of these chapters, so the possibilities continued to grow. I am convinced now more than ever, that through the analysis of precomposed music there is enormous potential for music therapy.

> Now, when you learn new pieces with your teachers, or when you study a piece of music, look at what's happening. Look at the life of the intervals as they weave and interweave, and change and work, and bring constantly new emotional experience into our lives. Become aware of this. This is the touchstone. This is a hypostasis, a foundation for the work we want to do. (Robbins & Robbins, 1998, p. 41)

Each of these chapters focuses on an excerpt from a particular work by Bach, Beethoven, and Cage. All of these composers, and in particular the pieces selected, have had a significant effect on my development as a composer/music therapist. They, along with others, informed the emergence of my evolving clinical musicianship that culminated in AeMT. The heart of these chapters is the analysis of compositional form in relation to clinical form. Exploring sections of precomposed music to the reality of sessions adds an authenticity that gives credence to these investigations. As the writing of these chapters matured so the links between artistry and therapeutic intent became more integral to the arguments of the book.

Chapter Two

J. S. BACH, *MASS IN B MINOR BWV 232:* THE CONTRAPUNTAL MUSICAL RELATIONSHIP

> Rhythm is in his every limb, he takes in all the harmonies by his subtle ear and utters all the different parts through the medium of his own mouth. Great admirer as I am of antiquity in other respects, I yet deem this Bach of mine to comprise in himself many Orpheuses and twenty Arions.
>
> – Johann Mathias Gesner
>
> Commentary on Quintilian's *De Instiutio Oratoria* (c.1730)

The *Mass in B Minor* contains some of the finest music of the Baroque era and stands as a monument to Bach's life as a musician and composer. It was compiled from diverse sources, spans a greater part of his composing career, and was written during his years at Leipzig. The Mass was never performed during Bach's lifetime and it appears that Bach never heard the work performed. The Mass contains a broad range of styles and forms: passacaglia, fugue, ricerar, ritornello, and stile antico. Over a third of the Mass includes arrangements from other compositions such as the Cantata BWV 191 (Butt, 1991). One of the most fascinating aspects of the Mass is its combination of earlier pieces worked and reworked to form a monumental piece of sacred music.

> Bach's transformation of earlier scores was a stunningly ingenious process. That he could take music of such high quality and lift it to further heights is a supreme testament to his creative powers. (Stauffer, 1997, p. 50)

The Mass is dramatic and impassioned (Staufer, 1997). It is set in five movements arranged in individual sections of choruses, arias, and duets. Tonally the Mass begins in B minor and ends in D major although D major predominates the work. If we look more closely at the seven keys of the Mass we find an exquisite bond between key selection and emotional depiction (Xinh, 2001):

- G minor – tragic consummation
- F# minor – transcendent suffering

- A major – joy and grace
- B minor – human pain
- D major – worldly power and glory
- E minor – crucifixion
- G major – blessedness

Bach's choice of keys to express the sensitivities of each part of the Mass is extraordinary. The beauty of his word painting (Swain, 1997) can be found in the "Crucifixus." Its expressive content shows an understanding of the human condition. In listening one is struck by the magnitude of Bach's compositional form. The balance between its architectural construction and the intense musical embodiment of the Catholic Mass leaves one with an impression of great spiritual intensity. The Mass was conceived over a long period of time, its content was considered and reconsidered in precise detail, and its emotional portrayal is transcendental and musically precise.

BACH, COUNTERPOINT, AND MUSIC THERAPY

Counterpoint as a compositional technique is a distinctive feature of the baroque era. When considering Bach it is counterpoint and the fugue that most often come to mind (Butt, 1991). The complexities of Bach's contrapuntal inventions are both artistically exhilarating and mathematically ingenious. It is this ingenuity that makes his music so worthy of detailed investigation. Through his study of the stile antico ("in the old style") Bach looked back to the 16th-century theory of contrapuntal composition. This retrograde view, along with the more contemporary styles, was Bach's attempt to include a wide variety of music (Butt, 1991). For Bach, the essence of composing relied on techniques that were regarded as antiquated. It was Bach's insistence on continuing his contrapuntal work–as a product of the stile antico–that guided his developing brilliance and secured his place in music history. Counterpoint can often seem dry, but in the hands of Bach it is elevated to some of the most emotionally striking music of his career (Kivy, 1990).

To compare the AeMT relationship to the contrapuntal relationship is to take an intriguing philosophical stance. When entering a musical dialogue with a client one instinctively takes a contrapuntal perspective. When a client offers melody the music therapist must respond and choose from various levels of melodic and therapeutic counterpoint. It is the musical one, however, that has the initial impact. Our choice of counterpoint with a client reveals our own understanding of the process and our response to the client's musical flow. Themes and their development are reflective of this relationship. How one melody leads to another creates musical direction. The therapist can make melodic inferences that will impel the musical discourse. Through the contrapuntal musical relationship the therapist can imitate and encourage a continued dialogue toward further musical ideas.

If we take Bach's Credo and contrast it with a contrapuntal section from a music therapy session we can begin to see similarities between compositional/improvisational processes. The counterpoint may seem from the score (see Figure 1) to be mathematical and devoid of emotional content. The balance of voice parts, the building of contrapuntal complexities, and the density of textures are precisely arranged. The continuo walking bass line provides stability that balances the interweaving voice parts above. Rhythmically, the fugal theme becomes more complex as it continues, adding new levels of counterpoint as each voice enters. The melody of the fugue is intriguing. It opens with a major third then moves stepwise and in the fourth measure opens to more spacious intervals. The combination of complex rhythms, increasing intervals, and walking bass line combine to produce a propelling musical effect.

What then could it mean to offer such an ordered yet passionate and active musical experience for a client? What therapeutic outcome might such music have? I believe that it is indeed possible to re-create such creative complexities. Therapists and clients have the ability to compose two musical lines by singing or playing. If we think of each as separate voices then we can indeed create complex counterpoint. Even though, for the most part, clients do not have musical training I believe it is possible to help facilitate a contrapuntal musical relationship. This is dependent on the therapist's knowledge of the repertoire and ability to understand, extract, and re-create contrapuntal invention within the clinical improvisational setting.

The example taken from a session with a client living with HIV (see Figure 2) contains a similar counterpoint. The client's free-flowing melodic contours are balanced with the therapist's ascending slow-moving chords. The third contrapuntal line (4) adds to the musical complexities and further illuminates the intensities of the relationship. The client comments on the impact of such contrapuntal invention:

Credo (Symbolum Nicenum)

fig. 1

fig. 2

> The music you improvised in response to mine was important. While I don't always want perfect music, there are times when I need you to support me with more complex structures than I can manage. Here you gave me a complex music that I could not have played on my own. This gave me the opportunity to express my feelings at a much deeper level. These times to me contain elements of beauty.

The therapeutic consequence of counterpoint is here clearly expressed. The client's invention is grounded with the therapist's chords. The ambiguity of tonality (D flat and C), the voicing and spacing of the therapist's chords further add to the emotional impact of the improvisation. Merging therapeutic process with aesthetic meaning is at the heart of AeMT and is no more clearly shown that in this contrapuntal musical relationship.

How might we compare–at what level and with what bias–Bach's Credo with the example of clinical improvisation? My argument is that there is no difference, nor should there be. That one comes from a great composer and the other from the client/therapist relationship is irrelevant. What is important is the musical and compositional aspirations with which both pieces were created. By separating music from therapy, by arguing that one is "art" and the other "treatment" and thus not contingent on the same level of artistic integrity, is to deny the true meaning of music. Studying the compositional procedures of Bach's B minor Mass can be related to the density of the musical relationship. It can inspire us to directly hear the client's creativity, to respond with more musical detail, and consider the implications of refining musical dialogue. If we listen to the Mass as a music therapist, if we begin to understand the spiritual source of Bach's genius and his beliefs, then the music will take on new light, one that could potentially deepen our understanding of music therapy. Studying the score will further illuminate our work. Extracting passages to extend our musical resources and understand the contrapuntal nature of relationships will reveal ever more layers in our future therapeutic encounters.

KYRIE, FUGUE, AND MUSIC THERAPY

> The first kyrie of the B minor Mass is so vast that it seems as if nothing could control its bulk; yet the listener needs no analysis to confirm his instinctive impressions that it reaches its last note with an astronomical punctuality. The foundation of this impression is that the form is such as well seem ridiculously simple when it is correctly described. (Tovey, 1935, p. 25)

The kyrie is spiritually intense. There is a feeling of enormity and granite grandeur in the fugue and its development. The opening four-bar adagio creates a gravity that sets the scene for the solemn nature of the unfolding Mass. There is a steadfastness in these opening bars, a certainty of B minor that portrays the nature of suffering. Music therapists must acknowledge pain and deterioration as central to the therapeutic process. Whether this is through our clients' personal struggles or the physical limitations dictated by pathology and illness…loss is central to therapy. This being said, what can the kyrie show therapists as they struggle to interpret and reflect clients' unknowing in the face of physical or emotional adversity? How can the strength in this music reveal the enormity of clients' predicaments and deepen the therapeutic relationship? If we look closer we may find some answers. The balance of the three settings of "Kyrie eleison" (see Figure 3, opening bars, full score), the thematic overlapping, and third extended setting provide stability, and add movement to the horizontal chords. Sopranos I and II interweave a cadenza-like passage that adds another layer of invention. Could not the austerity and forward-moving movement of these opening phrases be compared to many clinical situations we face as therapists? The monolithic opening makes one catch one's breath with expectation. If we can capture a similar musical grandeur in clinical improvisation then what of its implications for therapeutic growth? The adagio has the ability to influence wisdom of music and music therapy as well as the many levels of listening.

The main body of the kyrie is a fuga gravis (Stauffer, 1997). The theme features motives that depict the magnitude and solemnity of the developing fugue (see Figure 4). The repeated B (a) provides a stability from which the melody unfolds. It also provides a clarity of diction for the word setting and contributes a chant-like feel to the music. As the melody develops from the opening tone two musical "sighs", g to f#, (b) capture a musical/emotional representation of intensity. These sighs are structurally important in the thematic development of the fugue and have potential implications for music therapy. The sigh as an embodiment of the expressive dialogue has a subtle yet significant impact on the music. Clients often expel their emotions through the sigh. There can be a sense of "letting go" emotionally and physically. How the therapist reflects these sighs and incorporates them in the musical dialogue is dependent on the level of clinical listening (see Chapter 5). Listening to the actuality of the sigh, its tone, pitch and timbre–is vital if the therapist is to accurately include it within the dialogue. Bach's use of the musical sigh here is delicate, carefully placed and fundamental to the overall melody. To experience and understand the detail of this musical interweaving is to understand the deeper meaning and precision of sound in therapy. As the sigh becomes a prominent part of the fugue its influence in the overall composition is acknowledged.

Kyrie
Adagio
Flauto traverso I.
Flauto traverso II.
Oboe d'amore I.
Oboe d'amore II.
Fagotti.
Violin I.
Violin II.
Viola.
Soprano I.
Ky - ri - e, Ky - ri - e e - le - i - son, e - le -
Soprano II.
Ky - ri - e e - le - i - son, e - le - i - son, e -
Alto.
Ky - ri - e e - le - i - son, Ky - ri - e e -
Tenore.
Ky - ri - e, Ky - ri - e, Ky - ri - e e -
Basso.
Ky - ri - e, Ky - ri - e, Ky - ri - e e -
Continuo.

fig. 3

Largo ed un poco piano.
Fl. I
Fl. II
Ob. d'A. I
Ob. d'A. II
Bsn.
Vln. I
Vln. II
Vla.
S. I
- i - son.
S. II
le - i - son.
A.
le - i - son.
T.
le - i - son.
B.
lei - son.
Cont.

(fig. 3)

The fugue's chromatic development (Butt, 1991) is another striking feature. The falling chromatic line (c) is followed by an upward leap that propels the music forward to the end of the theme. Ending on the dominant, the music is open for the evolving fugue to develop. Three potential clinical techniques are noted below:

- chromatic movement
- melodic leap
- phrase endings on the dominant

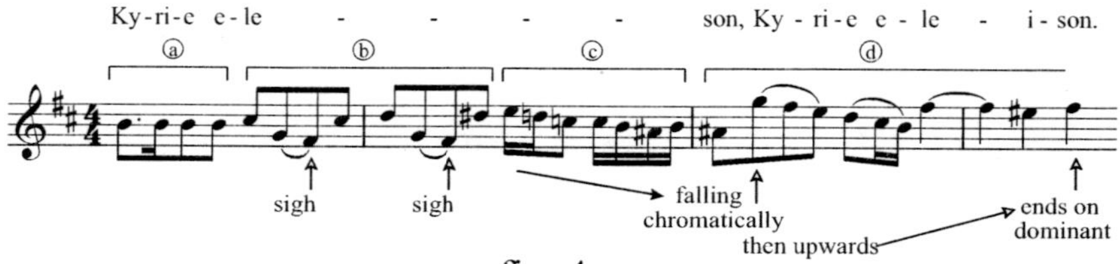

fig. 4

The fugue proper is an immense study in structural and contrapuntal design. The intricate themes and subthemes are interwoven to produce a fugue that is complex yet on hearing is simple in devotion. As the fugue becomes more complex, as ideas move from instruments to voice, the building of strands raise the music to ever greater heights. Achieving this level of musical intensity may never be possible in clinical improvisation. Music therapists should, however, strive to capture the essence of Bach's commitment portrayed in this fugue. To offer such an experience may give clients the musical empowerment they need as partners in the musical relationship.

COMPOSITIONAL DEVICES AND SPIRITUALITY

> Bach's music, like many of the things affording the deepest, most abiding pleasures in life, yield their delights to those who work for them. By no means are all listeners prepared to expend the effort of meeting the challenge posed by Bach's more complex works, or by the similarly "difficult" works of other composers. (Davies, 1994, p. 355)

The B minor Mass is an intricate work and to fully understand its subtleties requires acute listening. Bach's contrapuntal inventions are often complex and it could be argued therefore that counterpoint has no place in musical communication with clients. The counterargument is that the clinical process is complex, and to reflect therapeutic intricacies musical structures such as counterpoint should be available. The two sections chosen to focus on in this chapter open parts I and II of the Mass. While many of its movements are solemn and serious in nature it also has sections that are triumphant and joyful. These include the addition of brass and timpani and offer injections of energy. The *Gloria, Et resurrexit*, and *Sanctus*, all in the key of D major, are examples of extreme joy and exhilaration. D major as a specific key for clinical improvisation can provide energy and optimism. It is also a key of stability and focus.

Another compositional device of interest to AeMT is how Bach moves effortlessly from arias and duets into choruses. A good example is the aria, Quoniam tu solus sanctus, which leads into the Gloria. This bass aria has an unusual scoring of a corno da caccia obligato with an accompaniment of two bassoons. At the end of the aria the music suddenly moves into a driven vivace of magnificent splendor. By isolating and studying this transition in detail it is possible to replicate the move from small solo music to larger more orchestral textures and transfer it to clinical improvisation. These and myriad other compositional devices are available to the music therapist from the Mass.

Lutheran belief advocated that the true purpose of music was to glorify God (Marissen, 1995). Bach was inextricably tied to the church and his religious connections colored every aspect of his music. How different therefore is Bach's secular from his sacred music and with what intent, if any, did he approach both forms of composition? It can be argued that Bach's secular music contains the same spiritual content as his sacred music. How different, for example, are the sophisticated instrumental inventions of the Brandenburg concertos compared to similar instrumental music of the Mass? Even though one is depicting the glory of God and the other was a commission from court, I believe both include music of the highest spiritual worth. The choice of the B minor Mass for this chapter was not chosen because of its theological content but because of the music and its potential impact for clinical work. It is impossible, however, to separate the religious source of the Mass and its influence on Bach's musical invention. Is music beyond theological context because it is man-made, or is Bach's music itself–apart from religious connections–the source of spiritual inspiration? Bach's music is relevant to AeMT because it contains a purity of musical invention, a clarity of form that links clearly to the clarity of the therapeutic process. If we believe that spirituality and music are equal then to reflect on Bach's B minor Mass as a source of learning for music therapy is invaluable.

Chapter Three

LIVING IN PLAYING: A GROUP CASE STUDY

They said, "You have a blue guitar,
You do not play things as they are."

The man replied, "Things as they are
Are changed upon the blue guitar."

And they said then, "But play, you must,
A tune beyond us, yet ourselves,

A tune upon the blue guitar,
Of things exactly as they are."

–Wallace Stevens,
"The Man with the Blue Guitar" (1937)

This chapter is an evaluation of ten sessions with a group of clients living with HIV/AIDS. The extracts from sessions on the accompanying CD emphasize the importance of musical reality in assessing AeMT. Music is the most important component of this chapter. Music holds the clues to understanding the therapeutic process and creative expression of living with HIV/AIDS. The words are a guide to help balance and provide a framework for understanding the musical and therapeutic form of this compelling work.

Music therapists tend to focus their energies on either group or individual work, the choice often coming from the exterior sources of the setting in which they work. The therapist's own preference–depending upon theoretical and philosophical orientation–is a more fascinating and complex subject. As my clinical work developed I became more invested in individual work. I found the musical elements of group work to be complex and challenging. Meeting and reflecting the many sounds of a group improvisation invoked a collective potency that needed intricate understanding of the process. During my formative years as a therapist I felt unable to provide the necessary responses, musically or verbally, this work demanded. Balancing musical and therapeutic meaning, especially with verbally articulate clients, I felt at the time would need further education in group psychotherapy. As my work became more immersed in music and with the inception of sessions with clients living with HIV and AIDS, I again returned to the potential of group music therapy.

This case - study is described from an AeMT perspective. The musical interactions come from a belief that the improvisational structure is based on an understanding of the musical qualities in each developing moment. While that is not to deny the potential for a psychotherapeutic perspective, as in *Music at the Edge* (Lee, 1996) I have chosen not to offer in-depth nonmusical interpretations. Rather, this case - study focuses on the immediacy of interpersonal contacts within the group and how they were reflected through the music. The precision and collaboration of discourse in this group was sophisticated and presented many fascinating conundrums in further questioning the musical processes of group improvisational music therapy.

THERAPEUTIC STRUCTURES AND MUSICAL INTERVENTIONS

Group work often takes the form of words-music-words (Priestly, 1994). Music is used as a means to access and promote verbal interactions:

> Through music, there can be a resonance of . . . thoughts and feelings. For many . . . , words are not sufficient to portray what they feel, so music becomes their mode of expression. Through the musical expression, new roads are traveled, new signposts seen, and answers come not only musically, but often back to the spoken word. Thus a full circle is realized in the process beginning with words, leaving the words to explore musically, and then coming back to find the right words for verbal processing. (Borczon, 1997 ,p. 9)

What then of group work that does not necessitate the need to begin or return to words? The potential form becomes silence-music-silence. To find the "right words for verbal processing" I believe places an expectation on music to be something other than itself. AeMT is concerned with finding the right music for the expression of the group rather than a means to aid verbal interpretation. This, I believe, places music as the core rather than as a by-product. The question often raised is that if the musical experience is not placed within the conscious logic of a verbal framework, then its clinical validity is questionable. I believe the insistence on words to interpret musical articulation to be equally questionable. To bridge the gap between the unconscious articulation of music and the conscious rationality of words is, I believe, a specific endeavor. Verbally articulate clients often express their desire not to talk through extended and potent silences. Does the therapist impose that to complete is to speak, or do they allow closure through the natural completion of music and silence? That AeMT is not dependent on verbal processing means that our understanding of clients' growth can be understood through the structures of music itself. For nonverbal clients moving between silence-music-silence; this can release the expectation of words that so often causes frustration in the therapeutic alliance. The challenge of "to speak or not to speak" is equal of "to play or not to play." To create music, hold silence, or verbally intervene is a clinical choice that should be taken individually and not theoretically. Thus music psychotherapy should be able to embrace purely musical expression and AeMT needs to include verbal processing when appropriate.

So what of the musical role of the therapist in AeMT and what interventions are clinically appropriate in group work? AeMT group work is based entirely on clinical improvisation. The following observations are written from an improvisational perspective. The ideas presented, however, are appropriate for therapists who also use improvisation as just one part of their therapeutic offerings. Taking a continuum from nonparticipation (playing little) to full - participation (playing fully), the therapist must decide when to intervene, on what level, and the intensity of music needed to reflect the moment-to-moment expression of the group. Typically in group music psychotherapy the therapist does not take a leading musical role. The therapist is physically connected to the group by playing similar percussion instruments and sitting as an equal member of the group. The therapists' musical voice in this instance is essentially non-directive. Therapists also use their principle instruments other than piano (e.g. flute, cello, guitar), as a means to mediate the dynamics of the group. The use of orchestral instruments in group work provides a balance for the therapist's role and allows group members to feel physically connected. The therapist's musical role here often has a greater impact on the overall texture and form of the improvisation.

The piano brings both problems and advantages to group work. Due to its size it is impossible for the piano to be an equal physical member of a group. Its musical potential, however, far outweighs its disadvantages. The piano can enrich the musical intricacies of a group. It has the ability to provide melodic simplicity as well as complex harmony, counterpoint, and orchestral textures. The piano can capture the embodiment of a group while allowing individual voices to be heard. Using the piano as a musical catalyst in group improvisations can enrich and help promote music therapy goals.

It is important to clarify the role of the therapist-pianist within the musical exchanges of the group. When facilitating a group from the piano it is the aim of the therapist to meet and communicate the musical expression of the group. The therapist may contest and confront the group dynamics if this is considered appropriate. Because the piano is potentially directive it is important that the group understand that the therapist's skills help determine the instrument's role within the group, and that the role of the therapist-pianist is to meet, reflect, support, and confront. The therapist may sense an experience the group is trying to reach that through specific musical techniques it is possible for the group to achieve. From an aesthetic perspective in group improvisations the therapist is concerned with the actualities of sound as they impact the process, thus providing for the group a musical experience they may not be able to achieve alone. AeMT differentiates itself from other nondirective group improvisational approaches with regard to the therapists input. Decisions and boundaries of the therapist are dependent on a balance between the aesthetic and the clinical, and clarity of group goals. Transforming the strands of individual voices is a challenging musical process that once attained can bring enlightenment to the group. Techniques and resources provide the necessary skills for the specific needs of AeMT group work.

The musical components used in group work are integral to the therapeutic process. The use of clinical music should be conscious and finely graded. Listening to the often disparate sounds of a group requires good clinical musicianship. To reflect and transform a coherent musical whole is one of the main aims of AeMT group work. While this does not negate the clinical relevance of containing and accepting chaos as a group expression, it is my belief that simultaneity is the first step in the developing therapeutic process. The therapist's skills in facilitating group improvisations is highly complex. Not only must the therapist be able to clinically listen to each voice and combinations thereof, he/she must also be able to respond and make sense of each of the intermusical and interpersonal representations of the group. Clinical listening in group work demands meticulousness and perception of response.

THE LIGHTHOUSE GROUP

London Lighthouse, a residential and support center for men and women affected by HIV and AIDS, was founded in 1986 (Spence, 1996) in response to the pandemic of these viruses. Most of the documented music therapy work detailed from London Lighthouse is based on individual work (Hartley, 1999, Lee, 1996, Pavlicevic, 1997). Group work with clients living with HIV and AIDS can be difficult due to the different needs of asymptomatic and symptomatic clients. My experience at Lighthouse was based on closed groups that ran for ten-week cycles. The maximum number in each group was eight and every self-referred client met with me, the therapist, individually prior to the commencement of sessions. Regular attendance was often difficult due to the changing nature of some client's health. The therapeutic process shifted accordingly. The three groups I facilitated at Lighthouse were influential in the evolving principles of AeMT. The musical sophistication and explosion of group dynamics can be heard in the accompanying audio examples of this study. They demonstrate the potency of improvisational groups with HIV and AIDS.

The clinical applications and aims of AeMT group work grew spontaneously during my work at Lighthouse. I had been offering individual music therapy sessions for almost a year prior to the inception of group work. I tried not to premeditate what the aims of this work might be. I guessed that the issues facing a group of clients with HIV and AIDS would be different from individual work. Some of the aims of individual and group work shown below highlight the differing needs for inclusion in each process:

Aims of individual work

- to express frustration and anger at living with HIV and AIDS
- to face personal loss
- to express nonverbally intense feelings and emotions
- to find healthy alternatives of coping and living
- to share individually with a therapist
- to face one's own death and dying

Aims of group work

- to share with other people living with HIV and AIDS
- to express collective feelings of frustration and anger
- to share personal loss
- to find collective musical rapture
- to build healthy group relationships
- to support peers living with HIV and AIDS

It is interesting to note that referrals to individual work mention the need to face loss, whereas in group work a need to share and support seems most important.

The following musical and therapeutic themes were crucial in the developing group work at Lighthouse:

- the use of descriptive musical textures
- the use of specific instrumental combinations

- the balance between words and music
- the meaning of one complete improvisation per session as opposed to several smaller ones
- the musical representation of loss
- the use of tonality and atonality to express the group process
- the use of untuned percussion in portraying frustration and anger

As these themes developed and grew within the group, certain characteristics of improvisational playing became evident:

- lack of rhythmic clarity–rhythms with little or no regular pulse and rhythms that were perseverative and lifeless
- musical aggression–loud playing, often over long periods
- the avoidance of melodic expression
- a preference for minor keys, modes, and atonality
- the use of the cell and seed motive
- musical representation of opposites

The balance between therapeutic aims and musical representation is at the heart of this work. The aesthetic content of sessions was often brutal and offensive (Lee & Khare, 2001), and the aesthetic consideration of group members and the process, intricate. Moments of introversion did appear as crucial experiences of musical rapture. These moments were significant in the cohesion of the group. The balance between words and music found a natural level as the improvisations became a clear representation of the groups' needs and direction. As with individual work the more influential the music became the less need there was for verbal processing. The move from words-music-words to silence-music-silence was witnessed in each of the three groups at Lighthouse.

THE SESSIONS

The four members of the group were:

- John (25)–a quiet retiring man who played and spoke only when he had something to say. His music felt like an accompaniment for the rest of the group.

- Ian (28)–came to sessions with vigor and determination to play. His music was often based around rock rhythms that were influenced by his experience as a young man in marching bands.

- Terry (20)–was immediately aware and sensitive to the group dynamics. His music was strong and rhythmic.

- Simon (23)–the least sure of the group, who missed several sessions. His place in the music was not always clear. His most personally influential improvisations were at the piano.

All were HIV-positive and asymptomatic though Ian began to show symptoms as the sessions progressed. John, Ian, and Simon had never improvised before. None of the group had received formal musical training and no one knew each other before the sessions began. Sessions were one hour in length. The group found styles of improvising that reflected the unique nature of each member and the group as a whole:

- fast, furious, atonal percussion playing
- melodic improvisations on tuned percussion
- the use of recorders as a means to "sing"
- long, slow tonal moving phrases
- rhythmically pulsed playing
- rhythmically unpulsed playing
- the piano as a vehicle for harmony (note: the piano was used not only by the therapist, but by all group members)
- improvisations with no piano
- long extended silences

A sense of chamber music permeated all the sessions.

The sessions were held in the music therapy room, Ian McKellan Hall at London Lighthouse (Lee, 1996 p. 5). Included was a grand piano and an extensive range of tuned and untuned percussion instruments. The following description, taken from my indexing and assessment notes, are written in a free-flowing format. This shows, along with the two audio examples, the sense of excitement and fervor this group entered into as a part of their therapeutic process.

Session One

The session opened with a verbal discussion on the possibilities for the group. Everyone introduced themselves and made a brief opening statement. Each member expressed their eagerness to explore through music. My role as therapist was defined as one who would musically and therapeutically meet, contemplate, and contain the revelations of the group as they occurred. Verbal reflections would be included if needed at the end of the session or directly after an improvisation. It was felt that words should be in a physically different space to music-making. A circle of chairs was therefore arranged next to the instruments.

The one improvisation of this session began with everyone playing fast, furious music. As is natural for a group of people who have never played music together, everyone improvised constantly, loudly, and frenetically. Underneath this explosion of sound there was also a sense of rumbling that was to become the cornerstone of Terry's emotional/musical contribution to the group. After approximately twenty minutes of continuous playing, where there seemed little or no sense of group listening, the intensity of the music suddenly ceased:

Audio Extract One: Session One, Improvisation One (twenty minutes after the opening)

- Ian/Terry–drums and cymbal, John/Simon–xylophone, Colin–piano
- A sense of quiet exploration
- (20:44) Xylophone and percussion explore the group musical relationship
- The therapist reflects the musical dialogue from a distance
- The xylophone initiates a clear rhythm in 4/4
- This theme moves the music into an exciting affirmation of playing
- A rock-based experience that Ian described as being reminiscent of the group Santana
- Listen to the excitement of beginning musical identities and group music-making

My assessment of this session included the following notes:

- huge musical experiences–organic and free
- an immediate sense of group
- improvisation influenced by drum and rock music
- a sense of energy and expectation
- a sense of gentleness and vulnerability
- a group that feels alive and running (I think I am trying to catch them!)
- carefully balanced texture of xylophone, drums, and piano
- a group with overwhelming promise

I left the session enthralled and astounded at the accomplishment five people, who had never improvised together, had achieved.

Session Two

The group entered and they immediately expressed their desire to play. The first improvisation (12'31") was firmly grounded in a rock idiom, and exhibited acute listening and shape with an already complex dialogue of musical voices. The second improvisation (32'02"), was bigger in architectural form; a slow and gradual build of emotional/musical form. The xylophone (John) introduced small almost imperceptible themes that would be taken as a group theme. These were interspersed with sudden intense explosions of drumming (Ian), that would come to the fore and then pull back–a sense of needing and breaking free. Toward the end of the improvisation (25'56"), the music became caught in patterns strongly reminiscent of minimalist music. There was a pause and a coda of quiet nonpulsed playing.

Session Three

The one improvisation (45'33") of this session was impenetrable. The structure was enormous and fell into the following form: A (forceful loud,) B (calm and gentle), A, C (without piano), A, D (Ian–piano), A. Words and phrases from my assessment best describe the essence of this session:

- musical exploration as therapeutic process
- complex dialogues–my role as therapist facilitating the organic growth of the group
- does this music portray the battle of living with HIV and AIDS?
- a balance between consonant and nonconsonant expression
- Ian's beautifully controlled and expressive piano playing was an inspiration

The group dynamics were becoming complex and stronger. In the discussion following this improvisation John and Simon expressed their feelings of acceptance: that although their voices were not equal in dynamic musical content, they felt heard and embraced by the rest of the group. Ian's musical voice was becoming stronger and more personal. Terry seemed confident in his playing and would always meet Ian's rock style of improvising.

Session Four

(Simon absent) The two improvisations of this session (16'37" and 11'39"), were structurally led and developed through the xylophone playing of John. The long extended silence held at the beginning of the session was broken by Ian's quiet solo piano playing. This felt like an extension of his piano improvisation from the previous session. As the music developed, a granite-like quality emerged providing music that was syncopated and forceful. After a huge climax (10'15'), the music subsided, building again to another peak dominated by Ian's piano playing. The second improvisation was calm and musically lead by John on the xylophone.

At the end of the session, even though Simon was absent, a discussion took place as to the developing relationships and group process. I wondered if Ian's growing dominance within the group, always supported by Terry, might in some way undermine or usurp John's more introverted contributions. The group indeed seemed more aware of their differing roles and levels. My sense that Ian was surprised at his developing place within the group was supported through his declaration that he was potentially becoming symptomatic. This news along with the possibility of a new drug regime had given him a new sense of creative freedom. Ian felt able to take musical chances, to dare to express parts of himself that he would normally keep hidden. He felt that even after four sessions the group was sufficiently supportive and able to allow him such personal release. The response from the group to this statement was overwhelming.

Session Five

The words that opened this session were important as they acknowledged Ian's testimony from the previous session. The silence that followed led into the one improvisation of the session (32'52"). The first extended section (A) was on untuned percussion without piano. This led (27'44") to an unexpected light and frivolous Spanish passage. The piano was initially played by myself and then Ian as he accompanied the wood block (John) and tambourine (Simon). A sudden menacing explosion broke across this music (Ian and Terry) providing a feeling of being on the edge of a precipice. The music unexpectedly returned to the lightness of the Spanish idiom. This idea was developed to the end of the improvisation. There was little conversation at the end yet a sense of struggle between the intensity of Ian and Terry and the lightness of John and Simon.

Session Six

The group entered and immediately began playing scattered frenetic music. As the therapist I tried to contain the disparate strands of their music. The sense of freedom and excitement was addictive. The music built and built and built . . . there were screams of excitement . . . complex rhythms appeared . . . the music momentarily stopped (8'41") and then built to an ever greater peak of total frenzy (9'31"). My assessment notes gave an indication of the fervor of this session:

- what's happening?–the wildest improvisation I have been a part of
- playing of extreme energy that gets more and more energized
- difficult to find my place and role in the music
- everyone is caught in the musical hysteria
- the improvisation gets faster and faster . . . wilder and wilder
- a sense of total musical and therapeutic cathartic freedom

There were no words at the end of this session, just feelings of exhilaration and exhaustion.

Session Seven

(Simon absent) A quiet session led by John, supported by Ian and Terry. A sense of quiet after the storm.

Session Eight

The opening verbal dialogue acknowledged the three sessions left before the end of the group. Following an extended silence the first improvisation (12'38") explored musical floating and glass-like textures. The improvisation was devoid of established rhythmic or melodic content. Supportive listening continued as the group attempted to find an equality of music-making. The second improvisation (19'55") was similarly calm and nonintrusive. The four members rarely played together, the two extended chamber music sections consisting of A) piano (myself), xylophone (John), and recorder (Terry) and B) cymbal (Simon) and piano (Ian). The musical/personal intimacy captured in this session was enigmatic.

Session Nine

This session contained the apex of our work. The one improvisation (42'31") was created with musical and therapeutic precision. It began quietly building through exquisite serenity and equilibrium.

Audio Extract Two: Session Nine (fifteen minutes after the opening)

- Ian/Terry–drums/cymbal/gong, John/Simon–xylophones, Colin–piano
- xylophones and piano explore melodic phrases
- Musical strands naturally interweave
- Gong and percussion appear as the intensity grows
- Music that is both sensitive and yet powerful

This is one of the clearest examples of AeMT I can offer in this book. It was a perfect example and union of therapy and art. My voice both leads and contains the emotional edge of the music. It was not subservient and yet was delicately poised over the group as clear negotiator. As the music became more and more intense the dynamics of the group melded and the five players became one.

The short verbal discussion of this session was limited to a few simple words that tried to help describe the intimacy we had all shared.

Session Ten

The group entered and immediately began improvising. There was a quiet determination from everyone. This improvisation was the longest we had created (58'32"). The structure was based around the opposing music that had been the hallmark of our work. Delicate music on tuned percussion was balanced with loud aggressive music on untuned percussion. The improvisation was grand and emotional. Small chamber music combinations balanced with elaborate orchestral textures. Toward the end of the improvisation an extraordinary event occurred: the music began to fall apart. It was as if the group tried to sabotage any sense of a coherent ending. An extroverted and playful rhumba (49'12") appeared that was menacing and cliched. I was initially surprised at this musical turn but soon realized that a balanced ending would be impossible for the group. Staying and holding their musical insecurity, here the intensity of four was far greater than the similar individual experiences I had encountered. It was difficult to stay and hold this intense and strange turn of events.

As the music concluded there was a long and uncomfortable silence. Each group member simply said "thank you" and left the room. Three of the group members self-referred themselves for the next set of sessions: John, Terry, and Simon. Ian did not return to Lighthouse.

REFLECTIONS

This group, the first of three at Lighthouse, was an important step in my analysis of the sophistication of a music-centered approach to group work. My role as composer/music therapist was tested to the extreme. What resulted was an eruption of artistic, clinical, and compositional connections that combined to present another approach to my developing work in AeMT. The musical components of every moment, phrase, and complete improvisation were intensive and complex, yet structured from the simplest and logical of ideas. The music shaped the therapeutic process with a different clarity from that of individual work. The many sounds introduced a complexity of musical/group dynamics that further validated the need to look at the musical structures of the process. Clinically listening to groups and attempting to find a form of indexing that acknowledged the complexities of group form continued as I attempted to delve deeper into my understanding of the link between therapeutic intent and musical articulation. Analysis of the therapeutic process is critical. To interpret music as an agent of change we must first understand the structures of music itself and how it is communicated between fellow human beings. In group work the precision of musical contact and analysis becomes ever more complex.

This case-study does not include the verbal reflections or my counter-transference responses. You will note that even though verbal processing did take place, it was not the central focus of the group. This material is presented as factual and unbiased in the hope that colleagues from different philosophical backgrounds may interpret and understand the group's meaning from their own perspective. It is my hope that through the description of the process the reader/listener will gain a sense of the emotional strength of this group. The power of the audio examples included attest to the potency of a music-centered approach to group work with clients with HIV and AIDS.

Chapter Four

TONE, FORM, AND ARCHITECTURE

> The single harmony produced by all the heavenly bodies singing and dancing together springs from one source and ends by achieving one purpose, and rightly bestowed the name not of "disordered" but of "ordered universe" upon the whole.
>
> –Aristotle (384–322 BC), *Metaphysics,* quoted in Watson (1994)

To a layperson, the word "clinical" conveys images of white coats and medical procedures. Considering the music therapy relationship as clinical seems at odds with one's usual beliefs and experiences of music. How can a music therapist provide clinical music and how can a therapeutic relationship be clinical? In this context, "clinical" denotes clarity rather than sterility. Clinical music is central to AeMT because it substantiates the importance of music in the process. To be a clinical musician is to be aware of every component, its content, and the potential it has to affect the developing relationship and therapeutic direction. Clinical music should have structure but also be structurally free, be able to move into any key, change texture and transform as the therapy dictates. Clinical interpretations, influences, and assumptions come from an understanding of assessment and ongoing evaluation.

What makes music clinical is the intent with which it is used. Whether using improvisational or precomposed music, the purpose of the music should be carefully directed toward the client's needs and the therapeutic process. Neither aesthetic quality nor clinical direction should be allowed to overpower the other under the therapist's conscious and directed use of music.

Balancing the aesthetic and clinical features of improvisation is no easy task. For these characteristics to be truly balanced we must know and understand both music and therapy. In our quest to understand the medicine of music therapy have we sacrificed our awareness of its art? Many music therapists read clinical literature at the expense of music writings because they believe that such literature is more important and relevant to their evolving work. Music therapists converse on clinical theories at many levels, but rarely discuss the musical makeup of their work.

Recent writings are now beginning to redress this imbalance (Aigen 2001, Austin 2001, Bonny 2001, Bruscia 2001, Hesser 2001, Soshensky 2001), although there is a long way to go before the research of music therapy is equally weighted between the art and science of its practice. Have music therapists failed to recognize that most clients naturally find this balance in their work? If indeed this is the case then are we perhaps not listening carefully or deeply enough to our clients?

Paul, a seven-year-old nonverbal client with Down's syndrome, taught me the significance of balancing the artistic and the therapeutic. Embracing his explosions of creativity within a clearly directed process was difficult. To find equilibrium between the freedom of inspiration and the precision of direction was a constant challenge as we negotiated the twists and turns of the therapeutic process. Paul would become caught in the discharge of his playing and resistive to change. Our relationship battled between the inventiveness of music and his resistance to any form of guidance. I could not move him beyond a certain point without his becoming controlling and disturbed.

The strength needed to move along and yet keep the innovation that was at the heart of our work came in the twenty-fifth session. After a long and thunderous improvisation on drum and cymbal, Paul spontaneously sat next to me at the piano. Continuing the intensity of his playing at the piano, he also began to vocalize–immense ascending phrases, which, along with hand-clapping rhythmic phrases, added to the musical energy. As the intensity of the music decreased I segued into his good-bye song. Paul immediately began to sing "Bye." This was the first time he had consciously vocalized specific words in response to a given situation. The experience was now one of acute learning and direct musical communication. For approximately ten minutes Paul and I worked at extending his vocalization to "good-bye."

We played with musical questions and answers and he experimented with being able to sing and play simultaneously. The experience became balanced between learning and the musical freedom that was the groundwork for his musical expression. My role in facilitating this equilibrium came through acceptance alongside a constant and step-by-step belief in Paul's ability to focus and to comprehend. The aesthetics of the music, our relationship, and his eventual enlightenment facilitated a genuine parity between the artistic and the therapeutic in our work.

THE AESTHETIC THERAPEUTIC RELATIONSHIP

Relationship is fundamental to music therapy. In music-making, the relationship between the players and the aesthetic outcome is fundamental to our understanding of the process. Just as my values and vulnerability as a human being affect my responses, so my musical perceptions of the therapeutic relationship influence the content of my improvisations. Boundaries and professional distance are necessary for the well-being of the therapist. Honesty and insecurity also play important roles in the responses of the therapist to the client. There is a danger in remaining too musically separate, making the client feel apart from the process; there is also a danger in being too compassionate so that the client feels overwhelmed by the well-meaning and often effusive style of the music. It is easy in music to over-identify and to find oneself caught in playing improvisations that are more reflective of the therapist than the client.

What then of an aesthetic relationship that is agitated and unbalanced?

> The aesthetic potential of therapeutic resistance and disturbance is equal to considering the rounded expression of the beautiful. Aesthetic here means both the offensive and the beautiful. (Lee & Khare, 2001, p.268)

The aesthetics of the music therapy relationship are fundamental to our understanding of the client and his or her music. To consider the client, no matter how disturbed or ill, as aesthetic and therefore see the relationship as fragile and elegant is to transfer to music a sense of the comely that is at the heart of music itself. Just as beautiful music is not dependent on consonance of sounds, so beauty in the therapeutic relationship is not dependent on conformity and refinement. Sometimes to be musically aggressive is to be liberated, free, and beautiful:

> The periods of wild free playing are very important for me and balance the times when the music is more controlled. It is at these times that I can lose control, be frenzied and let go of all my inhibitions. To be angry, violent and not worry about what I do musically. I don't think however that we are ever completely chaotic. We accept the chaos of our relationship but we don't want it to be chaotic, (Eddie, a client living with HIV).

The aesthetics of all relationships have the potential to metamorphose. The therapeutic relationship through music finds a balance, one that is reliant on yet free from the constraints of pathology and illness.

Clients often refer to the release of musical expression as being like flying. The aesthetics of musical flying and the therapeutic relationship can transcend the bounds of living and dying:

> Through music I fly. In improvising I leave behind the realities of my illness, my tumor and the degeneration of my living. I portray my anger and feelings of hopelessness. The music we make is not pleasant and often feels intolerable. We do not try to "fix it," we explore it and let it be. (Carol, a client with cancer)

Flying in music is, I believe, an ultimate experience. Musical flying can suggest a progression in the developing process and the therapeutic relationship. Flying in improvisation can be organized yet free; it is a representation of the client's growth and a need to express cathartically.

There are many ways that people make music. In the classical style there is orchestral, chamber, or operatic music; pop music is created through singers and bands; in jazz through small and large combos; and in music therapy through group and individual work. All of these are comprised of common elements and yet ostensibly music therapy would seem the odd one out. Why is this? When we enter music-making we leave behind the laws of realities and conscious logic. Whether there is union through a Beethoven violin sonata, a pop song, a jazz duet, or an improvisation in music therapy, the dialogue between players can be seen to be of a similar nature. Is music-making in music therapy dissimilar to other forms? I would suggest not. The intertwining of clinical direction and aesthetic value in music therapy is a manifestation of musical direction and freedom. If we truly hear our clients in music, then the aesthetic flying in the process may be the same as that of the string quartet's spiritual connections in Beethoven's Op. 132 as analyzed in Chapter Nine. If we enable our clients to experience the musical-spiritual connection, then perhaps in some small way we have added to the richness of their existence.

In AeMT the role of the therapist is that of both clinical musician and composer. All music therapists who improvise are composers and all music therapists who think intensely about their work are clinicians. Does this also mean that all clients are potential composers and clinicians? What distinguishes AeMT is the idea of first understanding the nature of clinical music before interpreting the process:

> Until we understand music itself we can never understand the effect it has to change people's lives. (Lee & Khare, 2001, p. 247)

The therapist's first and foremost attribute is to be an accomplished musician. Once musical fluency has been achieved the therapist can start adapting music to the specifics of clinical situations. In AeMT it is music that is the genesis and which remains the guide for the therapist's developing work. Musicality is not placed second to music's clinical application. In fact, the emphasis on music becomes stronger as the therapist perceives with greater detail the balance between the art and the science of their practice. The role of the clinical musician is thus to:

- listen musically
- listen clinically
- evaluate sounds as part of the process
- respond to sounds as a musician
- respond to sounds as a clinician
- have a clear perception of musical aims
- have a clear perception of clinical aims, and
- respond with quality and aesthetically embodied music.

ASPECTS OF PROCESS

The process of music therapy has been researched and discussed at great length. What is the music therapy process, how do we define and quantify it, and how will our greater understanding of it increase the value of the work being done in both the medical and artistic communities? The following subsections are contemplations about areas that have been important to the development of AeMT. They are aspects that have been developed through my teaching and clinical practice. The answers to the mysteries of the music therapy process are to be found in the music dialogue and relationship. The process is dependent on a comprehension of the realities of musical structure, shape, and form.

If we allow for the intricate balance of the artistic dimensions that client and therapist bestow on the process, then music and therapy will become an integral characterization of the client's aspirations as creative musician and composer. To understand the process of AeMT is in essence simple because there is clarity in its musical intent. Taking music as the essence does not however, negate the potency of clinical analysis. In fact, it heightens it. Once a clear comprehension of clinical music is established then extramusical theories can be investigated with solidarity and insight. Analysis of the process without understanding of the musical underpinnings that informs it will, I believe, be inherently flawed.

Musical Choice

Why do music therapists use specific intervals, tones, melodies, rhythmic patterns, or harmonic progressions? What is it about the therapeutic relationship and ongoing aims of therapy that dictate the therapist's musical choice? Musical choice is a combination of assessment, inventiveness, structure, relationship, and process. Why and how do we repeat musical themes and what learned resources enable the therapist to improvise, remember, and repeat? Therapists must be clear in their musical choices and be able to justify their specific musical/clinical choices. Musical choice should not be indecisive but a finite decision made with precision and insight. During every moment of an improvisation the therapist and client are faced with musical choices. As the parameters expand, so do the minutiae of musical dialogue that are open to creative and informed possibilities. The client's choices are dependent on the therapist's ability to offer a range of musical opportunities. As therapists develop their improvisational skills their proficiency in facilitating choice will expand. The intersecting of musical abilities enables the strength of the process to influence the developing relationship and thus the course of therapy.

Therapists will initially offer wrong musical choices. This addresses the importance of ongoing supervision. In supervision and through indexing the therapist is able to look specifically at the musical paths taken and to reflect on the clinical reasons for the choices made. Through guided reflection the therapist will understand the significance of musical choice. Analyzing specific moments and using them as a base to extend musical resources will result in an enrichment of ideas that can be taken into future sessions.

Taking Risks

To live is to risk. Every therapeutic encounter contains risks. To enter a music therapy session as client or therapist is to risk the unknown. To wait for the client, to hear their first sounds, and to respond through spontaneous improvisation is full of musical and human risks. If therapists decide they fully know their practice and work only from the bounds of that approach they will soon become stagnant. The strength found in acquiring knowledge and then relinquishing it to risk is a mystery. Like the process of therapy itself, risks are balanced through knowledge and understanding. The music therapist must always be prepared to take risks from a base that is clinically clear and focused.

Taking musical risks is challenging and can be liberating for both therapist and client. Preparation allows the therapist to bring to a therapy session that which has been derived through assessing the direction from previous work. The therapist's need to rely on familiar music should be balanced with sections of openness, unpredictability, and that essence of "not knowing" that is at the heart of clinical improvisation. This does not mean that music should be unprepared even in the freest of improvisations. From detailed evaluation of previous sessions the therapist is given a myriad of themes and ideas to practice and consider. The therapist should come to a session with a mental and aural encyclopedia of music that has been acquired and that is appropriate for the particular client. Having this vast range of music available, the therapist must then be prepared to relinquish these conscious themes and to place them in his or her subconscious. Only then will the resulting music be a true reflection of the moment-to-moment expression of the client.

Cues

Aural and visual cues in clinical improvisation are a sophisticated form of nonverbal communication (Smith, 1998) necessary to balance the evolving musical structure. The need for cuing comes from the belief that therapists should never verbally converse with clients during music-making. Therapists working together must refine their relationship to include cues that are acutely sophisticated. Nordoff and Robbins's (in press) articulation of the roles of therapist and co-therapist include sensitive cues that are central to the tripartite relationship of individual work and the more complex dynamics of group work. Therapist and co-therapist communicate through sophisticated visual cues that include the glance of an eye or the nod of a head. The evolving relationship between therapist and co-therapist, therapist and client, and co-therapist and client, is heightened by the subtleties of visual cues. Once the client becomes aware of the potential for nonverbal visual direction they too will include visual cuing as a part of their communication.

Musical cues are equally refined. As the structure of an improvisation develops so musical form becomes clear for the direction of therapy. Cadencing, pausing and tonal and melodic direction can all herald the segue into a new section or the recapitulation of an idea that has already been developed. Each of these acts as a cue that does not detract from the overall flow but help participants to understand their place within the music. The therapist must be keenly aware not to exercise his or her ego within this context, as was previously discussed. The combination of aural and visual cues provides a level of nonverbal refinement that is essential for the complex musical manifestations of AeMT. Just as jazz musicians use aural and visual clues to challenge their creative playing so the client and therapist(s) will use cues in the moment-to-moment expression of their therapeutic intention.

Keeping Going

One of the greatest fears for any improviser is the possibility of paralysis and the inability to keep going.

> Keeping it going means that something has to be there to do next. And since what is there is not concrete or written down, it must be something remembered and reproduced intact on the spot, or something created extemporaneously by recombining stored musical information in a new way that is appropriate to the music situation of the moment, (Slawek, 1998, p. 336)

The art of clinically applied improvised music is dependent on repertoire and exacting assessment. In music therapy the music is kept going through: a) developing resources, b) responses and creativity of the client, c) the aims of the moment and overall design of the session, and d) incorporating previous material. I have found from experience that the music will rarely lose direction if the therapist is knowledgeable about the music needed for the therapeutic partnership and is free from inhibition.

Every therapeutic musical contact does, however, contain the possibility that the therapist, for whatever reason, may not be able to keep going. Is this a consequence of the therapist's musical inability, the client's resistance, a reflection of the therapeutic relationship, or the need to musically rest? If the therapist is unable to keep going these questions should be addressed during assessment and supervision. What if the client needs to keep the music going but is unable to do so? What role does the therapist play in facilitating a musical experience that will allow the music to establish direction? The therapist must listen to the strands and reconnect them so that the client can return to the musical dialogue. If the music fails because of the client's lack of technique then the therapist must improvise themes that will reestablish the music seamlessly.

Musical Equality

The Venda taught me that music can never be a thing in itself, and that all music is folk music, in the sense that music cannot be transmitted or have meaning without associations between people (Blacking, 1973 pp. x–xi).

Many folk, jazz, and pop musicians who do not have formal musical education are adept and skilled. In light of this, clients can often be the musical equals of the therapists. Music therapy challenges the hierarchical implication that musicianship is about knowing and education. To envision clients as inherent artists is to respect their creativity as equal to those of trained musicians. AeMT derives its approaches from the musical equality of client and therapist. Its philosophy is based on the assumption that music translates equality and that a therapeutic dialogue in music is founded on different human principles and logic rather than on the consciousness of words. A musical relationship will find a level of human contact that cannot be premeditated in therapeutic terms from the rationality of conscious and verbal logic.

Musical parity does not, however, mean that the boundaries of the therapeutic relationship are in danger of disintegrating. Rather, it emphasizes the need to look beyond the inequality of the therapist as learned and the client as uninformed participant. Music therapy does not require an educational imbalance, yet it requires much education on the part of the therapist. I believe that to fully understand therapeutic interaction through improvisation, we must look further to what it means to be musically equal with our clients.

The myth that fully understanding music is for the intellectual few is a view that has corrupted Western classical music. The concept that an autistic child can create music comparable to that of a trained musician may at first seem ludicrous. If we accept the possibility that a person with a disability can contribute to music as much as a trained musician then where does this place music therapy within the development of music? What does this also say about Western "art" music and the lack of spontaneous creativity and improvisation placed within the education of musicians?

Music therapy has helped broaden the definition of what constitutes being musical. When Blacking (1973) asks "How musical is man?", he raises a fundamental question for music therapy:

> We need to know what sounds and what kind of behavior different societies have chosen to call "musical"; and until we know more about this we cannot begin to answer the question, "How musical is man?" (pp. 4–5)

Are all human beings–and therefore clients–musical, and to what level of musicianship can our clients aspire? The music therapist must hear every sound and nuance of the client as being intently musical. If we are not clinical in our musical listening then we will miss crucial components of the therapeutic process. A musician would probably not consider a spontaneous scream to be musical, but music therapists will consider the scream as containing tone and musical inflection. They will attempt to place the quality of its sounds within the overall structure of the music.

That all clients have the potential to be great musicians is what makes music therapy such a driving force for the future of music and medicine. Maggie, a thirty-year-old, nonverbal, quadriplegic blind woman, taught me that disability and musical genius are not mutually exclusive concepts. Her musical expression through voice and delicate cymbal playing was of the highest compositional order. She instinctively knew form and was able to create music that was exquisitely crafted and designed. I believe that if Maggie had been born without her profound disabilities she might have been a great musician. The privilege and responsibility of considering clients as musical equals are the characteristics that bestow upon music therapy its unique characterization and contribution to society.

TONE

Tone is the genesis from which all possibilities of AeMT develop. The tone as an intangible yet grounded experience helps to define the potential for the therapeutic relationship. By considering the nature of the tone, its relation to the client, the music, and the therapeutic process, the therapist begins to understand the complexities of clinical improvisation. "Tone is described here as a single pitch that may also be described in terms of its quality, character, timbre, color, and intensity of singing and/or playing" (Lee & Khare, 2001). As the tone provides the beginnings for composition, so in clinical improvisation it presents endless possibilities for the musical and therapeutic alliance.

The tone exists as a question that calls to be answered and placed in context by other evolving tones. The change that comes through the introduction of a tone and the musical direction that ensues is dependent on quality, duration, and pitch. The tone immediately searches for balance and development.

> The tone seems to point beyond itself toward release from tension and restoration of equilibrium; it seems to look in a definite direction for

> the event that will bring about this change; it even seems to demand the event. (Zuckerkandl, 1956, p. 19)

The single tone, then, cannot survive unless it is placed alongside other tones, leading to melody, harmony, and structure.

> Tones seem to incline towards each other, fall away from each other, as though they were complete entities which are magnetized by their neighbors and eager to cling to them. (Scruton, 1997, p. 52)

The opening horn theme of Brahms Second Piano Concerto in B flat major, Op. 83, that moves so effortlessly away from the opening tone and the seemingly disparate relation in Webern's Konzert Op. 24, show the scope of possibilities for the beginning tone.

In music therapy tone heralds the beginning of the process. Ansdell (1995) describes how tone by succession leads to other tones and eventually larger musical frameworks.

> Each tone is not separate but contains a "force" (both melodic and harmonic) which gives it direction towards and connection to the next tone. Groups of tones then organize themselves into motifs and phrases, which are themselves "nested" within larger phrases and periods. (p. 139)

As the music then moves into compositional form an interpretation of the beginning tone is essential.

> The starting point for clinical listening is the identification and qualities of the "tone" itself and its effect on the ensuing musical structure. Once the opening tone is ascertained others can then be identified as the evolving intervals become apparent. (Lee & Khare, 2001, p. 252)

From the foundation of the opening tone, the musical structure evolves creating a "force" that has a life of its own. This act of creation, however, is not possible without acute listening and response.

The client's opening tone can often be embedded in complex vocal textures or nonspecific instrumental playing. Spontaneous sounds reflect the emotions of the client entering the session. If the therapist is improvising music as the client enters, the opening tone either vocally or instrumentally will often be related to the music being improvised. The therapist should therefore improvise music that is open and tonally noninferred since the musical relationship begins the instant the first sounds are created. Precisely hearing, reflecting upon, identifying, and moving forward from the tone into the core of the session is the therapist's challenge. To reflect the interpersonal links between creativity and expression that emerge for client and therapist in the evolving relationship.

Tension and release are integral components of tone. As tone moves toward melody and composition there are elements of tension. Where does the musical direction need to go? How does tone speak to the developing music? What aims are being evolved as tones emerge? The tension of an opening tone is often followed by release; tension and release reveal the flexibility of the therapeutic process. Paul Nordoff's exploration of tension and relaxation (Robbins & Robbins, 1998) gives us a wonderful insight into the specifics of musical construction and how this can affect musical direction in clinical practice.

> The music you use in therapy must begin to have tension in its harmonic form, and both harmonically and melodically, a sense of urgency in the tonal direction . . . Now, there can be more or less tension, depending on the kinds of chords and the kinds of intervals you use. And there can be more–there can be less–relaxation, depending on the kinds of intervals and chords you use. (p. 111)

Just as human relationships contain equilibrium and disparity so the therapeutic relationship is balanced between fragmentation and union. The tension and release of music is displayed through the human/musical contact of improvisation.

If we look at a distillation of the opening moments of an improvisation with a client living with HIV (see Figure 5) we can see how the therapist answers the clients' opening tones. The tension and release of chords in response to the client's repeated B provides a sense of harmonic direction and openness. To answer the tone with a consonant chord would have implied tonality and therapeutic direction reflective of the therapist and not the client. The opening 7th (1) allows for many different tonal directions. The following chord (2) moves closer to tonality and yet retains a sense of ambiguity by overlaying an implied F# minor and G major without the thirds. The therapist's choice of harmonic stability and release (3) is interestingly a firmly rooted C major against the client's B. This provides consonance and release yet retains a sense of musical divergence. "Meeting" a client's sound, however, does require that the therapist play musically the same:

> By "meeting" a client's sound we remain separate, presenting our own identity, our own voice, which ultimately supports the client but does not impede or step upon their individual voice. (Lee & Khare, 2001, p. 259)

The movement from tension to release is repeated (4-6) through F# minor, G major–with the added ambivalence and spice of D #–to C major. As the client's tone moves away from the B (7) the F#/G major overlay is repeated moving to the opening 7th and then toward a two-part melodic invention (9-10). This example demonstrates how the tone can be colored to reflect ambiguity and subtle stability that was an expression of the shifting musical/therapeutic relationship.

T = Tension R = Release

fig. 5

FORM

Form surrounds all aspects of music and therapy–the form of the complete music therapy process, the individual session, the improvisation within the session, and every moment within each piece. How we perceive musical and clinical form, how finitely we are able to hear, understand, and interpret reflects our understanding of form. This in turn informs our response to the client and the musical style we use to translate form into clinical intent (see Figure 6).

Levinson (1997) in his study on listening and form suggests that:

> The judgment that a piece has good musical form,...cannot rest directly on the presence of this or that large-scale formal relationship. It must rather rest directly on registration of moment-to-moment satisfyingness or cogency. (p. 161)

He argues that a listener does not need the comprehension of large-scale form to understand the overall form of music and that "music's real form, . . . is continuational and successional, not spatial and architectonic." The deciding factor that differentiates the client in music therapy from a music listener is that the client not only listens but also actively responds. The client instinctively comprehends the nature of form dependent on the moment-to-moment realization in conjunction with an overall sense of large-scale form. If, as Levinson suggests, a global understanding of structure is not needed, then the therapist's understanding of the process and the client's place therein may become misread. When talking of new form Scruton (1997) puts forward the view that:

> New forms in music cannot be created by fiat or convention. They must grow from a new musical gesture, which means a new style–a new way of hearing tones, and their organization. The successful invention of form is a rare achievement. (p. 341)

AeMT requires a comprehension of the relationship between clinical tone and clinical form. This is what differentiates music therapy philosophy from musicology; AeMT is indeed a new way of considering form in the clinical context. The level of maturation of the therapeutic process determines the form of an improvisation, as well as its ingenuity, spontaneous structure, and development.

Landscape of the Conscious Music Therapy Relationship

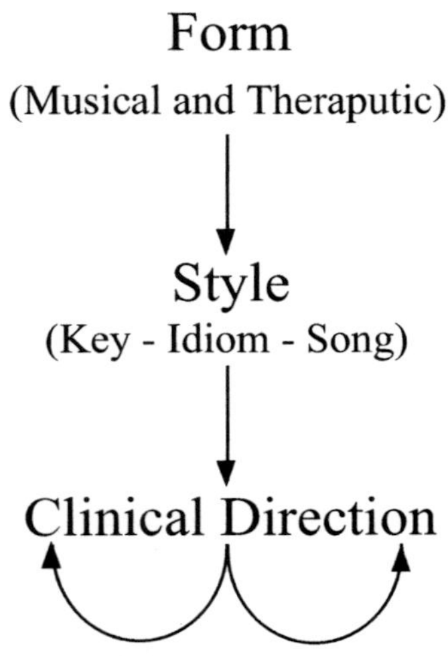

Figure 6

Pavlicevic's Theory of Dynamic Form (1997 & 2000) "clarifies the interface between music and emotional form in Music Therapy improvisation (MT improvisation)." Paralleling Daniel Stern's (1985) "Vitality Affects", Pavlicevic explores the stylistic and spontaneous qualities of music communication:

> Dynamic Form is elicited within and as part of the clinical-musical relationship, and needs both therapist and client to be engaged with one another through jointly created sound form. Thus, the music therapist generates Dynamic Form jointly with the client (rather than play music with the client). This means receiving the client's musical utterances as a direct presentation of the client-in-the-world; and listening to the improvisation with a therapeutic mind–that is not allowing (conventional) musical dictates to interfere with, or override, interpersonal ones. (Pavlicevic, 2000, p. 276)

Dynamic Form is an important MT improvisational theory because it identifies the need to consider the link between being expressive and being musical. Exploring further, Pavlecevic suggests there are similarities as well as distinctions between the mother-infant relationship and the client/music therapist relationship. In Dynamic Form the therapist seeks to answer the client's music through a balanced appreciation of the musical and therapeutic responses inherent in music.

A music-centered approach to clinical form is derived from an understanding of musical form. The interface between the two is crucial, but the musical essence of awareness is the element that differentiates AeMT from Dynamic Form. Until we know and understand the musical form of improvisation we cannot link it accurately to clinical form. Illuminating our knowledge of the client and his or her musical responses within the framework of musical form requires clarity and awareness of musical structures. Comprehending a client in a holistic manner will be achieved only by understanding and accurately interpreting his or her music.

ARCHITECTURE

What do we understand as the therapeutic process? What does it mean to progress therapeutically? What influence does music have on the therapeutic process? Throughout my writings and research I have spent a great deal of time considering what is meant by "the therapeutic process" and what impact music has on this phenomenon. The music therapy process is intricate and delicate; like music itself it is reflective and is illuminated through macro- and microstructures which constitute the basis of its power. The process is unique to every individual's growth, every session and moment; it is dependent upon the moment of contact, what has gone before and what may happen in the future (see Figure 4). How can we, at the moment of contact, know what will occur in a piece of improvised music? We can't, of course. What we can know, however, is the impact of that which has gone before and how it influences each moment for the future. By understanding the past in context of the present, we can allow the process to happen instinctively and insightfully.

Levinson's (1997) argument that music needs only to be experienced in the moment may be true from a client's perspective, but for the improvising music therapist it is not. The therapist's sense, realization, and ongoing appreciation of musical and therapeutic architecture are critical. Learning to distinguish the moment in relation to the whole is a precise technique that comes from detailed assessment, ongoing practice of musical resources, and direct experience from clinical work.

Analyzing the architecture of precomposed music with which the therapist is familiar, then linking it to improvisation, will help to clarify the clinical structure of ongoing sessions. Taking significant pieces of music and interpreting their composition, as is the focus of Chapters 2, 7, and 11, will further highlight the music-centered focus of musical and clinical architecture. Music therapists as improvising composers must know the musical structure and architecture of their work; just as composers learn the art of orchestration and compositional form, so the music therapists must learn to craft the architecture of music to suit the needs of the client and the process. The creativeness of the therapist in the moment is balanced with the precise knowledge of universal structure. We cannot break free from that which we do not know. The appreciation of Dynamic Form and architectural clinical form is dependent on study and therapeutic insight.

Philosophical ruminations of life and what it means to share music are the lifeblood of our work and influence our understanding and sense of the process. While music therapists all share in the rich heritage of musical speculation, learning, and personal debate, philosophical stance is influenced by training, theoretical preference, individual bias, and musical motivation. As one's clinical work matures, so too the musical knowledge of the therapist must broaden. The awareness of musical shape and form in the therapeutic setting is a crucial foundation of AeMT.

All great and influential music is written by composers who are prepared to take risks. New critical music therapy theories have come and will continue to come from those who are able to challenge the status quo. Music therapy as art needs innovation and speculation, whereas music therapy as science needs stability and replicability. That is the paradox. Pioneers of music therapy should be educated, yet free in their thinking. Pioneers of music therapy should be affirmed not only through research and writing but also through the practicalities of clinical work. Pioneers of music therapy should justify their status by sharing work that will set future standards of musical excellence.

> See, if you put a musician in a place where he has to do something different from what he does all the time, then he can do that–but he's got to think differently in order to do it. He has to use his imagination, be more creative, more innovative; he's got to take more risks . . . So then he'll be freer, will expect things differently, will anticipate and know something different is coming down .. . . Because then anything can happen, and that's where great art and music happens. (Davis & Troupe, 1991, p. 220)

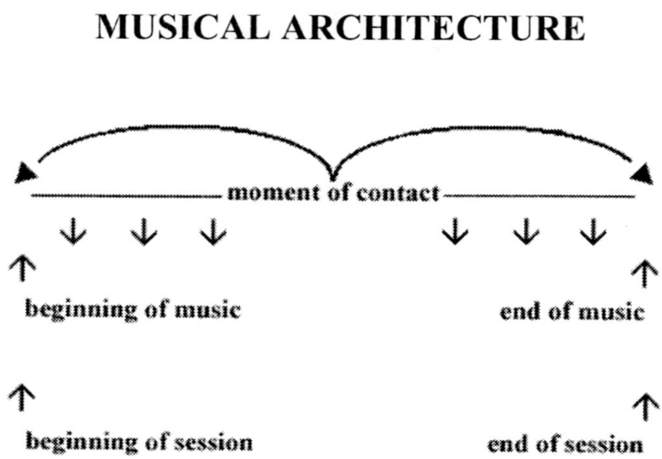
MUSICAL ARCHITECTURE
moment of contact
beginning of music
end of music
beginning of session
end of session

Figure 7

Chapter Five

CLINICAL LISTENING

> If your mind is empty, it is always ready for anything; it is open to everything. In the beginner's mind there are many possibilities, in the expert's mind there are few.
> –Shunryu Suzuki,
> *Zen Mind, Beginner's Mind*

Listening is at the heart of human relationships. How we listen reveals our sense of the world. Listening to music can be inward experience as a means for personal reflection, or external experience as a means to relate to others. Clinical listening is the art of the therapist's attunement to the client's sounds, listening to reality and beyond; listening to every nuance from the client's first utterances to the final sounds as the session ends. Every sound, musical contribution, of an improvisation is a moment of clarity and emotion that should be heard with exactness and insight. Steele (1988) eloquently expresses the view that:

> Perhaps the most primary service we offer our patients within space and time of the therapeutic environment is our willingness and ability to listen. (p. 3)

Our musical responses to listening determine the level we endeavor to attain as therapists. Through the meaning of listening, music and its potential for healing can become ever more discriminating:

- Listening to the client, their music, our music, and the musical relationship
- Listening behind and beyond the music
- Listening to silence
- Listening to the client as personhood and musichood
- Listening as musicians and therapists
- Listening as sound and community

(Lee & Khare, 2001, p. 268)

The musicologist Roger Scruton (1997) makes two interesting observations:

> Music begins when people listen to the sounds that they are making, and so discover tones. Of all musical experiences, there is none more direct than free improvisation (whether vocal or instrumental): and this should be understood as a paradigm of listening–the form of listening from which music begins. (p. 217)

Improvisation was used long before precomposed music appeared. Tones that combine to form melody, harmony, and rhythm were reflective of the listening necessary to form relationships at their most fundamental and mysterious level. Listening in improvisation is precise and finite. In order for an improvisation to make musical sense player(s) must be attuned to the sounds being created in the moment-to-moment evolution of the improvisation. When more than one player is involved there must be a community of listening for the music to make sense. Improvisational listening and developing relationships reveal the origins of music therapy as a nonempirical phenomena:

> Music is heard as though breathed into the ear of the listener from another and higher sphere: it is not the here and now, the world of mere contingency that speaks to us through music, but another world, whose order is only dimly reflected in the empirical realm. (Scruton, 1997, p. 489)

Expressive listening holds spiritual significance and provides for clients a depth of experience that is beyond rationalization. Listening to specific levels of musical contact can inform our understanding of a client's existence.

All musical relationships involve what Ansdell (1995) describes as listening-in-playing. To listen to another person, to accommodate another's voice is to be a part of a musical relationship. In clinical improvisation listening-in-playing is even more essential for a successful musical and therapeutic outcome. In Creative Music Therapy (Nordoff & Robbins 1977) listening is integral to an understanding of its philosophy and theory:

> Creative Music Therapy is able to use to therapeutic advantage both music's natural cultivation of the art of listening and improvisation's special emphasis on listening-in-playing. (Ansdell, 1995, p. 158)

Listening in Creative Music Therapy is further explored by Pavlicevic (1997) who suggests that:

> . . . we all listen differently as different times. During the act of playing, our listening is colored by the immediate movement and physicality of the act, which feeds that acts of playing as it unfolds. (p. 162)

Performing a precomposed piece, a musician must know the content and detail of the music as it unfolds. Listening to the moment-to-moment interpretation is influenced by the listening quality of both the player and their interaction with the audience. An audience that fails to listen with insight can dramatically affect the performers' ability to present the layers of content that will produce a worthy expressionistic interpretation. The act of listening-in-playing during performance is therefore just as intricate as that of the dialogue in music therapy.

Listening is complex and hierarchical. Recreational listening colors one part of our consciousness whereas clinical listening demands every facet of our consciousness. When I listen intently to music I allow the music–its feeling and design–to affect me at many levels depending on my state of mind. Listening to a dense orchestral piece by Schoenberg requires a different kind of concentration than a Schubert piano sonata, yet both may have the same emotional impact. For a client the act of listening-in-playing should be natural whereas for the therapist it requires insight and sensitivity. Playing an instrument requires a client to listen and physically respond. A client's sense of physicality, as Pavlicevic (1997) suggests, will influence their listening and therefore their level of creation.

The therapist listens before, during, and after music. Sounds that preempt the improvisation reflect the significance of the opening tones.

> . . . the principle of waiting and listening, both at the beginning of and during the musical dialogue, is of paramount importance for the therapist's attunement. (Lee, 1996, p. 89)

As an improvisation ends the therapist listens to the closing sounds and beyond. Listening to the concluding silence, its quality and intent, can reveal the significance of the session itself. Listening is not bound by the music and extends throughout every second the client is in contact with the therapist.

In AeMT the following questions are raised: Why is it important that clients are heard through both music and sound? What is the difference between hearing and listening? How is clinical listening different from our general experience of listening? How do we identify levels of listening that will give a greater understanding of the therapeutic relationship? These underlying questions point to the need to listen ever more deeply to our clients, the music, and the timbre that lays between the notes. Clinical listening is both precise and sonorous. Being heard is one of the most powerful experiences two human beings can share. For a client who has not had the experience of being heard, the music therapist's responsibility is to attempt to find an opening that will allow this. The therapist should pause, wait, and allow an opening that will enable the client to reevaluate their sense of themselves in relation to music and people. Listening to both sound and silence can support an equality of relationship that is inherently therapeutic. To hear can be abstract whereas to listen requires accuracy.

LEVELS OF LISTENING

The six levels identified below show the intensity necessary in evaluating listening skills in clinical improvisation.

1. Surface Listening–identifying fundamental musical form and therapeutic relationship
2. Instinctive Listening–identifying and interpreting further complexities of music form and therapeutic relationship
3. Critical Listening –identifying fundamental musical resources
4. Complex Listening –identifying and interpreting further musical complexities of musical resources
5. Integrated Listening–identifying and interpreting links between therapeutic and musical
6. Listening Beyond–identifying the incorporeal nature of the music and relationship

The following clinical example (see Figure 8) shows an assessment of the therapist's levels of listening and response. The extract, an improvisation from the eighteenth session with a client living with AIDS, comes 15:05 minutes after the opening. Prior to this section the client explored different instrumental textures on drum, cymbal, and bongos. Moving to the xylophone the improvisation became gentle and delicate. The aims for the ongoing work were to: a) explore personal defenses at receiving an AIDS diagnosis, b) translate feelings into musical expression, c) use improvisation as a means for catharsis and thus stress reduction, and d) enjoy the act of music-making with another person. The case illustration contains information taken from the assessment and indexing notes.

fig. 8

Level One –Surface Listening

- client: explorative and focused playing
- therapist: simple supportive accompaniment (1-6)
- structural development of an earlier theme
- relational listening, based on the melodic song-like qualities of the xylophone (client), supported with the piano accompaniment (therapist)
- the musical dialogue between between players is sensitive

Level Two–Instinctive Listening

- the client's melodic invention develops from motives (1-5) moving toward recitative-like phrases (6-8)
- the therapist's suspended chords (6-8) provide a background for the melodic development of the client
- an acute sense of listening and response between players
- the musical and therapeutic relationship is refined
- in discussing this passage the client remarks: "our playing is together and yet separate . . . this perhaps reflects our (therapeutic) relationship?"

Level Three–Critical Listening

- client: upward phrase (1) followed by two downward phrases (3 & 4); (6-8) free-flowing melodic invention with broader spaced intervals as the phrase develops
- therapist: syncopated accompaniment (5/8) based on 2nds and a descending bass line (1-5); suspended chords (6-8) around a tonal center of G

Level Four–Complex Listening

- client: major 2nds followed by minor 3rd (1-2); 2nds followed by descending major 6th (3) repeated with descending minor 7th; (6) semitone and tones (6) move toward displaced intervals (7-8)
- therapist: descending bass line starting on B flat (A #) (1-5), moves to a tonal center of C (5), resting on D (6), and finally settling on G (7-8)
- the compositional form is sophisticated–tonally and rhythmically the passage moves between a consonant accompaniment and melody followed by a recitative
- musical interpretation reveals a sophisticated and intricate compositional form individually and collectively

Level Five–Integrated Listening

- this section meet the aims of our work and highlighted the link between musical and therapeutic expression
- the quiet, tender, yet syncopated nature of the music was antithetical to the more normal forthright dialogue–a powerful expression of the clients intense emotions
- the music allowed a balance between simple structure and freedom that reflected the developing relationship and the client's need to find different forums of musical expression to translate his precise feelings of helplessness and pain

Level Six–Listening Beyond

- the music held a transcendental quality that mirrored the inner expression contemplating an AIDS diagnosis
- the movement of themes and exploration of melodic lines show the spiritual nature of emotions being expressed
- a sense of deep listening pervaded this section of the improvisation
- listening to and beyond the sounds themselves

These observations hopefully give a clear and detailed picture of the levels of listening available in one section of music. Through detailed listening our understanding of the moment-to-moment structure in relation to the complete improvisation of the session and overall therapeutic process will become clearer. Reflecting on these statements and interpretations will further color and affect the empirical and reflective elements of listening and analysis.

CLINICAL LISTENING IN SUPERVISION

Clinical listening is the first of four levels in the supervision process of AeMT (Lee & Khare, 2001). The other levels, clinical evaluation, interpretation, and judgment–unfold from this core concept. The description of clinical listening is initially presented by the supervisor:

> One of the main tenets of music-centered supervision is hearing objectively and precisely the musical constructs contained within the musical relationship. Music as a complex and multilayered phenomena in music therapy should be precisely evaluated, considered, and analyzed at all levels of its experience. Separating what we think we hear from the reality of sound, music and the interrelationships can provide a new basis and understanding for our work. Living in the knowing of music can dramatically transform our sense of the process. Music then is the starting point for our greater understanding; not words or exterior clinical theories but the pure phenomena of music itself.
>
> Listening to audio recordings of sessions enable greater and more detailed study of the musical building blocks in improvisation. Clinical listening is the ability to determine the balance between the actuality of music and the potential therapeutic constructs that constitute the musical/therapeutic dialogue. The supervisee must extend their aural skills to describe what they hear without bias–listening without interpretation or reflection to describe chord progressions, melodic lines, client's responses, and their musical combinations. The first stage of supervision is fundamental in providing the base from which the supervisee can then move into more interpretive assessments. In clinical listening there is re-examination of the boundaries of knowing and understanding. Knowing the musical exchange as pure data will give a greater sense of where the therapeutic relation-

> ship is beginning and the possible clinical pathways that lie ahead. The supervisee must learn to hear precisely and clinically before he or she makes choices that are truly balanced and therapeutically informed.
>
> This stage of supervision is usually challenging, as supervisees will instinctively feel the need to interpret. Indeed, the education of a music therapist is built on postulates of observation, interpretation, and clinical orientation. Music therapy could not survive without the therapist's ability to critique, interpret, and proceed. Supervisees may wish therefore to select passages of improvisations for musical discussion that are therapeutically significant and that relay to the supervisor work that they feel is effective. As supervisor it is important that these assumptions are challenged.
>
> Initially, the most important segments of a tape to explore are the beginning passages of the improvisation. The reasoning is that these beginning passages will normally contain simpler musical patterns. Here, therapist and client explore a musical groundwork from which the ongoing musical relationship may develop. By accurately describing these musical beginnings the supervisee will begin to understand the importance of clinical listening and responding. These opening moments also often contain generative musical seeds from which improvisations develop. If we explicitly hear these generative musical cells expressed from the client, therapist, and musical relationship, we may begin to unravel the complexities of the ensuing therapeutic and musical direction. As the supervisee develops his or her ability to clinically listen to these opening moments, so will this be transferred to the ongoing work. (p. 251)

This is followed by reflections from the supervisee:

> Music as emotions, is immediate. I never perceived these experiences as separate. It was during supervision that I first began to understand the clinical implications that my lack of conscious separation was creating. In "clinical listening" the "I feel . . ." and "I think . . ." are removed. The clinician's personal and musical biases are stripped away to reveal the musical intention and clinical direction. By directly dealing with the factual experience–what is actually happening musically, rather than one's own perception–the focus is shifted from therapeutic presence to musical presence.
>
> Initially it is frightening to listen at this level. Feelings of self-doubt and inadequacy are shamelessly experienced. But that is not the purpose in listening in this capacity. To listen "clinically," not per-

> ceptually or even therapeutically, is shocking. We have rules and fundamental concepts of the inherent nature of the medium, that when disregarded can lead to a situation not unlike playing with fire. The aesthetic of music is a combined effort of profound emotions and fundamental clinical aptitude. Knowing the geography of one's instrument can only support knowing the geography of one's emotional landscape. And in supporting a client's growth toward self, we must know the precise application of the music that affects the emotions.
>
> Clinical listening brings you to the basics. What is the timbre of the client's instrument/expression, the pitch, the duration of the tone? What is the attack, the phrasing of their rhythmic/melodic work? Here is where we separate from style. We do not ask the "feel" of the expression, but the precise measurement of it.
>
> The next question for me was not "How can I match the sound?" but rather "How can I meet the sound?" This concept is the key in that I believe it is what helps the clinician continue to separate clinical listening from perceptual listening. By "meeting" a client's sound we remain separate, presenting our own identity, our own voice, which ultimately supports the client but does not impede or step upon their individual voice. By "matching" we tend to "do the same" which neither indicates our intention as clinicians or provides direction for our clients. Matching can at times simply be repeating, whereas meeting is a conscious choice. Meeting supports co-creating, it motivates independent thinking and awareness of the present, immediate moment. Listening can be cultivated. (p. 259)

Clinical listening can be learned and developed. Supervision is an essential process in the therapist's acquisition of the skills necessary to acquire precise clinical listening. As illustrated in the above evaluations it demands discipline and commitment. Cultivating clinical listening can also be liberating and creative. Hearing yourself being "heard" is one of the most dynamic forces client and therapist can experience. To be heard is to be understood and to understand being heard is to gain human insight. Once the exactness of clinical listening has been mastered the therapist can move beyond pragmatic knowledge toward Listening Beyond (see: Levels of Listening on page 90) that holds the essence of therapeutic truth. Hearing the client as musical essence is to hear their resonance as they survive and mature in the world. Listening to the actuality of musical existence will therefore inform our appreciation of sounds as expression and discrimination. Through the exactness of clinical listening the therapist's creativity will radiate.

Through supervision the music therapist must acknowledge that listening is one of the most critical components in understanding clinical practice. If clinical listening is compromised then interpretations and clarity of outcome may also be compromised. Listening acutely will clarify our understanding of music, the client, and the interface between musical expression and therapeutic outcome. To listen clinically is to listen with every fiber and nuance as responding musicians and therapists. In and through supervision the exactitude and inspiration of clinical listening can be explored and matured.

CLINICAL RESPONSE

Clinical listening requires a clinical response from the therapist. A reality response is a factual identification of musical, physical, short-term, and long-term aims. An intuitive response is a more hermeneutic identification of the client, music, and the overall therapeutic situation. How the therapist perceives their intuitive response will result in their reality response as the session unfolds. The intuitive response may also suggest something that is in direct opposition to the therapist's reality responses. When do we and when should we allow the intuitive response to outweigh the reality response? Are there times when one category is more important than another, and when and what grounds do we base that decision? The ideal process is (a) clinical listening and (b) response which leads to (c) developing dialogue and (d) clinical refinement. But therapy is rarely that neat or tidy. Even the most accomplished therapist can misinterpret the actuality of the moment and experience is not always proof of an accurate response. How we respond discloses our professionalism and respect for the client(s). Listening requires space and time. It is important never to crowd expression and response. The quality of clinical listening and responding will result in the potential for quality reactions from the client. Through the therapist's intent of playing and listening the client's contribution will become ever more decisive in the developing musical and therapeutic dialogue. Anything less will preclude the essence of true innovative involvement.

So what of the client's response? What happens when we respond in a way that does not fulfill the expectations of the client? The therapist must identify and acknowledge this experience and make the necessary decisions to counteract the predicament. There are times when the therapist is clear in their response but the client struggles or is unable to find their place within the unfolding therapeutic structure. Response is based on understanding but we should also know that we can often be wrong. This is natural in a healthy developing therapeutic relationship and should not be misinterpreted as failure on the part of the therapist. The therapist should, at these times, return to the theories of clinical listening as their anchor for reassessment and continuation. The therapist may misinterpret the client's musical responses if they are not open to the originality of composition in clinical improvisation. Confusing musical responses of the client and being unable to find a clarity of direction are elements that become clearer as the therapist continues to challenge their insight and understanding. Supervision and assessment are the keys to developing perceptive clinical responses and ultimately the client's response will be reflective of the therapist's insights into the therapeutic process.

ACTIVE LISTENING

There are certain situations where either therapist or client do not come to play. Their role thus becomes one of active listener. The reasons for active listening can be many and complex and varies depending on the client focus and stage of the process. For some clients active listening becomes a potent sense of activity that, while silent, can be as creative as the actuality of a precise musical response. In active listening it is possible to be connected yet apart from the music. In performance there is an inherent distance between player and audience that provides a foundation to be initially detached. The listener can move personally closer as they feel comfortable. Thus I can experience listening either passively or actively depending on my mood and willingness to invest. In music therapy intimacy is more integral to the experience. The client can feel exposed within the ongoing potential exposure of musical expression and may feel the need to pull away to the role of active listener.

The therapist as active listener is not common. *In Music at the Edge* (Lee, 1996), I describe my thoughts when the therapist becomes an active listener:

> . . . gradually I learned to understand the importance of the receptive role–not receptive in a passive sense, but as a real and continuing part of the music, mute perhaps, but actively resonating (p. 156)

When the therapist becomes an active listener they revoke their active musical role in favor of musical stillness. This dynamic can test the therapist's role in terms of input and therapeutic balance of power. It can also allow a direction in the process that is innovative and necessary. Learning to be musically passive and yet directed in the relationship can seem a daunting task, especially as in the case of Francis, when the client is articulate and sure in their need to play alone:

> The realigning in my relationship with Francis was simultaneously unsettling and liberating. . . . (Lee, 1996, p. 156)

Francis explains how he considers his solo improvisations to be more influential than our improvisations together:

> When I'm improvising alone I'm entirely following my own rhythm. My own inspiration. When you are working with someone else you can unlock different doors that wouldn't have been available on your own. When we are improvising together I pick up some of your rhythms. The sum of the two gives a different result: in a sense doing things together, rather than the increased energy by support and solidarity. Ultimately, I think that duets are less of a personal document. They are less revelatory because if I'm working on my own it's a very personal statement. (Lee, 1996, pp. 86–87).

The client as active listener is a more common occurrence. Through reflective improvisation music can be offered that does not necessitate a response but that reflects the inner world of the client. Examples of this approach can be found in Chapter 12 and the case studies of David and Lisa.

CLOSING THOUGHTS–LISTENING AND LIFE

Listening as relationship is the apotheosis of life. How we listen determines our understanding of the emotional impact of living. To listen clinically means to focus on the client's revelations as a precise manifestation of their inner world. It is the music therapist's duty to listen on many levels:

- Listening as musicians
- Listening as therapists
- Listening as human beings
- Listening to music
- Listening to silence
- Listening to actuality
- Listening to creativity

If the music therapist listens deeply and creatively then they will hear the client as a free musical spirit, and will respond with an informed balance of organization and freedom. If the music therapist is only able to hear peripheral sounds, however, they will only be able to respond at a surface level. Learning to clinically listen is a process that takes dedication and insight. Clinical listening skills can be learnt. Taking one small section of a session and focusing on repeated hearings will help the therapist find ever complex levels of music.

Mark, a client with HIV, improvised on the piano in a consistently perseverative style. Perseveration is normally considered a "block"–dull, lifeless playing that needs to be changed. The question, however, should not be "How do we break perseveration?" but rather "What is perseveration telling us about the therapeutic process and how will our understanding of it help us to hear the client more clearly?" I consciously improvised with Mark's perseveration and did not attempt to break his playing. Even though on an exterior level the sounds were regular there was a quality in his playing that called for more detailed listening. I attempted to hear behind his surface perseveration, and found to my amazement a level and clarity of expression that Mark could only have expressed through these continuous sounds. It was only when I accurately heard and accepted his perseveration that Mark allowed me in and behind his music. Once this had occurred I found that his playing wasn't as stuck or fixed as I had originally heard. There were qualities, subtle changes in texture, that kept the music alive and creative. As the clarity of my listening increased so Mark's responses became ever more refined. This culminated in an eventual disintegration of his perseveration. This happened not because of a direct intervention to challenge his playing but because I had accepted and intently heard his music. Once this had happened Mark was ready to relinquish and move his perseveration and move forward.

AeMT is based on the premise that the musical relationship is an essential component of the therapeutic relationship. Being able to listen precisely without inference is a further foundation of this approach. A common argument of this book is that until music is understood in terms of itself then our interpretations of it will remain flawed. Interpretations therefore only become valid if the phenomena itself can be accurately and precisely described. In terms of AeMT this means delineating the nuts and bolts of music. Once this has been achieved it is then possible to relate this knowledge to our ongoing understanding of the therapeutic process and the balance between music and words.

"Something sacred there is about listening
when the whole of our Being is tuned
to resonate with all that
enters our field of experience."
(McMaster, 1995, p. 72)

Chapter Six

CASE STUDY–MICHAEL: MUSIC AND LOSS

> The mellow touch of music doth wound the soul, when it doth rather sigh than sound.
>
> –Robert Herrick, *Soft Music,* (1891)

The strength of music to express loss is inextricably a part of the AeMT process. Loss is fundamental to living. As we face beginnings and endings our need to overcome the trauma of loss becomes necessary if we are to live. To face the intense catastrophe of death is not to mend or overcome but rather to provide an opportunity to reflect and realign with the reality of living. Finding a path through the maze of bereavement can be both intense and illuminating. The music therapist working with bereaved clients must guide, through music, the anguish of surrender and grief. Confronting and acknowledging the expression of loss is ultimately therapeutic. Music therapy is able to give voice to the meaning of loss at its most spiritual level. Music has a beginning and end. It exists in time, then dies. Is the composition of music similar to the composition of living and dying? If so, how do we link music to the cycle of life? Some of the greatest music was inspired by loss. Composers such as Dvorak, Berg, and Poulenc composed from their personal experiences of bereavement, producing works of heightened emotional intensity. Is it possible then that the nature of music can translate the gravity of loss in a way that is not possible through the explicit nature of words?

Through musical examples this case - study speaks from sessions alongside reflective interpretations from client and therapist. It does not aim to give an exhaustive summation of our work but rather tries to capture the essence of our musical relationship in helping Michael to confront his grief. This was one of my first experiences of working with a bereaved client and as such my frame of reference came from my ongoing supervision without which I would have been unable to continue this work. The uncertainties of the developing process were not unlike my previous work in palliative care and I struggled with every therapeutic decision as it occurred. In terms of AeMT this is perhaps the clearest example of the therapeutic process immersed in the essence of music. As the work unfolded so the music became ever more central to the process and understanding of Michael's search for balance. The quality of the improvising on the accompanying CD provide a glimpses into a dynamic representation of music therapy in the face of loss.

THE CLIENT SPEAKS

I first met Colin through the referral of a music therapist who supervised my voluntary weekly music sessions with an autistic girl. When hearing the recordings of our music, my supervisor would often wonder why I didn't seem able to match the intensity of musical expression which this little girl of five brought to life. When finally I told my supervisor about my mother's recent and unexpected death she immediately understood that I had not worked through the grief of this bereavement and suggested that I should meet Colin.

Little more than one year before, my mother's body had been found frozen in a lake near her home on January first. Nobody knows how she got there and whether she committed suicide or not. She had suffered from manic-depression for several years, never having found herself the help she would have needed. Being her only child in a divorced family, her death meant both grief and relief to me. On the very day before she was buried, my father married his second wife - emotional support from his side was not to be expected.

I was in pain and loneliness when I met Colin. My first impression of him was that of a very skilled pianist and able music therapist who, nevertheless, would not be able to face the emotional intensity I needed to express. Luckily, Colin took on the challenge of this rather misguided assumption.

THE THERAPIST SPEAKS

Michael was referred through my supervisor. I had little information other than that his mother had died some years earlier and that he was interested in exploring the potential of music therapy. I knew my first impressions of Michael, during our assessment session, was of a quietly determined and expressive young man. He spoke with precision and clarity even though English was his second language. Michael explained that he was curious to experience music therapy and the potential it could have to explore his life at this time. We talked of improvisation and that this would be the potential focus for our work. I explained my approach came from a belief that music was at the center of the music therapy process. In discussing music and words we agreed to find the balance necessary for the changing nature of each session but that I would not attempt psychodynamic interpretations of our work. We agreed on an initial series of ten one-hour sessions to be held in my room at the Hospice. It is interesting to note that we did not discuss Michael's bereavement during this assessment session. After he left I remember being both excited and apprehensive at the potential work that lay ahead.

BEGINNING COMMUNICATIONS

Some years after our work, and since beginning this book, I contacted Michael to see if he would be interested in collaborating with me on an evaluation of our initial ten sessions. Having used this case study extensively in teaching and presentations I thought it would make an ideal contribution to my developing philosophy of AeMT. I proposed that we meet and listen to the sessions together. We would then both comment freely about our feelings now and how we recalled the sessions. I was aware this may be a difficult experience for Michael, so wanted to be sure he felt strong enough for such a undertaking. We agreed to meet for two days at Berklee College of Music, Boston, where I was teaching at the time.

Through our initial correspondences Michael reflected on the potential for our evaluative work:

> I am interested in working with you and reflecting on our sessions, but more in terms of personal exploration. If I am to address again the pain through this work, that is undeniably still entangled with my mother–and always will be–it will be in my interests first, and in everyone else's second. Thinking back to the sessions themselves, I had doubts at first if you would be prepared to accept my emotions. Would you be willing to deal with my pain? I knew that in working with you I would have to address emotions that you may not have been able to work with because they were so intense. During the sessions I knew you heard my pain and accepted it, though as I suspected you could not become it. This was one of the fundamental principles of our work and was one that helped me to understand my grief.

> One aspect of our work that I appreciated was that you only played when I did. It took getting used to. Your attention and intention was always clearly directed toward me. I felt uncomfortable in the beginning because I could not hide from you and be without you. You were always there with me. Once I understood and accepted this I began to appreciate your musical support and reflection. This made an impression on me in several ways and I am still thankful for this approach and what I discovered from it. I remember you saying you considered me courageous. But I wouldn't have been able to do this with just anyone. Having had this experience with you, I am only now able to consider such a crazy thing–courage seems to be a two-way process. I also believe in admitting to one's vulnerability. I am still learning this but now seeing it as a source of strength. This is one of the key reasons that I now dare to look deeply into what the music therapy experience was for me. I now see that not knowing may be essential to the therapeutic process.

MUSIC THERAPY SCHEMA

Michael described how he remembered the ten sessions falling into the following six sections:

1. Setting the Scene (sessions 1–4): Anger, grief, and how to deal with it. Ways of interacting with Colin.
2. Negotiating Relationship (sessions 5–6): Struggling for common ground. A modus operandi.
3. Pain (session 7): Question: 'can I take Colin to the painful place?'
4. Reaching Out: (session 8) Colin listens to my song. It is painful and it is beautiful. Something profound is happening.
5. Plateau (session 9): What is there left for us to do?
6. Music (session 10): Whistling–without emotional urgency–mainly music.

GENERAL REFLECTIONS

Our observations were based on listening to the ten sessions. After this we identified sessions seven, eight, and ten as appropriate for more detailed analysis. During this meeting the intent was for Michael to review his therapy, for me to ask questions about aspects of the process, and for him to remember, as well as possible, his feelings about certain pivotal parts of the work. Michael also made notes which have been incorporated within the text where appropriate. The qualitative nature of our meeting allowed our conversation and listening to be free and improvisational in nature.

Pulses

M. I remember there were times when you followed me and I followed you . . . that's really interesting. And then there is the opposite . . . it's almost like you suggest something. I'm also interested in the pulses and tempi that I initiate. In the beginning the music was very fast and then it became slower and slower as the sessions progressed. I think I played a constant xylophone pulse throughout and wondered how that may have related to all the other pulses.

C. Your xylophone-pulsed playing was a common thread throughout the sessions.

M. I remember thinking that I was giving myself a structure, giving myself some unity, something that I could hold onto.

A constant or changing pulse either within the confines of a single session, or as a motive taken from session to session, can tell us about a client's need for stability. By its nature, music falls into structures and patterns. Improvisation has the potential, however, to be free from formation and shape. In my experience it is rare for a structureless improvisation to be therapeutically appropriate. Most clinical situations require some shape or form for a musical dialogue to take place. In describing how his overall tempo became slower Michael gives an indication of the intensity of his developing expression as the sessions progressed.

Sorrow and Sadness

M. One thing I want to hear are the different gestures and emotions. In the beginning I remember a sense of acting up . . . and then there is a point where I justify my grief and sadness. To hear unlimited amounts of energy and anger . . . well, maybe anger is not the right word . . . just high energy. The amount of time that I can bear to be in these different emotions is limited.

C. Improvising with you was tiring yet invigorating. You always propelled the music.

M. The music propelled itself. It's like the pulse goes on and on and on. Something that suggests . . . that long after . . . and then just when you suggest something like a root . . . but I say to you: "I'm not having it!" I didn't know how to get out . . . that bothered me.

C. You wanted to get out?

M. At the time I'm not sure . . . I started singing . . . I remember thinking how long it took to find my voice. My singing was like struggling for words. I had an idea of what I wanted to express and the way I wanted to go . . . but I was very shaky.

C. My worries were to do with facilitating that space that would allow a clear expression of your confusion and anger. What musical and clinical decisions and interventions would be appropriate? I was respectful . . . though at times fearful of what you were expressing. There were times when I had to pull back from your expression . . . both in terms of our therapeutic alliance and my personal safety as a therapist. My perceptions of your expression were different than yours, I think . . . that was the enormity of your challenge to me as therapist.

M. Yes I became more aware of that dynamic as our sessions progressed… and then in the years that followed our work. I wanted to be able to touch on sorrow and sadness . . . but then be able to draw back from it.

C. I remember times when I wanted to meet your musical expression but couldn't bear to be with your rawness and pain.

In music therapy we aspire to meet a client's expression simultaneously as it is experienced. Through music the truth of that expression can be authentically touched. There is danger, however, that the therapist may become too embedded in the client's intensity. Michael's musical manifestations of loss and pain were at times overwhelming in terms of the actuality of sound and meaning. It became dangerous for my personal safety to continue building with his expression of anger and pain. I had to distance myself musically and emotionally. This establishment of personal boundaries became a clear part of our therapeutic alliance. How best could I be a therapist for Michael within these musical volcanic explosions? How could the enormity of his loss be transferred to such an intensity of improvised musical expression and how should I facilitate this? I felt as if I were stepping into the unknown.

Music

M. Everything you did was what I needed. I feel it says something about who I am. I have contemplated suicide a lot of times in my life, but never for real . . . at some point it was like a method for giving . . . for setting the boundaries.

C. You were forceful and would let me know when I did something musically you didn't like.

M. This is true. I sensed your respect from the beginning. These sessions were about me and that I had the right to speak to whatever I needed. This is what made the whole experience so valuable . . . because I knew this was my space . . . and I knew that you would go along with whatever I needed. I completely trusted and still don't doubt that. I think I always did.

C. There were times when I was apprehensive and wondered if I could come up with the goods you needed as a therapist. I didn't know at the time that you trusted me so much.

M. It had to do with your musical expression . . . how you made music . . . how you responded to my playing . . . because you were up to it. There was never any point where I felt this man can't improvise . . . in the first session maybe . . . I wasn't sure . . . but from the second or third session I knew there was no place on this earth musically that I could go that you couldn't also. I'm still absolutely convinced that musically speaking that I could do anything and that you could respond to it. This is also the miracle that once we had established this relationship that I never felt absolutely unsupported. Well, there was one . . . that is the funny thing . . . but that wasn't because you were unable to meet with me but rather that I felt I didn't want to go with you.

C. Did you realize how enormous your musical expression was?

M. No, I couldn't perceive how big it was from your perspective, I just knew from my point of view it was gigantic.

C. I was constantly amazed at your musical expression.

M. I still feel unable to give an impression of the enormity of it . . . the significance of it . . . that it would be possible to just take a part of it and spend time really analyzing just one section. There were times we made musical contact. They were on one level affected by how we interacted as therapist and client . . . but that's not the real stuff we are talking about . . . the musical relationship. It's unbelievable where these moments come from.

Michael raises the need for music therapists to be musically competent. Is it important that music therapists are strong musicians as well as therapists? I believe that if a music therapist does not try to support and develop musically they will not be able to support and develop therapeutically.

Music and Words

C. Do you think we could have expressed these ideas and concepts to the same level in words?

M. It was so valuable to do this in music. Words are the way in which everybody relates to each other in this world. At some point I had a verbal counselor at college. What she always said is that we need to find, live, and experience the emotion . . . without giving any sense of actually experiencing it. I find that outrageous. This is perfect and in hindsight I can see a huge difference between the music therapy we did together and the sort of therapy I did in words. What we did was right because it wasn't about a method of living . . . it wasn't about how to deal with my life. It wasn't pragmatic . . . it was pure emotion, and that was so necessary for me. Even today I can't put words to it.

Boundaries

C. What boundaries do you think there were in our work?

M. I think you said at the beginning of our work that you were happy for me to say whatever I wanted to say but that you wouldn't interpret my music.

C. Were you happy about that?

M. Yes I was. I think it happened more than once after a session, it became almost meaningless that we were trying to talk and verbally interpret…it didn't add to the experience . . . it would have detracted.

C. This is against psychoanalytic theory.

M. Yes, I know, but our musical expression was beyond words and so to try and put it into words would have diminished what I was exploring.

> Everything happens in the music. The emotional work . . . you need to establish the climate and relationship every time you meet. If you go and see a therapist and talk to him you probably won't get through the real issues until further into the sessions . . . whereas in music it happens faster and more dynamically.

Relationship and Reich

M. I remember thinking: "I'm going to music therapy" . . . I was trying to find an alternative. We both knew that what needed to be said would be said. It happens . . . it could be the most profound thought. Here is another person, the therapist . . . if I want him to swim with me I have to get him used to the water. You take my hand and even though you don't want to go there yourself, you are leading me to the water. It's intriguing, the achievement of knowing there is a place that you–the therapist–doesn't want to go because it's not yours, but at the same time you encourage someone else to go with you. You lead and I immediately follow.

C. When I think of your music I think of the composer Steve Reich.

M. I love Steve Reich.

C. Reich enables individual players to become one.

M. This musical parallel tells you a lot about me.

Steve Reich as a leading figure in the minimalist movement had a significant impact on my work as a music therapist and composer. Minimalist composition is controlled and has ostensibly little connection with the process of improvising. The merging and development of small figures, can however have direct applications on the developing clinical/musical relationship. By focusing on minimal patterns as the core of musical development an intimate merger can appear that can have important consequences for the developing relationship (note: for further discussion see Chapter sixteen). These patterns, often initiated by the client, can also be introduced by the therapist as a direct clinical intervention. Once a minimalist merger has occurred it is the therapist's responsibility to understand and interpret the nature of such a musical union. The danger is that as individual players unite the music can also become relationally and musically redundant. The therapist must know how to move toward and away from such a musical dialogue in a way that is pertinent to the direction of the work.

Following the Path

C. I'm amazed at the intent of our musical dialogue.

M. It's like looking for the path . . . we both have a serious intention to find significant music . . . important things need to be expressed. Sometimes you need time to pause. I can only get help if I make myself available. If I talk in a foreign musical tongue to you . . . if I decide I am going to scream at you and yell at you it won't work . . . the only way I am going to get something is to find a way of talking to you. I can only relate to other people if I don't run, crush, or smother them.

C. Did you feel at times that you where trying to smother me?

M. Yes, and I think that's valid therapy and social learning therapeutically. It's like rebellion because at times I had an image of a place I wanted to go. When you didn't always go there it frustrated me and I would rebel.

C. There were times when I would test you musically.

M. This is what makes our work therapy . . . we could very justifiably claim that this is music psychotherapy. For the record I think an analytic therapist would talk about everything that's happening here in terms of narcissistic personality. That the client is expressing intense emotions and yet he's not talking about it. Musically we are communicating at a deep and intense level . . . that is the paradox. To communicate with you I had to offer something you could embrace. I have tried to qualify different types of grieving in sorrow. I believe there are different areas of emotion and expression . . . and then there's anger and other kinds of grief . . . another kind of sorrow. There are musical leitmotivs that help us find these modes of expression.

After the opening general dialogue we move to a more in-depth analysis of sessions seven, eight and ten.

Audio Extract Three: Session Seven (ten minutes after the opening)

- Michael settles on a repeated A (xylophone)
- The therapist plays the same tone on the piano
- Michael begins to vocalize and the therapist joins him
- A vocal dialogue develops alongside the repeated A on xylophone and piano
- Michael starts to play the cymbal

- Michael finally moves from the A and the therapist begins to introduce a harmonic accompaniment
- Michael's vocalizing becomes more impassioned
- The music builds in intensity
- Michael's singing turns into screaming/shouting
- A section of extended cymbal playing
- The improvisation finally subsides

M. What we are doing here is totally liberating . . . it's like flying. The cymbal playing with piano is commanding and yet it doesn't divert attention. I started using my voice and wrote: "What is there about this music that so evidently points to the fact that I am vulnerable?" My vocalizations sound fragile and vulnerable whereas everything else is so forceful . . . not everything . . . but so much is determined. And when I heard the repeated "A" on the xylophone I wrote: "What song is this? . . . what are we singing? . . . I don't know." You were only playing an "A" too?

C. Yes . . . I made the decision to stay on the same pitch as you.

M. We started the "A," hovering with our voices. I haven't an image of what this song was about. I couldn't tell you . . . I'm full of questions… and then I play the cymbal again. This helps me. It's an aid for my expression. My voice grows stronger and higher. The cymbal is ambivalent. In one way it helps and in another it detracts. The cymbal has a role . . . it's like setting the scene. It's a contradictory role even though it's serving a purpose. Then I do lots of playing that sets the scene for the scream that never leaves my throat. I make an effort to set the scene but I can't do it. I don't think I fully screamed . . . I'm trying but I can't fully express it. The cymbal is like a anchor to express what I otherwise can't. It's almost petty . . . until we get to the real expression. And then you reintroduce the funeral march and I say: " No one would want to listen to this!" This session seems to be like a diagnosis where you can see the real issues and the aim of the therapy. The pathology. And then there is the gong and I remember thinking that it's like a reminder of the enormous emotion that is threatening and looming in the background. It's a threat because there is a rhythm that goes on forever.

C. This experience for me was totally embodied.

M. There were moments in this session when I did things in spite of myself, as if I didn't mind doing it even though I didn't know why.

Audio Extract Four: Session Eight (fifteen minutes after the opening)

- Michael sings quietly–long sustained phrases–the therapist accompanies
- The therapist begins to sing also
- Michael begins to sing the therapist's name: "Colin"
- He sings part-sentences "I . . . , I have . . . , but I have . . . , yes I . . ."
- The music builds in intensity
- Instrumental climax one
- The music subsides–Michael and the therapist sing quietly together
- Michael sings: "Now listen"–the therapist stops singing
- Michael continues singing: "Listen to my song. Listen to me. Listen to my song."
- Instrumental climax two
- The music subsides and Michael continues singing: "My song it is sad . . . and my song is long . . . it is sad and it is long… and my song it had a beauty . . . yet it is sad, so sad."
- Instrumental climax three
- Michael's cymbal playing becomes loud and free
- The music subsides and Michael continues singing: "And my song, it is high and low, high . . . low, high . . . low . . ."
- Instrumental climax four
- The music becomes quieter and more gentle

M. It's interesting to see how we were developing our conversation in close contact right from the beginning. Unlike the previous session when we took nearly half - an - hour to negotiate our relationship. In this session it was there immediately. Listening now I am struck by how much of your music is in the dialogue. You are taking a more confident musical role. Even though I play musical tidal waves you are still prominent. You are not retreating.

C. Our relationship is different in this session. I am musically more prominent and directive. It was a conscious decision because of our developing relationship and the nature of the musical expression at this time. When you started to sing my name I was shocked. This was the first time a client had done that in therapy. It felt uncomfortable . . . like being in a dream and being called to. I remember thinking: "Why are you calling me?" "What do you need from me?" . . . so many emotions raced through my mind. Do you remember this as clearly as I?

M. I find it hard to reconnect with the emotion or the intent of my singing. I really don't know. I'm perfectly sure it did mean something to me then . . . but couldn't tell you what. I remember this moment when I had an idea of calling your name. I was hesitant because I knew it was daring. It was like standing across a boundary . . . even though we had never agreed there would be this boundary. It's something to do with connecting to another person. We were playing music together on an equal basis, even though it was understood that I was the client. We were two equal people expressing through music. From the second session it was clear that we were musically standing on the same plane. Your musical ability and technique was better, larger, and more sophisticated than mine. But in terms of what we expressed together it was an equal contribution.

C. I felt honored to be an equal musical partner.

M. I know I have pain, loneliness, and depression. I am in this world and I can engage in some kind of communication that enables me to look outside. But at the same time I say: "Hey, look at this . . . It's me . . . listen to me." Reaching out to another human being. It was one of those scarce moments when I was in a position to let someone in and openly share. This was more distinctive and intense than anything else we had shared before. What implications would this have to sing your name?... and yet it seemed so natural. In the music you were following, you were reacting to me . . . this is why it was so extraordinary.

C. Then came the moment when you started to sing.

M. I don't know what to say.

C. Do you remember?

M. I wanted to express that my song is both sad and beautiful. There is beauty and there is sadness. This is what I was struggling to express. It's a powerful example of how important words can be with singing. The last time I sang, I sang that my song was both high and low . . . they are just words.

C. For me this was a stunning experience.

M. It's absolutely profound I'm sure . . . it's not the words themselves. I wanted to use words to try and acknowledge the fact that life is challenging and that it's hard and sad and yet it has beauty . . . I guess that's all.

C. That in itself is profound.

M. I was more struck by the intervals that we were using . . . the musical things that happened between us more than the words. The recorder was a substitute for my voice. It was painful and like weeping but that was the closest I could get to the actual expression of weeping. Then I introduced the cymbal. It was such an integral part . . . it was always there. I'm amazed at how I keep it going. There is a loud passage and then the constant pulse. Throughout this session the balance between us is wonderful. There was only one moment when you didn't go along with me . . . one brief moment until I got to my senses and we could take it from there. You follow wherever I went except for a very few instances.

C. This is a perfect example of AeMT.

M. In retrospect I know this expression was good for me but I can't say more than that. Maybe it's like a security mechanism for me now not to be able to reconnect . . . because it's history.

C. Perhaps it would be too much if you did?

M. Exactly. If we had to tell anybody what an experience these sessions were and why they were so profound I would have a really hard time. I've been talking about our sessions to a lot of people and I'm completely convinced that it was absolutely profound and yet people have asked: "What did you do?" "What did it do for you?" "What was the point of it?" These are hard questions because it was so intangible. The core was that I was able to express my pain, to address it and then finally transcend it.

Audio Extract Five: Session Ten (ten minutes after the opening)

- Michael sings alone
- Michael whistles disembodied music
- Michael play the recorder and the therapist sings
- The therapist stops playing the piano leaving voice (therapist) and recorder (Michael)
- The therapist resumes playing the piano
- Voice (therapist) and recorder (Michael)
- Two voices a capella
- The music subsides leaving Michael singing on a chant overtone
- Both players eventually rest on the same note/chant tone
- The music dies away to nothing

M. How equal do you think the musical relationship is here?

C. Totally equal.

M. That's what I felt. I have written: "simply music." We were simply playing music, I don't think it,s anymore than that.

THE THERAPIST CONCLUDES

In articulating clinical work where music is the essence, there is the potential for misconception even more strongly than through the written word. Music can be our ally but also our nemesis if we do not, as therapists, clarify its role within the process. Music-centered approaches to music therapy, I believe, are still misunderstood because the role of music in therapy itself is misunderstood. Clinical improvisation continues to inspire yet perplex. Structure and freedom balanced within the framework of intrinsic personal creativity is a complex yet liberating phenomena. This case study as a clear example of AeMT, shows how music as a therapeutic force can be a process that is complete within itself. Michael's musical clarity and reflective analysis shows his belief in the potential for music to expressively articulate loss. His words give support and accuracy, but it is in his music that the kernel of therapy is born and cultivated. Improvisation is at the core of his therapy and to understand his journey we must understand the nature of his musical persona. Thus the audio examples hold the key–returning always to the music–in realizing his musical journey through bereavement.

Michael's presence in my life during the sessions and now as we prepare this work has been considerable. The musical challenge he set me as our work began often felt overwhelming. Could I meet this challenge and what it would mean to musically translate the intense pain of his mother's death? In asking him to meditate on our work some years later, I was equally aware that this could be very painful to reflect upon. Had I the right to suggest such a venture and could this work become in itself another therapeutic process? For me the opportunity to analyze our work was indisputably therapeutic. As we unearthed ever more complex aspects of our alliance I began to further appreciate the nature of our musical relationship. I hope the outcome, not only for Michael but for music therapy as a profession, has been worthwhile. Clients teach and define a music therapist's practice. Michael's sessions were pivotal in helping me further realize the balance and interplay between the "art" and "science" of improvisation and that neither are mutually exclusive. The "science" of creativity is equal in stature to the "art" of empiricism. It is how we define their limits that provides the necessary opening for each individual's conception of music and therapy. This case study highlights this developing balance and search that is concrete and yet inherently creative.

THE CLIENT CONCLUDES

When listening to the music, I immediately understand that what is being negotiated in sound reflects a therapeutic process that has taught me something very important. With hindsight, I understand that the mere expression of emotions in the presence of a therapist is not necessarily therapeutic.

When I first listened to the extracts Colin had chosen for this case study, I thought: "There isn't enough of the furious gong-bashing in it! People won't really understand just how great my pain and suffering was!" Only later I realized that the sheer loudness and sustained drum beating of mine was not very meaningful at all. Only now I understand that what Colin's unfailing presence offered me was this: to reach out to him from my remote point of loneliness. Rather than making a big noise so that he would reach out to me and comfort my wounded soul, my only chance to find help and comfort was to reach out to him! Naturally, less imposing music that leaves more room for refined interaction was what I needed to offer him. I am glad I did. Because what I found was a therapist who was every bit as passionate, courageous, and humourous as one can only wish for, when a client really needs help.

Chapter Seven

BEETHOVEN, *STRING QUARTET IN A MINOR, OP. 132*: CREATIVITY, MUSIC, AND ILLNESS

> Beethoven's last quartets are not the justification of modern music, but modern music has reached the point at which it justifies the quartets.
>
> –Marion M. Scott, *Beethoven* (1934), quoted in Watson (1994)

Immersing myself in music as a young man I was challenged to find innovative avenues of contemporary sounds that would keep expanding my awareness. Because I belonged to the 20th century and avant-garde, I wanted desperately to know all recent trends. Alongside my thirst for new music I also looked to the great composers and their greatest works . . . to find the essence of what had made them great. If I could understand the psychology of musical greatness then I misguidedly thought perhaps I too could be great! When I bought my first recording of the Beethoven string quartets I felt as though I was holding a testament. The substantial box that held the twelve discs somehow seemed both immense and impenetrable. I remember wondering why this music was regarded so highly. Carefully extracting each record and moving from the first to the last quartet, I listened and studied each from the score. There was a sense of responsibility to listen to every movement, every phrase, and every note with precise detail. As I entered the realm of the late quartets I was unprepared for the impact these works were to have on me. Indeed their grandeur shone; listening repeatedly I tried to fathom what lay behind the notes and immersed myself in the beauty of their sound. In this music I felt a sense of responsibility that deeply affected my relationship with music. The fact that I could not fully understand their meaning made them ever more intriguing. I knew then that my alliance with this music would be a lifetime commitment. To this day I listen to the quartets with awe, to the sounds that Beethoven captured, the beauty of form, the serenity of melodic textures, and the inner personal struggle they portray.

Beethoven's late string quartets are regarded among the most perfect, profound, and spiritual music ever written. They stand as a testament to perfection and are the most personal and revealing of all his compositions. In these works

Beethoven's soul is bared. His pain is evident; pruned to the essentials of life and psyche. Their musical construction is near perfection; complexity of form manifested through a simplicity of content. Can we define the music behind the notes that are so clearly a part of the late quartets? Just as the essence of music is beyond rationalization so this music defies the ultimate logic of analysis.

The influence of the late string quartets on my evolution as a clinical improviser has been considerable. Beethoven passionately shaped my growth as a musician. Upon becoming a music therapist I again looked to Beethoven's clarity of form to help in my development of musical resources. I renewed my relationship with the piano sonatas, playing them now as both clinician and artist. Considering a connection between the two, I speculated how themes and ideas might be transported to work with clients. I also heard his symphonies anew and felt ever more connected to the beauty and struggle portrayed through his opera *Fidelio.* This renewed alliance culminated in my reestablishing a connection with the string quartets. I listened again from the first quartet to the last, marking on the score possible musical ideas that could be used as themes in clinical improvisation. This music I transcribed, practiced, and then tentatively dared to take into sessions. Apart from the practicalities of musical content I looked to the inward nature of the music. Working in palliative care had changed my sense of life, endings, and suffering. What now was my personal relationship with these works? Why did they affect me so acutely? What spiritual connection had I made and how could I utilize this personal connection to aid my maturing work as a music therapist?

As I began to find new meaning in Beethoven's music a clinical encounter occurred that cemented a link to music therapy. Margaret was referred to me as a client in the final days of her life. She was in a wheelchair and silent. Taking Margaret quietly to the music therapy room I placed her next to me at the piano. We sat in silence. After what seemed like an age suspended in time, I gently took her hand and placed it on the keys. Margaret began to play with a sense of inner quiet. She caressed the keys, creating a hushed and ethereal musical atmosphere. Whether or not she had played the piano before was immaterial. What was important was the quality of her sounds placed behind and beyond the notes themselves. It was as if she was expressing something more than the music itself. I knew my response would have to be of an equally penetrating nature. I struggled as I heard the incorporeal nature of Margaret's music. How best could I meet the beauty of sounds and of the musical embodiment she was inwardly portraying? An essence of Beethoven's late quartets seemed the exact response. I focused on the four-part precision of Beethoven's string writing, particularly the slow music. I did not use a transcribed theme, but instead attempted to capture the inward quality of Beethoven's music. I began to improvise string-like parts in response to Margaret, attempting to share with her my own passionate love of the quartets. By offering her a sense of my clinical/musical relationship with the quartets–as a type of musical countertransference–the relationship immediately opened. This was my first clinical application of Beethoven and proved to be the beginning of a new relationship with the composer and music therapy itself.

BEETHOVEN'S LATE WORKS AND AESTHETIC MUSIC THERAPY

Beethoven's late style has been discussed at length in the literature. It is not always the case that a composer's final works are their finest. Adorno (1998) suggests that the distinctiveness of Beethoven's compositions lay in their enigmatic nature and constantly changing styles:

> If asked for the true reason for Beethoven's greatness I would probably answer first of all: that he did not simply produce one good Beethoven piece after another, but he incessantly–virtually infinitely–produced new characters, types, categories of music. (Adorno, 1998, p. 159)

To create and re-create, to produce new ideas and new sounds, to challenge that which has already been acknowledged, and to move forward incessantly are hallmarks of greatness. The "timelessness" (Dalhaus, 1991) that permeates Beethoven's late works is a true aesthetic of his genius. His music transcends the time in which it was written and is as contemporaneous now as the day it was written. Because of this timeless quality Beethoven's late music has the potential to shape the principles of AeMT on many levels.

Beethoven's late works hold an interesting position in music history. His final period of creativity is the standard against which all other composers are compared. It is as if Beethoven's final works are sacrosanct. This is due not only to the extraordinary clarity of the music itself but also to his developing deafness. The impact of disability on his composing is undeniable for the listener and is even more significant when we realize many of his late works were written when he was supposedly totally deaf. What effect did Beethoven's deafness have on his music? There appears to have been a decline in piano music and an increase in other areas (Cooper, 1990). Listening to his late music as a therapist, one is struck by the underlying pain and despair balanced with music of great serenity. What of the man that bought this music into being? We tend only to see the genius and not the fragility of the person. What inner personal crises must he have faced? Knowing this to be true if we revisit his music as therapists, if we listen as an expression of disability, then what implications could this have for clinical practice? Beethoven's late works are the pinnacle of creativity. They are also the pinnacle of adversity in the face of decline. If we separate one from the other–similarly, if we disconnect a client's musical ability from their illness–then our picture and understanding is incomplete. Music therapists need to consider Beethoven's music clinically not only for our own learning but also to shed light on this explosion of creativity in the face of illness.

What does it mean for a person's genius to flourish when confronting loss? Music therapists working in palliative care may experience this phenomenon regularly. A clients' creativity often becomes more tangible and authentic as their health declines. Francis eloquently expresses this in *Music at the Edge*:

> I sit here and think "How can I?" on one level–the level that I'm amazed at the continuity, richness and absolute security of what I'm doing. I'm not amazed at myself. It's a rather . . . it's so natural, so automatic that it doesn't amaze me. I'm delighted by the validity. It seems as though it is good and that it does convey expression. It does convey meaning and certainly it speaks back to me–and I think it speaks to you. So on one level I'm amazed it happens, but on another it's naturally a part of me . . . It's what is behind this desire to give concrete form to something. I suppose it really is an instinctive expansion of the soul. (Lee, 1996, p. 136)

Francis's exploding creativity indeed spoke to me on many levels. His dying and the growth of his music were indeed extraordinary phenomena.

Begbie (2000) suggests that "perhaps there is a link between the temporal extremities of Beethoven's late quartets and the extremity of his own impending death" (p.117). The late quartets do have a sense of ephemerality that could clearly support this argument. If Beethoven was aware of his approaching death and if he used his compositions to express personal despair, then what can music therapists learn about music and loss?

Beethoven's depiction of peace is also crucial in our overall understanding of his music (Lockwood, 1992). Listening to the variations of the fourth section of the string quartet No. 14 in C# minor, Op. 131 (Andante ma non troppo e molto cantabile), we hear music that is exquisitely serene. This is music of clarity and equilibrium. Just as clients often express themselves through opposing styles so much of Beethoven's late music is contradictory and enigmatic rather than a direct expression of frustration.

For Mahler and other composers their composing was a means to reflect on their impermanence and their anguish at confronting death. Historically then, Beethoven is not alone. However, the complexities of his personal situation and his compositional representation of it were, I believe, unique. Listening to the "Hammerklavier" sonata, the 9th Symphony, or the late quartets one hears emotions balanced with exaltation, tranquility, and torment. That we cannot fully know his anguish means we will never fully understand the daily obstacles he faced. What we can hear, however, is a sense of uncertainty, of a man not knowing his future. That these styles combined to reflect a complex personality is a further testament to Beethoven's greatness. If we listen anew to these works–if we hear more than the notes themselves–then perhaps we may better understand the meaning of music, emotion, and therapeutic intent.

As Beethoven struggled with his declining health so he yielded to his escalating genius. His music became ever more an explicit translation of the human condition. Through the string quartet medium Beethoven captured a complex range of emotions that had alluded him in other genres. From the serious contrapuntal opening of op. 131 to the strident measured intensity of the Grosse, Fuge op. 133, Beethoven's understanding of compositional structure became ever more discerning. The late quartets draw the listener into the inner workings of his music.

Beethoven's late quartets reveal a musical precision that is at the heart of AeMT. AeMT strives to find a similar level of musical meticulousness in clinical improvisation. Just as Beethoven refines and eliminates extraneous musical expression in these works so clinical improvisers aim to remove the irrelevant from their musical response to clients. To study Beethoven's late quartets as clinical theory will help to establish true potential of music therapy. Through the exacting study of musical components, the relationship of players, the overall infrastructure of movements, and Beethoven's psyche it is possible to relate compositional theory to clinical awareness. The connection between Beethoven's late quartets and AeMT is thus a challenge to the development of clinical improvisation.

"HEILIGER DANKGESANG EINES GENESENEN AN DIE GOTTHEIT, IN DER LYDISCHEN TONART" ANALYSIS OF OP. 132, THIRD MOVEMENT

Beethoven's *String Quartet in A Minor, Op. 132*, was written after a long illness of jaundice (O'Shea, 1990). It was composed between February and mid-July of 1825 and was commissioned by Prince Nikolas Galitzin (Imeson, 1996). The quartet is divided into five movements: Assai sostenuto, Allegro ma non tanto, Andante, Alla marcia, Allegro appassionato. This was the first quartet to be written in five movements and contains the structural use of paradox that includes:

> . . . melodic surprises, unusual harmonies, atypical sonorities, incongruities of genre, juxtaposition of sharply contrasting musical events, and frustrations of expectations on various levels, . . . (Imeson 1996, p. 125)

Compositional devices include the use of intervals and motives that work independently from the overall structure of the quartet (Dalhaus, 1994). The music is constructed so that it gives a sense of improvisational freedom.

Listening as a music therapist one is struck by the tension and release in the quartet's construction. The music moves between dark austerity and subtle sophistication. There is a tautness in the sudden and unexpected polarity of ideas that catch and draw the listener into the strength of the piece. Slow obscure music is contrasted with clear melodic lines. Is this quartet a reflection of Beethoven's struggles with his own health? A portrayal of suffering and restlessness? While it may not be possible to conclusively answer these questions there is an overt sense of yearning. What the exact nature of this yearning is, we may never fully know. What is important for music therapy, however, is the translation of Beethoven's sentiments. What therapeutic gains might he have made through the writing of this quartet? How important was it for him to face his immortality and to translate these emotions into musical expression and meaning?

The translation of the heading placed in front of the third movement is: "Hymn of thanksgiving to God of an invalid on his convalescence, in the Lydian mode." Beethoven's articulation of illness here is passionately expressed. The music is austere, yet ethereal. There is a sense of emotional concentration set against a backdrop of lightness and sophistication. The music has two starkly opposing themes (ABA′B′A′′). The first is a simple hymn (A) in the plagal mode based on F. This is balanced against the second florid and dancelike theme (B) in the key of D major.

Placing the opening bars of the three versions of the hymn (A) side by side (see Figure 9), it is possible to analyze Beethoven's treatment of melody and ornamentation and consider the possible connections with AeMT. The first statement (see Figure 9a) of the hymn is a simple yet perfectly controlled statement. Beethoven uses uncomplicated music to portray complex sensitive intentions. Music therapists must strive to find the simplest of music to communicate for and with the client, as well as the most sophisticated emotional shared responses. The carefully placed open intervals, the gently moving upward phrases, and the grounding balance between C and F combine to produce music of immense elegance and sophistication. The second recapitulation (see Figure

9b) contains suspensions and added passing notes, giving the music a greater intensity, while retaining the serene nature of the upward intervals and phrases. It is the third and final reiteration of the theme (see Figure 9c) that is the most heartfelt and potent. It is marked "with the deepest, most intimate feeling." This final version of the hymn is one of the most profound sections of music ever written in Western music. The interweaving and complex stretching of melodies produce an inspiring and intimate chamber music experience. The moving of parts and suspensions become more complex yet the serenity remains. The countermelodies and gentle syncopations give a sense of emotional rocking. As the movement comes to an end it becomes lighter and more transparent. The music makes one hold one's breath; a musical capture of the utmost mystery.

This principle of developing themes is relevant to clinical improvisation. Playing the three versions of the hymn, listening clinically and artistically to the interweaving parts, considering the impact of suspensions, and passing notes on the emotional impact of the music will provide a richness of ideas for improvisational themes. The clarity with which the simple yet spontaneous harmonies move can be a framework for coherent clinical improvisations.

The opposing theme (B) is by contrast light and dancelike (see Figure 10). The key is D major and the time moves from four to three. The staccato octave movements of the lower strings give a light delicacy to the texture. The third beat of the viola and cello remain silent, providing a lilt and strength before the following down beat. The opposing dynamics between f and p provide an element of constant surprise, the syncopation created by the second violin further adding to the glasslike quality of the music.

What then of the sharply contrasting themes and how can Beethoven's work be linked to clinical techniques and the philosophy of AeMT? Never before had Beethoven set such strongly opposing musical ideas (Imeson, 1996).

fig. 9

Violin I
Violin II
Viola
Violoncello
Vln. I
Vln. II
Vla.
Vc.
cresc.

fig. 10

The exploration of opposites in music therapy (Lee, 1992; Aigen, 1998) is an interesting study. Therapists may use strongly contrasting themes to offer a sense of ambiguity and lack of expectancy. Musical unfamiliarity is as important in the musical relationship as predictability. Beethoven, I believe, wanted to provide that exact same sense of opposites. It shows the serenity and sparseness is more powerful if compared to lightness and dance. This presentation of opposites can be important for clients who need a musical framework that is dependable but not predictable. Beethoven here teaches us what it means to move from one emotion to another. Studying the score we see that the transitions between the two styles of music are simple, direct, and uncomplicated. We could also hypothesize that emotional opposites provide a potency that can be crucial for the therapeutic alliance. That the second theme (B) is not repeated at the end of the movement highlights the spontaneous nature of the quartet and the potential of openness and uncertainty. At the end of the movement we are left suspended and unsure.

BEETHOVEN AS CLINICAL GUIDE

Susan, a 30-year-old, blind, nonverbal, quadriplegic client, had lived in a group home all her life. Our first meeting was during the group music therapy/physiotherapy session held weekly at the home. Susan's creativity radiated. Her response to improvised music was startling in its sensitivity and understanding. Even though Susan was physically immobile and unable to play instruments without assistance, her voice was free and communicatively sophisticated. I felt an immediate musical connection. Individual music therapy sessions were soon arranged. The work consisted of free vocalizations and instrumental improvisations with the aid of a co-therapist. Our work was alive and vital and was deeply embedded in the musical experience.

Beethoven's late string quartets were to have a great influence on our music. As with Margaret, my understanding of Susan's invention necessitated improvisations that had clear musical lines and powerful content. Susan's vocal contributions were phrased with precision and her awareness of our developing musical relationship was acute. As Susan and I entered themes and ideas from the quartets so our quickening musical alliance grew. An example from session nine shows the inclusion of a skeleton theme taken from the third movement of Op. 135 (Lento assai, cantante e tranquillo) (see Figure 11). Taking the underlying harmonic progression, I improvised chords directly from the quartet. The reason for this choice of linkage came from various factors. First, from my experience, D flat major is a key of stability and strength. Many of Susan's vocalizations were spontaneously centered around black keys (E flat minor, G flat major). Second, this section of the quartet has a serene quality and sense of suspended time. Third, the simple yet gently moving harmonic sequence felt appropriate for Margaret's quiet demeanor in this session. Lastly, this short section of the quartet has a simple and beautiful melody. The stepwise movement balanced with the unpredictable moving sequence gives unexpected balance. Susan's response to Beethoven's musical resource came from, I believe, an innate understanding of the spiritual and enigmatic nature of the music and its source. My role was that of the catalyst between Beethoven and Susan. Taking Beethoven's music into clinical improvisation I was able to provide Susan with a direct link to his music. In my role as composer/music therapist this is one of the most therapeutic and significant experiences I can offer a client. Throughout this improvisation Beethoven was a potent and exacting clinical guide for both Susan and myself.

Understanding Beethoven's nature of composing and allowing it to directly influence clinical work is a gift for all clients. Just as music therapy cannot separate the musical from the therapeutic, so understanding Beethoven the man is as important as understanding Beethoven and his music. Our interpretation of the influence between emotional and compositional processes comes from the music and available historical information. The images portrayed of Beethoven are of a man disheveled and emotionally unkempt. We think of Beethoven as a composer enraged with his ensuing deafness. This simplistic view becomes more apparent when listening to his works as music therapists. What we infer is indeed a man in mental anguish. We also discover a man of sensitivity and gentleness. In Beethoven's late music there is an astute articulation of oppression and yearning for freedom. These feelings are musically translated through an eloquence of style. Beethoven creates intense yet delicate music that opposes the nature of his personal agony; an artistic translation of the struggles in facing the unknown.

These same situations face many of our clients, and as therapist we try to alleviate them and place them within a broader musical context. Facing the unknown and traversing life through a maze of emotional dilemmas is a familiar music therapy occurrence. As our clients grapple to make sense of the world so their musical impression is similarly complex. I believe that Beethoven made sense of his physical limitations and deterioration through the stability and coherence of composition. The opportunity to offer clients a similar balance is evidence enough to warrant a complete investigation of the clinical applications of Beethoven's music. If we acknowledge this analogy between Beethoven's psychological dilemmas and the clients we work with, then what implications could this on the future of music therapy?

Original

Session

fig. 11

Chapter Eight

ANALYSIS AND ASSESSMENT

> The purpose of music is to draw toward a total exaltation in which the individual mingles, losing his consciousness in a truth immediate.
>
> Ianis Xenakis (1922–) in *The New York Times*, 21 April 1976

The musical content of music therapy has always been under debate. In music therapy why is the music considered secondary to psychology, medicine, and psychotherapy and how can we raise the musical standard of clinical practice to accommodate complex musical theories? The argument that to consider musical quality is to detract from an understanding of music therapy is, from a music-centered perspective, inconceivable. In the analysis and assessment of AeMT an understanding of music theory is essential. The recognition of musical and therapeutic structures is critical for a balanced perspective. Does musical analysis destroy the essence of creativity? Is it possible to analyze music therapy in exclusively musical terms? The answers lie in our ability to describe and analyze music. Does the resistance toward a detailed understanding of music in music therapy therefore come from unfamiliarity with the theories of music? If the quality and intent of music becomes diluted then its effectiveness in the clinical setting will become diluted also.

Charles, a man living with AIDS, taught me the importance of balancing the musical and therapeutic makeup of clinical improvisation equally. My work with Charles was based on attempts to make musical contact that would reflect his life and illness. Themes were developed from motives initiated from both Charles's own musical creativity and in response to my clinical improvising which contained ideas taken from previous sessions. These themes became the leitmotifs (Carter, 1990) of our work and were used freely as a structural base for each session. Assessment, interpretation, and analysis came from the hierarchical shaping of ideas. In our twenty-fifth session during a four-hands piano improvisation, Charles began to develop an accompanying theme in C minor over which I improvised an open melody. Previous to this section his music had been hard, driving, and brutal. His improvising seemed a direct reflection of his emotional state. My role was one of both support and challenge, as I pushed to keep the driving music constant and propelled. This sudden change in musical direction felt significant and therefore worthy of detailed investigation. The texture and key was developed to form the musical argument for the final stages of the improvisation. On closer inspection through a three-level analysis (see Figure 12), I found underlying tones that formed the core of musical dialogue. By studying the three levels and extracting the core tones I was able to ascertain a relationship between Charles's C minor harmony and my response of D flat (A) and an implied E minor melodic outline (B). The intricacies of our therapeutic relationship are clearly shown in the ambiguity of our musical connection. Charles commented afterward on this section:

> I felt as if this section should have been separate. That we came to an end after an emotional peak. Then it came down into this quiet section. It was felt like that was enough of that life story and after reaching such heights let's express another side of my emotional coin.

In my own notes I make the following observations:

> At this point our therapeutic roles have now reversed, he is allowing me to improvise a melody. It feels like a relief because we are now playing together. We turned a corner. The restlessness of Charles's playing stopped. This music was a point of focus. The music then went in a different direction. The music is more expressive and gentler, not necessarily less painful, but different.

What can we deduce from the above analysis and what do the core tones of level three in relation to levels one and two tell us about Charles's growth as a client? The essential tones that form the core of this improvisation are central. The semitone relationship between client and therapist can be interpreted on several levels. When a core tone is established by the client and heard by the therapist, the therapist must decide upon a response that is appropriate. This means hearing the tone in relation to musical form and as a manifestation of the client's inner world. The semitone was chosen to reflect both closeness and ambiguity. The correlation between C and D flat was based on the close tonal proximity alongside the harmonic core of white and black tonal centers. Therapeutically there was a sense of standing next to, but not smothering Charles's meaning. Thus the therapeutic response from the therapist takes into account levels of music, therapy, and the interface between the two.

It would seem logical that in order to understand the process of clinical improvisation that we should also have an understanding of the musical processes that constitute its makeup. Bruscia (2001) states:

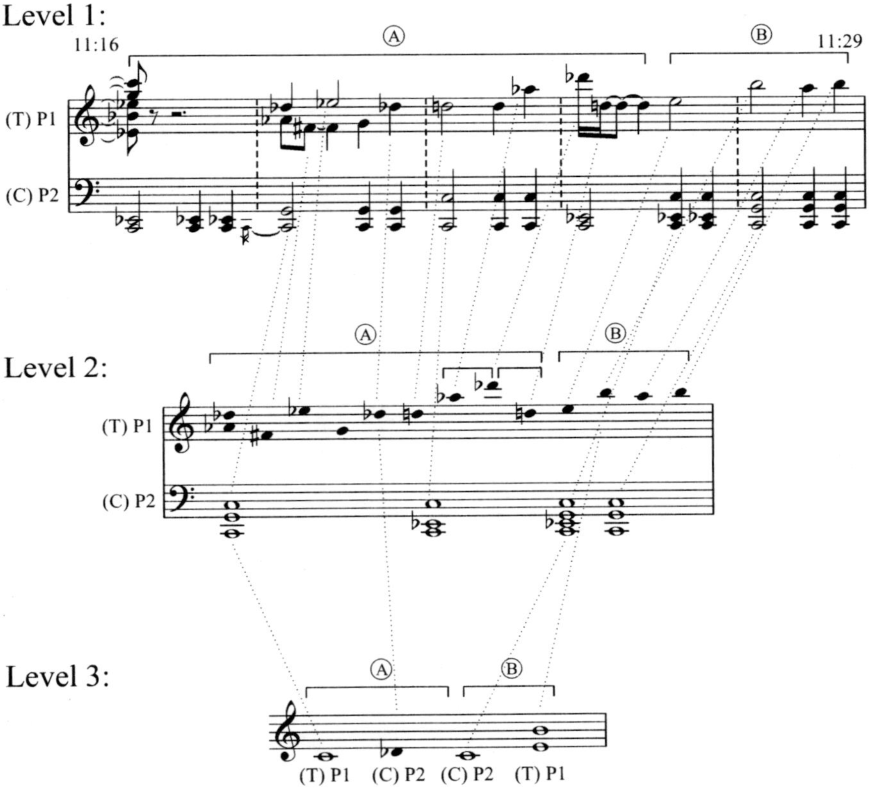

Level 1:
11:16
Ⓐ
Ⓑ
11:29
(T) P1
(C) P2
Level 2:
Ⓐ
Ⓑ
(T) P1
(C) P2
Level 3:
Ⓐ
Ⓑ
(T) P1
(C) P2
(C) P2
(T) P1

fig. 12

> Without methods of music analysis, the improvisational therapist has no focus or frame for listening to the client, the researcher has no methodology for studying the process and outcome of improvisational therapy, and the theorist has no basis for explaining its clinical rationale. (p. 7)

Analysis as a means to gaining greater awareness in music therapy is complex. Comparing divergent theories of "art" and "science" means we must make quantum leaps of knowing that often give rise to theoretical tension. One might argue that music analysis is too embedded in music, that psychotherapeutic interpretations are too subjective, or that music medicine is too scientific and therefore links will be impossible to find. Links, however tentative, must be found if we are to discover a music therapy theory from within.

MUSIC NOTATION

Finding sympathetic and relevant methods of notation become paramount in defining questions that will evaluate musical intent and therapeutic outcome. The graphic notation of clinical improvisation (Bergstrom-Nielsen, 1999) is an important development in making available evidence of sessions other than audio or video recordings, a means of transcribing music therapy diagrammatically and pictorially. Through various stages of notation, small-scale ("stenographic notation") and large-scale, it is possible to provide notational depiction of a session:

> If one or more sessions are to be studied, one can create an elaborate notation. This forces the therapist to make up his or her mind as to how the music is perceived, to go into details and perhaps throw new light on them. This can enable new structural relations to stand out, thus helping the therapist to "look beyond" their subjective bias. (Bergstrom-Nielsen, 1999, p. 14)

Graphic notation provides information that is insightful and creative. It focuses on a free, creative, and musically non-theoretical approach to the analysis and interpretation of improvisations.

The musical notation of improvisations is specific and raises controversial issues on the link between "traditional musicology," music analysis, and music therapy. The following arguments show a resistance to including musical notation as a valid form of assessing music therapy. It is interesting that Smeijsters (1997) loses the core of music itself when he states that;

> classical notation does not capture the essence of the musical-psycho-social processes that occur during improvisation (p. 197)

When discussing this author's work in music analysis describes "problematic cross-currents" and obstacles of methodology and philosophy in attempting to link "musical content and personal (therapeutic) significance" (p. 11). For Ansdell (2001) the translation of "musical form" into "therapeutic content" focuses on the problem of "the way the translation is being made" (p. 12.) Bruscia's (2001) view that the analysis of music is a "common language for music therapists to communicate with other musicians" (p. 15), is considered alongside three shortcomings. First, that traditional methods are too focused on tonal harmony, second, that music analysis is too organized to include the more random features of improvisation, and third, that improvisations are not easy to aurally notate and thus not accurate. The few therapists who have included traditional musical notation, apart from myself, in their work (Aldridge 1996, 2000; Ansdell 1995) are critiqued by Ansdell (2001), including his own work, when he discusses traditional musicological methodology "which tends, despite the most stringent efforts, to turn processes into structures, and to be insufficiently sensitive to contextual" issues (p. 12).

In defense of musical notation and my research in this area (Lee 1989, 1990, 1992, 1995, 1996, 2000), I would like to propose a five-point counter-argument. First, music notation is a standard form of depicting music and is understood by all musicians. Second, if adapted and used creatively it can provide the flexibility necessary for analysis of improvisation. Third, there are now available computer programs that alleviate the necessity to transcribe aurally. Fourth, there are many forms of music analysis that cover aspects of both tonal (Schenker, 1979) and atonal (Forte, 1973) harmony, melody, and rhythm. Fifth, that the divide between "musical form" and "therapeutic content" must come first from an understanding of the nuts and bolts of music itself. Understanding this within the therapeutic context is the essential dilemma. In the current trends of the new musicology traditional methods of analysis may seem outdated and irrelevant to music therapy. I believe, however, that music notation should not be ignored as outdated. Rather, I believe we should be attempting to discover what aspects of music analysis and notation can help us in our further understanding of the divide between music and therapy. Recent work addressing these issues can be found in Arnasons work (2002) analyzing improvisations based on the work of Ferrara (1984, 1991). This research balances narratives from clients' processing, their journals, the therapist's musical analysis, and "analytical notes based on transcriptions of audiotaped sessions" (Arnason 2002, p.17).

THE GENERATIVE CELL

As my experience and proficiency in clinical improvisation grew and as I began to study more intensely the therapeutic and musical processes, I began to suspect that the musical core of many improvisations were based on small recurring motives. My initial aural sense was that motives originated mainly from melody. Through subsequent listenings I also noted rhythmic and harmonic cells. It appeared that these themes, or groups of notes, were initiated from either; a) the client, b) the therapist, or c) a spontaneous union between therapist and client. My hypothesis was that if I could extract these notes and study them in relation to the therapeutic process that it may help in my understanding of the subtleties and intricacies in the developing musical relationship. The clinical significance of a small melodic group of notes was first identified by Carter (1990):

> In the early stages of the work a small melodic phrase emerges which comes to assume a significance which is not immediately noticeable when it is first played. It is often discovered on reflection, for it is not until I have given sufficient time and thought to the musical process that the importance of what has been sounded becomes apparent. This small melodic phrase comes to be heard as the Leitmotif of the individual. In all cases I was to find that Leitmotif, as it came to be called, embodied either the nature of the presenting, or to be a realization in sound of an aspect of personhood by which the individual waited to be recognized.

In my research I noted that small groups of notes potentially provided the evidence for specific representations of clinical meaning. This concept became to be known as the generative cell and was defined as:

> . . . the germination of the improvisational procedures from a small group of notes; the seed motif: small musical themes that form the core of the improvisational procedure. (Lee, 1995, p. 49)

One of the four hypotheses of my ensuing research included an evaluation of the generative cell, stating that:

> . . . specific musical themes and/or motifs are employed (consciously or subconsciously) as a generative basis for the therapeutic improvisation as a whole. (Lee, 1995, p. 44)

It was through my doctoral research (Lee, 1992) and subsequent evaluation of work with Francis (Lee, 1996) that the generative cell became an identifiable force. Francis's evaluation of the cell prompted me to consider with greater weight this fascinating phenomena:

> The cell for me is the closest representation of how I am feeling. It contains an intensity of expression that is both limited and expansive. This duality is crucial, though I am completely unaware of how complex the cell became in the overall make-up of what I consider to be these certain crucial improvisations. The cell provides me with a structure in which I can focus my feelings, particularly when exploring death and dying. (Lee, 1996, p. 57)

To investigate the significance of the generative cell I took the improvisation discussed above and analyzed it within the following categories (see Figure 13):

- Pure–the cell in original order
- Inverted–the cell in reverse order
- Transposed–the cell starting on a different pitch
- Permutated–the cell in any order
- Harmonic–the cell as a basis for harmony
- Concealed–the cell hidden within the structure of the improvisation

I found to my amazement that the generative cell formed the essential backbone of the complete improvisation. The cell (A flat, G, E) provided a link between therapeutic intent and musical outcome. The semitone balanced alongside the minor third and the overall interval of the major third suggested an avoidance of tonality. The complexity and dense use of the cell, in all its combinations, showed the importance of a small group of tones in the therapeutic process. Downward intervals like these illustrated were common in work with people who were ill. The carefully chosen displacement of tones and their relation and subsequent development were crucial in a client finding a musical representation of their illness. In AeMT improvisation originates from a musical core that develops toward a union of music and therapy. The consequence of the generative cell in AeMT is of significance not only as a means for understanding improvisational musical structure but also in the evaluation of therapeutic and musical meaning. That a client without musical education has the ability to establish complex cells warrants further investigation in the intent and meaning of the generative cell.

Examples of the Generative Cell:

The pure cell

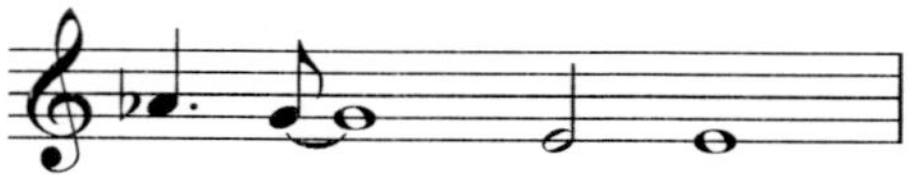

The inverted cell

The transposed cell

The permutated cell

The harmonic cell

The concealed cell

fig. 13

INDEXING

Indexing is a form of ongoing assessment that evaluates the complex strands of the therapeutic process from audio and video recording. It is mainly applicable to individual work but can also be adapted to group work. Indexing was first introduced by Nordoff and Robbins (1977) in their individual work with children:

> An Index Sheet should be made which describes the course of the session by listing each significant clinical detail against the appropriate counter number on the tape recorder. Noting some specific musical facts about the child's response will be important: the tempo range of his beating, his pitch range in singing songs, the tones of any free singing he does–the information should be sufficient to give a clear outline of his response. (p. 92)

In the recently revised edition of *Creative Music Therapy* (Nordoff & Robbins, in press) Robbins further highlights the importance of noting specific music facts such as the character of the child's beating, rhythmic order in the child's use of the instruments, and the character of the child's singing The detailed examples of indexing that follow give a clear sense of the intricate nature of detailed assessment in this context.

Indexing in AeMT was developed from the work of Nordoff and Robbins. The nature of indexing and its potential for illuminating our understanding of the therapeutic process is balanced alongside the time-consuming nature of its detail. There are no limits to the amount of time one can spend indexing a session, the individual therapist(s) determining the importance of the session, and/or sections that require more or less detailed analysis. Indexing is an effective form of assessment because it can be used on many levels to assess the moment-to-moment experience of the session. Indexing is the most musical and interpretive form of assessment and yet also the most objective and behavioral. Information can be counted, interpreted, and adapted to meet the needs of the client group and the therapist's clinical orientation. If two therapists are working with a client then it is advised that indexing should be completed as a team.

Because it is impossible to index in detail the many clients within a music therapist's work load, two levels have been formulated. In Surface Indexing (level one) the therapist(s) evaluates the session without stopping the tape. Comments are made on the index sheets as the session unfolds. At the end of the session the therapist(s) will make connections and recommendations. At level one the therapist(s) only records events that were striking and/or important.

Musical notation will be simple, such as sketched melodic or rhythmic themes and/or simple harmonic outlines. Inner Indexing (level two) is more intricate. It is a time to listen clinically and to reflect on the complexities of the process. Here the essence is on making connections between the music and the therapeutic aims of the session. The therapist(s) should make their musical notation as detailed as possible, the therapist(s) normally finding that the more experience they accrue the more adept they will become with aurally transcribing music. The therapist(s) is encouraged to listen to pivotal passages more than once. As in level one, at the end of the session the therapist(s) will make connections and recommendations.

There are three classifications of indexing:

1. Behavior

Include only factual information. All nonmusical observations: the clients, their posture, the way they enter the room, any verbal comments, etc.

2. Music

Include here everything musical. Try and transcribe aurally as much as you can. Extract important musical moments and/or passages and attempt an interpretation of how the music fits into the overall process.

3. Interpretation

Include your interpretations of the session and your personal reactions to the process. Make connections between the objective observations and your impressions of how these affected the outcome. Thoughts on your role as a therapist should be included with perceived successes and failures.

Connections and Recommendations

In your concluding notes it is important to consider links between the three classifications and how the objective, musical, and subjective material interrelates.

Making concluding notes on generalizations, insights, and thoughts will help focus the following session. It is important to end indexing with: a) thoughts on the long-term and short term aims in relation to the session, b) pointers for the following session, c) what the therapist should be working at musically, and d) musical themes and/or ideas to be carried forward and practised.

Please refer to examples of Surface Indexing (see Figure 14) and Inner Indexing (see Figure 15).

Indexing as Self-Assessment

Indexing provides a clear mirror of the therapist's role in the process. It helps clarify interventions and gives a clear indication of the therapist's growth. Indexing highlights the use of clinical music and what the therapist needs to develop musically. Extracting themes and ideas from sessions and using them as resources will give the therapist greater confidence in their developing musical palette. Questions should be: "What musical interventions did I make?" and "What other choices could I have had made?" Often at the time of contact we envisage only a few musical/therapeutic choices whereas after indexing and reflection we may realize that there were in fact hundreds! Indexing keeps you in check as a clinician, musician, and therapist. It is most effectively used in conjunction with supervision.

	Name: St.	Date: 11/1/00	
	BEHAVIOR	**MUSIC**	**PERSONAL**
0.05	St. enters + approaches piano	Humming loudly. I respond by humming on different pitches	Wearing her "angry" face
0.26	I encourage her to play		
0.38		I being Puccini theme	
0.49		St. plays drum (w/hand) I sing H + play S hums!	She seems to be in her own space
1.19		S "ma" + H + continues hums	
1.44		S makes more sounds	
2.05		I try "e i e i o"	It doesn't work S ingnores
2.42		S "splatters" on piano + hums	
3.03		I try "ba ba"s	
3.19		S responds w/ ba ba ba + we exchange "ba"s	
3.46		S plays piano + sings "ba"s	
4.05		I try "e i o"	NO! Fairly unresponsive
4.48	I suggest drum		
4.53		S plays drum w/ sticks	
5.03	I tell her sit + give her drums		
5.23		S sings short H + plays drum + sings ba's	
5.50		Fast beating–I make a din + we sing ba's	
6.10		A very loud sound + continued drumming	
		I accelerate but S stops–then continues at faster tempo	Very energetic drumming

figure 14: Surface Indexing

	BEHAVIOR	MUSIC	PERSONAL
8.30		S adds cymbals	
8.42		I try new theme	Really dumb
9.00		I try M.E.	
10.10		Get with for a second	
10.43		Hits drum 20 times (15)(20)(7)	
12.22		Lots of humming	
12.30	I invite S back to piano–she hands me sticks	Humming	
14.20		Loud expressive sound Gutteral–very loud	
15.30		A very expressive H	
16.23		Expressive humming + loud sounds	
17.32		I try Sp. Mode	
18.00		Try "e i e i" Loud sounds + humming Almost "keening"	NO A crying sound?
20.50	I suggest song		
21.48		S plays gong + hums + loud sounds	
23.00		S stops + I play Puccini softly	
23.25	I invite her back to piano		
23.50		S plays drum Loud + sustained	

Figure 14: Surface Indexing (cont.)

	Name: Jordan	Date: 2/16/2000	
	BEHAVIOR	**MUSIC**	**PERSONAL**
0.06	I play Greetings as J enters room	Change harmony + tempo–J sings to me	Singing weak
0.25	J sings + stands beside me as I---	J sings it in minor ----change to D minor	
0.40	w/o speaking or stopping I move-	----into a D ostinato  **etc…**	I messed up the melodic phrase because I forgot to breathe
		J joins in 3rd bar: 	I try to duplicate pitches on piano. He is reaching for a good idea, but too loud!
1.52		J sings (1st time in <u>steps!</u>) 	
2.17	J smiles as we do this	Imitate each other w. Descending 5ths	
2.43		I change to ostinato + then move back in	Ostinato works well
3.15	J laughs quietly w. pleasure		
3.34		J ends on high F#. I follow with same, on piano.	A 3" improv

Figure 15: Inner Indexing

Tr.3	J laughs quietly w. pleasure		
0.05	J suggests gong next	J ends on high F#. I follow with same, on piano.	Good–he usually wants to stick to drum 1st and gong last.)I think he was "moved" by the mood we had created)
0.10		J hits gong–I respond w. loud organ	Perhaps too loug? Also I was affected by mood + continued in same key
1.45	J stops + goes to drum	J starts w. cymbal	Piano not always "spot on"
		Steady beat on cymbal and drum: ♩♩♩♩♩♩♩ I imitate rhythmic pattern + try to stay w. him J does cadenzas	11 times–nuts?
2.50	J stops	I suggest we play softer I try Spanish	I flounder a bit
3.44	J stops–says he hurt finger + comes to piano for me to kiss it		I suddenly realize what a little child he is!
	I suggest softer	Continue w. Spanish, trying to match J beats very steady	Not so good!
4.28		I switch to M.E. + then "take off"	I am not so good at this (too stuck in music to listen to J)

Figure 15: Inner Indexing (cont.)

4.50		I try matching better + we get back on track. Bass is open 5ths ♩♪♩♪ etc… with M.E. melody	Lose the music (play Eb 7ths and Bb 7ths)
7.40	J yells (?) + hits under cymbal + stands on chair. We stop!		Not as chaotic as I thought, but had the feeling he might be on edge of losing control + he glared at me questioningly– (should I allow him to lose control?)
7.52	I direct J to piano to sing but---------	-------J starts to play softly on white keys–I respond w. chords (Debussyish?) + imitate his rhythmic pattern ♪♪♩♪♪♩	Is this bad, or is it better? Colin, listen please.

Figure 15: Inner Inexing (page 3)

Indexing as Professional Assessment

Indexing is known primarily as a tool for a music therapist's own work. It can also validate work for fellow professionals. Indexing demonstrates the intricacies of the process. Sharing examples of Inner Indexing is evidence of a precise and insightful profession. Indexing can also be focused toward multidisciplinary assessment. Objective classifications can be presented in a format that is behaviorally factual and pragmatic. Precise examples of Surface Indexing can also be used alongside other more formalized styles of music therapy assessment. Analyzing musical structures as an essential part of assessment will highlight the importance of the "art" of music therapy. To focus on the musical dialogue, however simple, is to validate the core of our work. Does the medical profession exclude diagnostic complexities from their conversations with music therapists because they are not able to understand the intricacies of their professional language? Subjective classifications should be interpretive, arising from the fundamental material presented.

Indexing as Clinical Clarity

Indexing as a factual yet imaginative form of assessment connects and compares all facets of music therapy. Its strength comes from the therapists desire for self-maturation in finding a connection between the musical and clinical in their work. Indexing can be creative, free, and revealing. The accuracy and proficiency of indexing, however, is dependent on the therapist's skills of reflection, observation, listening, and musical notation. Assessment attempts to find a path through the complexities of the therapeutic process. Indexing as a music-centered and humanistic form of assessment combines the specificity of other more precise forms of assessment (Hintz, 2000; Scalenghe & Murphy, 2000) with a sense of creative interpretation that is at the heart of AeMT.

CLOSING THOUGHTS

Analysis and assessment is fundamental in contemplating the balance between music and therapy. What can analysis tell us about the music therapy relationship? How do we articulate music therapy, understand, assess, interpret, and then return it to our clients with a greater understanding of the process? Evaluating perceptions of music and clinical communication provides a balance that is ultimately illuminating. The complexities of music when combined with the complexities of the human psyche provide an almost limitless range of possibilities and connections. It is these possibilities that make clinical practice such a mysterious yet tangible challenge.

AeMT as a music-centered approach to music therapy provides a guide for analysis and assessment that is experimental yet free. Finding musical constructs, such as the generative cell, as a basis for clinical enlightenment makes an essential paradigm shift–that of taking evaluations from the source of music itself. Problems of musical notation–transcribing from audio and video tapes and the complexities of computer-generated music–can often give the music therapist reason to look to other nonmusical forms of evidence. There is no substitute for studying the actual music of an improvisation. To see and consider the complexities of melody, rhythm, harmony, and texture will provide detailed information that is available in no other form. Music is a specific art and music therapy even more so. If we ignore the nature and constructs of music then we may be in danger of ignoring the essence of music therapy itself.

Chapter Nine

MUSICAL FORM AND CLINICAL FORM

> There is no real creating without hard work. That which you would call invention–that is to say, a thought, an idea–is simply an inspiration for which I am not responsible, which is no merit of mine. It is a present, a gift, which I ought even to despise until I have made my own by dint of hard work.
>
> Johannes Brahms (1833–97), quoted in Watson (1994)

What does it mean to consider music therapy in terms of musical form? What are the links between clinical form and musical form? How can musical form inform clinical form? Will a detailed understanding of musical form help us unravel the enigmas of music therapy? Why is it important that music therapists understand musical and clinical form equally? In research music therapy takes methodologies from quantitative and qualitative sources (Wheeler, 1995), in music psychotherapy from analysis (Foulkes & Anthony, 1990), transference (Bruscia, 1998) and imaging (Bonny, 1978), in didactic practices through data collection and analysis (Bruscia, 1998), and in music medicine through clinical trials (Standley, 1986). These exterior influences have defined the field and provided validation for music therapy as an established and credible profession.

But what of music therapy influenced by theories of music? Paul Nordoff, in his clinical applications of music and musical idioms (Robbins & Robbins, 1998), takes music as the essence of the process. In the editor's introduction music is clearly stated as the core of his teachings:

> The musical foundations of clinical musicianship in therapy concerned Paul Nordoff deeply. These lay not only in each student's clinical ability and musical skills, but in his or her musical awareness, in the experiential knowledge of music and the understanding-feeling for the expressive dynamics of its melodic, harmonic, and rhythmic components. He believed such a perceiving knowledge to be indispensable to the responsive, creative application of music in therapy. (Robbins & Robbins, 1998, pp. xix)

For Nordoff music was the inspiration and culmination of every nuance of music therapy. How the child responded, the overall aims of the work, the expressive qualities of music, and the child's musical connections were all influenced by an understanding and clinical appreciation of musical form. Nordoff's influence on this book is significant. Through the inspiration of clinical work and musicianship, his teachings showed that music and human potential are inextricably linked. To consider music as therapy (Bruscia, 1998) is to know and understand music. Therapeutic and musical both advocate precision and yet both contain the creative freedom of living and relationship.

Through the countenance of illness and disability AeMT proposes a musical link between human condition and experience. As clients explore their life situation the therapist must unravel a myriad of emotions. The therapist will not find the musical articulation of autism per se until they explore the client's own autistic music. Until then the music will conform to the therapist's perceptions of autism. The autistic child occupies their worldview of music and in order to understand their inventiveness the therapist must attempt to meet and find the innate musical expression of autism. Autistic music then is dependent on different factors:

- individual character
- clinical diagnosis
- musical preference
- emotional stability and instability
- cultural experiences
- life experiences

Just as Beethoven's compositions are dramatically different from Mahler's so one client's music will be different from another's. Eddie, a client living with HIV, used sophisticated complex music whereas Cory, an adolescent with autism, used music that was uncomplicated and sparse. It was not the complexity or sophistication that connected the two but the intent and clarity both bought to their music. Cory's music was equal to Eddie's and as such the therapist met both with the same sense of deep, active listening and response. Even though Cory was a young autistic man the music in response to the therapeutic relationship was no less complex than the musical manifestations of Eddie. It is a mistake to separate the musical and therapeutic work of differing clients. Cory's single note on the piano was equal to Eddie's complex atonal drum and piano playing. It is the depth with which the therapist hears the client that separates the relational content of music and not illness or disability. An understanding of the client's musical form must ultimately influence the therapist's response.

THE "TRISTAN" CHORD: CLINICAL IMPLICATIONS

Wagner: Tristan und Isolde

fig. 16

Wagner's Tristan chord (see Figure 16) is the most debated and analyzed harmonic sequence in the music literature. Its attention comes from its chromaticism, lack of key center, and potential move toward atonalism. The melodic line moving from leaps (1) to chromaticism is underpinned with a sophisticated harmonic sense of tension (2) and resolution (3). There are many different investigations from Schoenberg's (1954) implication that the chord was a precursor for atonalism to Chailley's (1963) analysis that focuses on the chord as the dominant of A minor. Analyses of the Tristan chord can be categorized into two groups (Nattiez, 1990): functional analyses where the tonal significance is based on a specific progression of chords and nonfunctional analyses where the chords structure is privileged above its function. The Tristan chord can be analyzed from a clinical perspective in three ways.

1. Harmonic Ambiguity

Improvisation should never be predictable. The therapist's musical searching can reflect the essence of the relationship and maturing therapeutic aims. Improvisation should also be open to limitless possibilities, these being evaluated as the therapist's understanding of the process deepens. Analyzing the harmonic ambiguity of the Tristan chord highlights possible connections with clinical improvisation. The suspension (2) of the F, B, D#, G# chord moving through the melodic A and A# to the final E major chord (3) provides a harmonic movement that is intangible yet grounded. Ambivalence followed by resolution can be a critical force in clinical improvisation. The harmonic uncertainty (2) provides a sense that the music could go anywhere, leading through resolution can be a critical force in clinical improvisation. The harmonic uncertainty (2) provides a sense that the music could go anywhere, leading through the chromatic melody toward the inevitable resolution of the E major chord (3). The Tristan chord as a harmonic resource and a basis for other progressions will give the therapist a sophisticated palette of ambivalent musical expressions. Clients often do not have the ability to move from ambiguity to stability either musically or emotionally. Utilized as a clinical resource the Tristan chord has the potential to redress a musical imbalance for the client and add continuity to the therapeutic relationship.

2. Melodic Movement

The melodic movement of the Tristan chord is interesting and directly applicable to clinical improvisation. As the melody moves upward the intervals become smaller. The opening 6th (1), presumes an F major tonality. This inference is thrown with the introduction of a major 3rdn (1-2) placing the melodic key clearly in E major. The chromatic movement (2-3) from G# to the B balances the broader opening. From a clinical perspective the balance between open and chromatic intervals shows an understanding that could be significant in reflecting a client's expressive melodic imagination. Aldridge (1999) expresses the significance of melody in music therapy:

> The experience of an unfolding melody is an experience of wholeness, a gestalt, a creation that possesses more features than the sum of its single elements would make up. (Aldridge, 1999, p. 151)

Taking Aldridge's view into account the Tristan progression therefore has the potential to illuminate our awareness of spontaneous melodic form. Thinking of melody as a sophisticated expression of the client will give weight to the therapist's musical thinking. The movement toward smaller intervals expresses a sense of openness that could have an impact if related to specific clinical situations. Studying, practicing, and directly relating significant progressions such as illustrated in the Tristan chord can help illuminate the minutiae of a therapist's clinical and music thinking.

3. Tension and Release

The immediacy of tension and release available in improvisation is a determining factor in reflecting, and if necessary, directing the musical articulation of clients. The Tristan chord is a perfect and refined example of moving from uncertainty (2) to the clarity of a clear tonal center (3). These chords can be used as a resource to initiate improvisations. Experimenting and exploring the progression will enable the therapist to find musical specifics that may be needed at certain junctures in sessions. The Tristan chord and its resolution can provide a musical palette for the therapist that can support and instigate aspects of tension and release that may be pertinent in the developing therapeutic relationship.

MUSICAL STRUCTURES AND THERAPUTIC STRUCTURES

In clinical improvisation creativity and freedom are essential, yet without structure music and the therapeutic process would not exist. Direction and organization form the backbone of clinical practice. How can our understanding of musical structures inform our understanding of therapeutic structures and vice versa? In AeMT the balance between the two is essential in understanding the therapeutic process. Music contains finite and controlled structures which are used in random and ordered combinations. Music must adhere to–and then break– rules that balance and give flight to the inventiveness of composition and improvisation. Therapy also contains theories which like composing are affected by, yet not reliant on, the outcome. The individuality of relationship is similar to the creativity enforced through ordered and free compositional thought. Just as the composer struggles to find his or her unique voice through the structures of music, so the therapist struggles to give voice to the client's eloquence within the bounds of musical autonomy and design. The musical theories of intervals, rhythm, harmonic balance, and tonal direction can all be related to the theories of the therapeutic relationship. Intervals, how they relate, the combination and direction of tones–similar and contrary motion–question and answer–can all be paralleled with the client/ therapist relationship in improvisation.

What does the dialogue in a two-part invention, for instance, say about musical connection and communication? When two melodic lines move apart, when they leap and then return to a tonal closeness, how could this correspond to the musical/therapeutic relationship? The connection between client and therapist in improvisation is a delicately balanced affair. Like a two-part invention there are gestural and personal cues as well as musical ones. It is structure, however, that makes both the musical and therapeutic direction: structure in music, structure in therapy, and structure in the relationship. Structure is what makes clinical improvisation an ordered yet free experience. Clinical improvisation takes it structure from various sources:

- the structure of aims and objectives
- the musical structure of each session
- the therapeutic structure of each session
- the structure of each musical moment
- the developing structure of each improvisation
- the developing structure and architectural shape of each session

The clinical improvisor must balance structure within the moment-to-moment development of the session. The therapist must pose the following questions when he or she is improvising:

a) what is the structural content of the music?
b) what is the structure hoping to achieve?
c) how will the structure inform the creative nature of the process?
d) how is structure being balanced alongside freedom?

Musical and therapeutic structures must be allies, each independent yet informing the other.

By analyzing musical structures the therapist can begin to deduce inferences about the connections between musical representation and therapeutic outcome. That a client may improvise consonant melodic lines and then suddenly move into atonal playing is an important indicator. What might this say about the developing relationship and the client's need to express within opposite musical polarities? What might this move tell us about the client's emotional state and how they are expressing it? AeMT is based on the belief that if the therapist turns to the deep structures in the musical dialogue–those that are not immediately aurally apparent–we may find important clues in understanding the developing process.

Is it possible that by understanding the compositional perfection of a Brahms's symphony and relating this knowledge to clinical practice, we may begin to better understand the connection between musical and therapeutic intent? This does not mean that we need to spend hours analyzing Brahms's musical structures. By consciously appraising his sense of form, his perfection of ideas and their development and the power of recapitulation we can gain a greater understanding of how the structure of music works. Allowing this knowledge to influence our musical reactions to clients in improvisation will provide an ever more detailed and sophisticated catalogue of responses. Brahms's dialogue, answering phrases, sophistication of harmony, and contrasts of shape and form all provide clues in understanding music and communication. If we listen to Brahms as therapists, if we hear the musical dialogue in terms of client and therapist, then one begins to realize that the gap between a Brahms symphony and music therapy is not that great. Brahms's music is both perfect in design yet is highly emotional. How did he achieve this balance and what can music therapy learn from his compositional designs? Music therapy has created a distance between composers' work and clinical practice, a distance that AeMT believes does not, nor should not exist. The study of Western music as shown in Chapters 4, 9, and 13 should be as natural to music therapy as the study of psychological theories.

CLINICAL IMPROVISATION AS SYMPHONIC FORM

The creation of an improvisation in music therapy is the same as a composer writing a symphony. Each begins with a blank page and embraces endless possibilities. As a symphony and/or session begins the composer/therapist must make choices from the vast horizons of potential. As the music/session develops so the composer/therapist makes decisions based on inventions that have passed and the influence these have on the future direction of the music/session. Each moment is a reflection of the music played and motivates the formation of what is to come. The inspiration of creativity and of artistic/therapeutic form in a session is akin to the first performance of a new symphony. How will the audience/client react to the music? What new musical perspectives can be offered to give a contemporary sense of inspiration and originality? Just as present-day music offers new and often contentious perspectives so each new client is a unique and demands new clinical and musical thought.

Analyzing the opening of an improvisation for piano four-hands from a session with a client living with HIV (see Figure 17), it is possible to consider symphonic potential. The opening theme of a symphony, like the beginning of a music therapy session, sets boundaries for the scope and magnitude of the work. The improvisation begins with a clear and forceful theme suggesting the music is to be large and expansive. The client's opening 7th (1) is underpinned against the therapist's strong moving bass that culminates in a spontaneously judged G from both players. A repetition (2) of this idea gives credence to what becomes an integral theme within the improvisation. The stabbing chord of the therapist (3) adds color and therapeutically challenges the client's single tones. The inferred key of D flat improvised by the client (4) is colored with an added G, the therapist again challenging the client by playing an accented white-note cluster in the bass. Both players end this passage resting on a B. The improvisation continued to develop this and two other counterthemes and was twenty-three minutes in length.

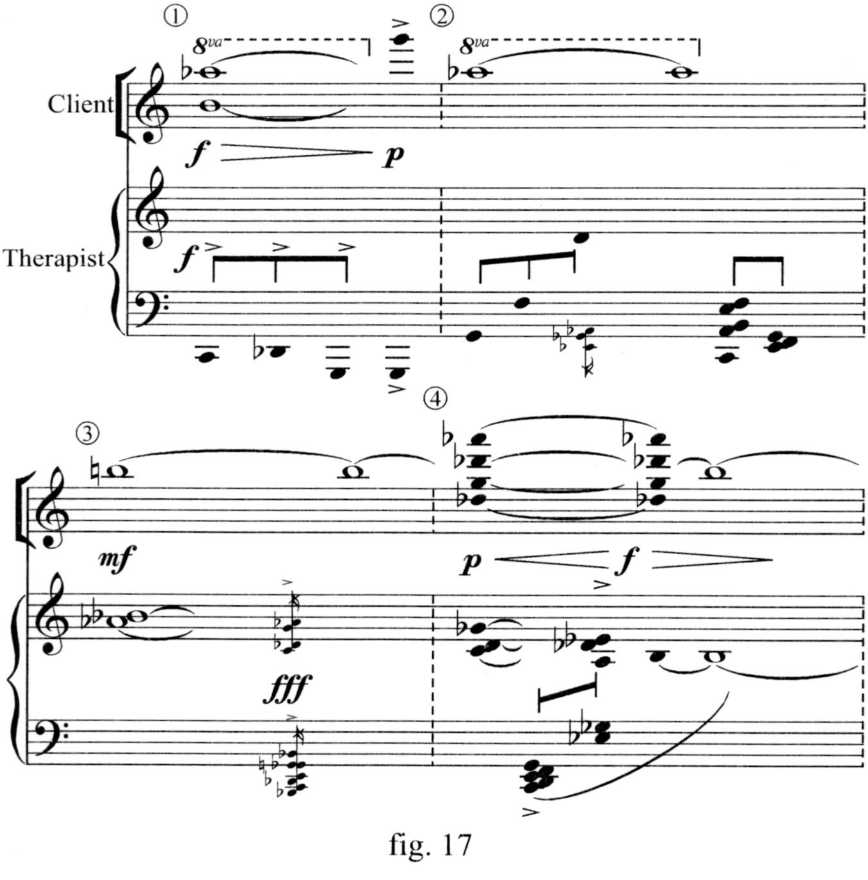

fig. 17

What can be deduced from this analysis in terms of musical meaning, symphonic intent, and therapeutic potential? The improvisational strength of the opening shows a link with symphonic thought. An opening theme is a genesis that yearns for development and clarity. This is not unlike the inception of the therapeutic process. The clients statement–musical, verbal or gestural–requires reflection and maturation. The client and therapist are partners in the evolution of emotions necessary for the client's growth. Music as a reflective agent strives to find a balance that will allow the client their fullest potential. In this example and in many others, therapeutic and symphonic process are not dissimilar.

As a composer and music therapist I consider every session to be like that of creating a symphony, each part of a session being like a different movement. Thinking orchestrally in my responses to clients I strive to create the perfect symphonic proportions within a session, emotionally and musically. As a composer I have found the symphony to be perhaps the most perfect expression of compositional craft. If I can transfer that knowledge of musical perfection to my clients then what could this potentially achieve? The problem that ensues is that music therapy is not only concerned with music but also the whole myriad of therapeutic and clinical intricacies that constitute the overall music therapy process. The idea that a session could be as complete as a symphony perhaps places too high an expectation on the music therapist–that a sense of attaining a musical Holy Grail may seem impractical and inconceivable. Attaining the highest musical and therapeutic standards, however, should be a natural evolution of the field. I believe this musical challenge should be faced for the future validation of the "art" of music therapy.

THE CLINICAL USE OF ORCHESTRAL INSTRUMENTS

The prevalence of the therapist's use of piano and guitar and the client's use of tuned and untuned percussion has resulted in a distinctive "music therapy sound." Many music therapists who study orchestral instruments in their music education often abandon them as they enter the field. How might music therapy have developed if the whole range of orchestral instruments and chamber music combinations had been available for expression? To imagine a string quartet, symphony orchestra or jazz band being able to respond as collective therapist, brings into play a whole new world of musical possibilities. While these may seem inappropriate speculations, opening the sound and textural world of music for clients should always be a priority. Piano, guitar, and percussion have many timbres available but there are times when we should look outside and find fresh and exciting sounds. AeMT urges that music therapy look to include all orchestral instruments in clinical practice. If a therapist has studied for many years and is fluent on the cello, then they should use and adapt that instrument clinically rather than trying to include instruments they are less comfortable and familiar with. In order to achieve this, orchestral players must start defining specific clinical techniques peculiar to their instrument.

Wind, brass, and string instruments offer immense possibilities for human contact. The quality of the flute is substantially different to the bassoon, the trumpet to the horn, as the violin is to the cello. Each of has the ability to provide the client with sensations of sounds and textures they may have never experienced. Hearing an orchestral instrument live can be a powerful and one that may have substantial significance for the therapeutic process. Moving a bow over a string produces tones, overtones, textures, and qualities of sound that can imitate and elaborate those of the voice. String instruments can articulate phrases providing human/emotional content. Wind and brass instruments are also closely associated with the voice. The breath needed to produce sounds are a direct human extension from physicality to sound. Clients' response to wind and brass instruments can be strong due to their temporal and flexible texture. What at first may seem a disadvantage for orchestral instruments–their ability to produce single melodic lines–can also be their strength. Music therapists can get caught in the need to offer full and complete music. This is often the antithesis of the transparent qualities necessary for good clinical improvisation. Single-line orchestral instruments have the potential to provide graceful clarity and simplicity of musical line. It is possible also to play harmonies on orchestral instruments which if used with precision can complement the impact of single lines. The physical presence of a bassoon or trombone can provide tactile stimulation that links the source of sound to the client's reactions and potential playing. Allowing a client to bow a violin or blow a trumpet or clarinet while the therapist fingers is one of endless possibilities for the clinical use of instruments.

Music therapy should accommodate all orchestral instruments as standard to clinical practice. Amplifying sound can provide instruments with more scope for volume. Purchasing work instruments so that your Stradivarius is not damaged is another important consideration! Taking certain musical and physical practicalities into account, the potential for orchestral instruments in music therapy is immense. Just as AeMT is drenched in the immediacy of music so every instrument has the potential to provide new and inspiring soundscapes. It is the innovative nature of these new clinical soundscapes, along with the developments in ethnomusicology and music technology, that will further open the doors to the limitless possibilities for the use of music in therapy.

THE ARCHITECTURAL TONIC

The process of clinical improvisation is intricate. How the music therapist combines music with therapeutic analysis indicates an understanding of the cumulative process. Sessions that include fundamentally clinical improvisation can seem daunting. To know and understand the design of a session while paying intricate attention to the detail of every moment is challenging. Recognizing and interpreting clients' music as music itself and then as a mirror of their psychological and emotional presence constitutes the "science" of the process. The therapist must practice, learn, and be free to take the many directions necessary for an effective improvisation. As described in the definitions of AeMT during Chapter one, clinical improvisation is based on the concept that the therapist must understand the architecture of the complete session before analyzing the parts. Through reflective supervision and assessment it is possible to interpret and deduce musical and therapeutic meaning. But what of the moment? How can we conceptualize musically the huge potential structures that an extended clinical improvisation demands?

Through AeMT I developed an approach to clinical improvisation that was based on an awareness of musical form. To describe and understand the musical constructs of an improvisation before attempting a clinical analysis became critical in this developing work. I began to consider and analyze how I musically approached improvisations. What techniques did I use to present the musical backdrop necessary for a developing musical dialogue? This question provided a springboard for much creative and tangential thought. The architectural tonic (AT) formed the main focus of my attention. I discovered during musical analyses improvisations often originated from a single core tone. There seemed to be a fundamental note which acted as an anchor in keeping a tonal sense of structure over the complete improvisation. It occurred to me that if I could identify this core note, then what might I learn about the client, the client therapist relationship, and the overall developing work. Was there a connection between the different ATs of each session and how did these affect an understanding of the therapeutic process? Just as the tonal center of each movement of a symphony reflects the core key of the complete work, so the tonal centers for a group of improvisations in a session or group of sessions could equally influence our understanding of the larger therapeutic picture. The AT became an essential and revelatory component in my continuing perceptions of clinical improvisational structure.

Presenting and identifying the AT during a session intensely changed my understanding of the emerging morphology of improvisation. The AT originated from either: a) the client, b) the therapist, or c) as a product of both players.

Once identified, the AT provided a structural foundation of stability and clarity of music thought. Pinpointing the AT while improvising meant listening intently and clinically as the music unfolded. Clearing extraneous sounds and hearing the essential core became clinically enlightening and enabled me to dialogue with the client at ever deeper levels. Identifying, generating, and creating an AT has become the hallmark of AeMT. It is a simple yet I believe significant way of thinking and articulating clinical improvisation. The AT provides security for the therapist and client. It permits freedom and liberation of musical thought because once identified the AT can easily be returned to, providing constant coherence and stability. Modulating to and away from the AT is an important technique because it develops other tones that are either closely or distantly related. The therapist can chose different ATs and then use them as a basis for developing their musical resources.

The musical form of the AT answers many of the questions posed at the beginning of this chapter. The "science" of music therapy is based on methodologies that explore the replicable and reductionist aspects of outcome. This theory is based on the belief that by condensing and quantifying the core components of music therapy it will be possible to understand how it works. The AT is a musical equivalent of this empirical view. By reducing the process to its skeleton form we can find why music and therapy are such close and effective allies. To reduce musical understanding and response to its essence shows the importance of fundamental tones in containing the whole. AeMT as a music provides a connection between musical form and clinical form that is both music centered and therapeutic.

Chapter 10

ATONALITY: CLINICAL INTENT AND AESTHETIC REALITY

> . . . dance to rhythms you've never heard before, don't experiment if you can't communicate and if you see a barrier, trash it.
>
> –Trans-Global Underground
> "Yes Boss Food-Corner" (2001)

In my formative years as a music therapist I was fascinated by clients who played in a pervasively scattered and nonstructured style. How did this playing color my understanding of their pathology and what would it mean if I directly met their musical unpredictability? Should I offer structure to help frame their expression or acknowledge and continue with their musical ambiguity? Listening back and indexing I discovered that what appeared to be passages of total freedom did in fact have structure and shape. Though more complex and intricate than overtly tonal music, nonetheless there was a finite sense of a client's creation that I felt more directly mirrored who they were becoming in the therapeutic alliance. I began to understand that as I responded to atonality in the moment and through assessment, so my understanding of the process and the world inhabited by the client intensified. We live in a world of predictability and conformity. For the most part our clients do not. Taking this into account, could atonality then be a more natural expression of a client's psyche than tonality and what would it mean to then place this expression in a more tonal framework? Even though now some fifteen years later I have a greater understanding of the role of atonality in clinical improvisation, I am still constantly inspired to understand the potential it has to both heighten tonality and to provide a musical landscape that is truly indicative of a client's expression.

I have found that although atonal improvisation is often used it is rarely discussed or analyzed musically in terms of its implications on the process and outcome of clinical practice. Atonality has come to signify a stylized approach where there is little or no musical direction. The experience is one of soundscape rather than complex musical form. Our understanding of atonality has become less dependant on the musical infrastructures and more on nonmusical analytic interpretations of the experience. This chapter will propose that atonality in clinical improvisation is indeed a precise musical resource that should depend on the client, the stage of therapy, and the immediate musical response. Atonality requires an intricacy of musical and clinical thought that is as far-reaching as tonality is. As we move between the polarities of tonal and atonal expression, our knowledge of each should be equal.

What are the implications, then, of improvising with no tonal center and what does it mean to offer our clients music that is theoretically devoid of structure or shape? Should atonality be offered with even greater diligence and care than tonality, or can it be used simply as a tool to meet and promote a sense of being scattered? Finally, how do we allow tonality to color our use of atonality and what does this mean in our understanding of the client and the therapeutic process? I have become increasingly fascinated and concerned by the use of nontonal music in clinical improvisation–fascinated by its potential and concerned that music therapists, for the most part, seem to draw upon atonality as a monotone resource; that it is similar to using a specific mode such as the Spanish idiom. It is my view that the gradient between tonal and non-tonal music is a complex yet simple phenomena that can have far-reaching consequences on every aspect of the music therapy process. How we evaluate and reflect on this musical balance between tonality and atonality speaks to our understanding of the musical/clinical philosophy we create for and with our clients.

UNDERSTANDING AND ANALYZING ATONALITY

Atonality has been defined in many ways by many theorists. Perhaps the greatest advocate for the veneration of atonality was Adorno. In his book *The Philosophy of Modern Music* (1973) he challenged that tonality and atonality could not coexist and denounced such composers as Sibelius for using atonality within a tonal framework. It may seem strange to us now with the return to the tonality of such composers as Gorecki and Tavener that Adorno spoke in terms of "vulgarity" and "cliché" when discussing tonality. His work is almost exclusively associated with the Second Viennese School and the formation of serialism. Schoenberg (1966, 1967, 1984) as the figure head of 'serial composition advocated a language of music where no one tone took precedence over another. The idea of "twelve-tone composition" is that one tone cannot be repeated until the other eleven have been played with equal weight. The twelve tones–the tone-row–"are arranged in a series, which can be inverted, reversed, and transformed in all the ways that are familiar from contrapuntal writing in the tonal tradition" (Scruton, 1997, p. 282). Two of his contemporaries and allies, Berg and Webern, interpreted theories of serialism differently. Webern acutely condensed his musical material into short yet intense compositions while Berg, more interestingly for music therapy, adding touches of romanticism and tonality in such works as his Violin Concerto and the opera "Lulu." If we are to acknowledge the link between tonality and atonality then the purist ideologies of Adorno and the theories of serialism are irrelevant and not applicable for the development of music in clinical practice.

More recently Sharpe's discussion that "when we turn to atonal music we find that audibly recognizable repetition of any sort is largely absent" (Sharpe, 2000, p. 191), is perhaps less relevant to music therapy than Scruton's definition that "Atonality may be unsystematic–a free use of musical elements in defiance of tonal organization. Or it may be founded in some rival musical system, and strive for a rival order to the tonal, a substitute for the organizing principles of the traditional language" (Scruton, 1997, p. 281). Here there is a clue; neither are mutually exclusive and atonality is another way of reciprocating tonality into a musical form that has its own language. If this is indeed true, that we are creating new musical languages of atonal tonalism and tonal atonalism, then this has implications for clinical improvisation that may be far-reaching and significant.

The recent writings on jazz provide other fascinating viewpoints in our understanding of atonality. Ornette Coleman stands as a leading figure in the developing dissonance of free jazz. He broke from the structures of diatonic thinking and moved toward a style that was free in structure, melodic design, and harmonic form (Heble, 2000, p. 56). His music is a testament to creative freedom and visionary musical thinking and has direct implications for the balance between freedom and form in clinical improvisation. Berliner, in his monumental book on jazz improvisation, shows how Dizzy Gillespie describes atonality as melodic lines "without any kind of harmonic reference" (Berliner, 1994, p. 225). He goes on to state that the "lack of harmonic and rhythmic reference allows players to create their parts without concern for moving from one predetermined harmonic goal to another or remaining within particular tonal centers for designated periods" (Berliner, 1994, p. 225). Here again there is a clue for clinical practice. How we conceptualize music will determine the music we can offer to our clients. If we think within tonal infrastructures then our music will reflect that concept. If, however, we can learn also to improvise within musical forms that are not bound to classical tonal theories then our music may become freer to more accurately meet the musical needs of our clients. As discussed in the previous chapter the architectural tonic can become the musical base from which exacting clinical improvisation can originate.

In analytic terms Forte (1988) proposed a method for understanding post-tonal music called "pitch class structure," based on the idea that "the notes within any given melody can be ordered into varying patterns and sequences for the edification of analysis" (Lee, 1990, p. 8). In the article from which the previous quote originates, I analyzed a section from a passage of atonal improvisation in an attempt to understand the intricacies of the musical process and therefore the music therapy process as a whole. What did I learn from such seemingly "dry" and intricate research? I think on one level this and other detailed musical analyses of clinical improvisation (Lee, 2000), and indeed the reason for writing this book, is to show how little we know and understand about music in music therapy. Understanding atonality brings with it a whole new set of complications and enigmas. Through this kind of analysis I believe it may be possible to begin to understand why a client's expression of atonality is so potentially important.

For music therapy the questions are:

- How are tonal and atonal centers constructed in improvisation?
- What is the clinical and aesthetic/musical balance between tonality and atonality and what is its effect on the music therapy process and relationship?
- How do we incorporate atonality into our palette of musical resources?
- When is atonality appropriate?
- What is the impact of tonal and atonal music on the therapeutic relationship?

TONAL DIRECTION, ANTICIPATION, MEMORABILITY, AND REPETITION

Tonality has a clear and formulated sense of direction and shape. All aspects of musical construction are manipulated to fit a clearly defined schema. The complex rules and theories of tonality, however, have changed over the centuries. Thus the harmonic theories associated with four-part harmony have little or no place in the current theories of tonality. The landscape of Bach's tonal grammar, for instance, is very different to that of Puccini's. Popular music and its predisposition to clear tonality and the move toward dissonance and atonality in serious music gave place to a musical divide between "popular" and "art" music. As tonality was stretched toward atonality in serious music so popular music became ever more rudimentary in its tonal outlook. If we consider the rich harmonies of Gershwin and then compare these with the basic harmonies of popular music today we can see a distillation toward an ever more simplistic tonal language. In serious music dissonance was stretched to its limit through composers such as Stockhausen and Boulez. In recent years there has been a return to more tonal parameters through the overt spiritualism of such composers as Part and Tavener, and the minimalism of Glass and Reich. The rich tapestry and fluctuation between tonality and atonality and its links to the development of popular and serious music is a complex yet engrossing subject. The connections between culture, societal needs, and levels of listening has given rise to parameters that are directly applicable and relevant to music therapy.

How we anticipate music, the nature of memorability and how it is repeated is crucial for clinical music. The reason that songs are so fundamental to music therapy is because all of these elements are included as integral to the process. The anticipation of tonal music is a much simpler affair than atonality. Chord sequences and melodic themes are repeated and recapitulated within a clearly defined framework. Atonal music has a different sense of anticipation, though all the elements as applied to tonality can be replicated into what I would propose as an even more powerful experience. The musical anticipation within a Mozart aria is very similar to that of a present-day popular song. Both use sequences and themes, and both have a sense of predictability. But how would we compare these with, say, a contemporary song by Harrison Birtwistle? There are elements in common though the area that separates his musical thinking is the freedom between tonal and atonal centers.

Improvisation is an altogether more complex affair. Anticipation, memorability and repetition are all the hallmarks of a good clinical improvisor. These elements though, in and of themselves, form only the initial backbone of clinical improvisation and the development of musical resources. They are elements that can be revisited but should never hinder the natural flow of the musical relationship. If an implied tonal predictability becomes more important than the natural freedom of musical flow then this will hinder the therapeutic partnership between client and therapist. The movement between tonality and atonality should be free and as carefully graded as the intricacies of the music therapy process itself. We have much to learn from other schools of improvisation, particularly jazz, and how they have balanced and developed musical structure and atonal musical thinking.

The argument that human beings are more naturally attuned to tonality and predictability (Lerdahl and Jackendorff, 1983) is one I would contest. I believe that we are influenced by what society informs us is natural. We are surrounded by tonal music: on the radio, television and in public places. Atonality has been safely withdrawn from community music. We live by rules of conformity and informed expectation–this is transferred clearly to our musical palettes. Is great music that which is memorable and instantly singable? Does a melody have less stature because one cannot immediately sing or remember it? One of the problems facing modern serious music is that the complexities of form often make it impossible to understand and fully understand its significance from a single hearing (Sharpe, 2000). As a student my obsession with Tippett came from the fact that initially I could not fully comprehend or be moved by his musical language. There was a sense that what he was trying to express was beyond me. On repeated listenings, however, his music would become dramatically illuminated. On reflection I was amazed at how much I initially missed and what the process was to find a more empathic sense of listening. To this day I am intrigued by music that does not immediately affect me. The challenge as listener is to look beyond. The challenge with our clients is also to look beyond. I would suggest that instantly memorable melodies or repeated harmonic sequence are crucial in music therapy, but melodies that are less easily remembered and harmonies that are less predictable are surely of equal importance in the musical/therapeutic relationship.

The other argument against atonality is that it is in some way perversive and uncultivated. We consider the "avant-garde" as unpleasant or unmemorable because it is new and alien to our ears. We listen to the music on the radio and have little demands placed upon us as listener, but if we attend the first performance of a new orchestral piece we know we will have to listen at a much deeper level. If we believe that the predictability of popular tonal music is artistically monotone then what does that say about music therapy's focus on the use of popular song?

Why has music therapy been influenced by popular music and for the most part untouched by the developments in present-day serious music? I believe this focus has misguidedly affected the development of music in music therapy and thus the possibilities and potential of clinical practice. I would suggest that music therapy has been colored by popular music because in tonality we can predict the musical structures, thus providing a safe environment for therapist and client. Would we ever think of offering an atonal greeting song? I think not. Why then would a music therapist consider an atonal greeting song inappropriate? In such activities we rely on the resolution of what Sharpe calls the gravitational pull (2000). The gravitational pull allows clients to know clearly their place within the structure of the music. Can this pull, however, be redundant in the dialogue if it is not balanced with freer musical inventions? If musical expectation is not realized, then this leaves the door open for other ever more dramatic and significant paths. This, I believe, is what makes improvisation such a powerful clinical tool. It provides that which is predictable and safe but also that which is unpredictable and unsafe. Therapy should not always mirror safety; it is about the risks of human potential and creativity. I believe the music we offer our clients should reflect that sense of potential and mystery that is central to clinical practice.

Our clients need musical anticipation otherwise they would not be able to traverse the musical and clinical landscape necessary for growth. Does atonality eliminate anticipation and what does that mean for the growth of clinical music? I would argue that carefully graded atonality can have an equal sense of anticipation. It is the musical style that changes and not the musical intent. In atonality it is argued that we cannot predict and be assured of the musical outcome. It is the retort of this chapter that atonality can indeed inhabit structure and consonance in the same way as tonality. Our clients are often unpredictable by pathology and nature. By offering predictable tonal music are we not satisfying our needs in bringing a client to the tonal stability and consonance that we regard as being "normal"? How long have we fought the limitations of this word as being confining, and yet in our musical discourse we use overt tonality as a base for crass musical normality. It is my contention that these are our musical insecurities and not our clients. Music therapy needs to drastically broaden its musical horizons from tonal predictably to embrace fewer tonal parameters.

ATONALITY AS HEIGHTENED EXPRESSION AND MEANING

Reflecting on the heightened moments of clinical improvisation I began to find common traits in the clients and my music. When sessions reached that sense of what I refer to as operatic clinical form, something compelling was happening. What contributed to this extraordinary pinnacle and how could I extract musical meaning from this seemingly mysterious experience?

Listening back to these experiences with various clients, a common musical thread began to appear–that of atonality. It seemed that when I was able to release myself from the confines of tonal infrastructures the client often became liberated in their response and connection with the music. Two factors became important in the consideration of this clinical atonalism. First, the decision when to break with the bounds of tonality and, second, the specific point on the tonal-atonal continuum that I, as therapist, chose to improvise. The second of these will be discussed in the next section of this chapter. The first is explored below.

In clinical improvisation we are faced with many musical challenges. When and how do we respond to our clients? Do we base our intervention on material from previous sessions or do we improvise in the moment? Do we play on the surface or do we offer serious musical responses that require a deeper level of listening and commitment? Do we improvise through song-form or do we play symphonically? All of these possibilities, and others, are dynamics that influence the musical/therapeutic relationship in the moment-to-moment experience of improvisation. So, when is atonality appropriate and when is it not? First, the therapist needs to understand the structure of atonality and its clinical intent, second, we should be fluent in improvising within atonal styles, third, the therapist needs to be conversant in moving between tonality and atonality, and last, we should have an understanding of our own emotional responses.

What then of the aesthetic qualities of atonality and how does aesthetic thinking impact the therapeutic process? One of the main arguments of this book is that aesthetic response is subjective. How we perceive and hear non-consonant music may be different from that of our clients. The emotional responses of dissonant music-making may be both unsettling yet invigorating. When working with Cory, a 16-year-old nonverbal autistic adolescent, atonalism served as the foundation from which the most heightened musical encounters occurred. The aesthetic qualities of nontonal and freely structured music gave him, I believe, the freedom to express the isolation and bewilderment of his existence. The wild nature of Cory's being was portrayed through our free dissonant playing. That is not to say that our improvisations were totally without key or structure. Indeed there was always an implied tonal center, rhythmic shape, and sense of form. What became the hallmark of these moments of heightened experience–operatic clinical form–was that Cory's playing and vocalizations were raised to a higher level of meaning. It was as if the freedom and intensity of atonal music enabled him to break free from the bounds of his autism. I believe the aesthetic qualities of atonalism for Cory were as natural as tonality is for us.

THE ARCHITECTURE OF TONAL AND NON-TONAL FORM IN CLINICAL IMPROVISATION: BALANCING THE CONTINUUM

As a composer/music therapist, the balance between tonality and atonality is at the core of my searching as a creative musician. My first analysis of atonal music (Lee, 1990) was realized through an in-depth investigation into one section of an improvisation with a client who had Down's syndrome. This seemingly dry paper utilized varying theories of 20th-century analysis. It struggled to make connections and understand the continuum between tonality and atonality and the possible implications this understanding may have for music therapy. The research concluded that:

> Analysis of musical content within therapeutic improvisation demonstrates that the improvised moment, however chaotic it may at first appear, can have a consonant structure in exactly the same way as a pre-meditated composition. An improvisation survives and exists for as long as it occurs, whereas a composed piece of music has been crafted and designed to a preconceived level by its creator. Perhaps the differences are not as great as they would first appear; both have an underlying unity of conception. One is acclaimed as being from the pen of an artist, the other as the chance product of a therapeutic situation. One is written by a supposedly "normal" person, the other is not. Are therapeutic improvisations then comparable to present-day works of art? To answer this question is not to compare quality of musical content alone, but also, musical intent and direction. A music therapist may have no wish to pose as a composer and *vise versa*, but if what both are creating and saying can be shown to be subject to the same structural considerations and inner relationships, then such analytical insights as these should be fundamental in the furtherance of music therapy. (Lee, 1990, p. 11)

Further in my doctoral thesis (Lee, 1992) sections of tonal and atonal improvisations were analyzed to consider the link between musical representation and the therapeutic process.

More recently in *Music at the Edge* (Lee 1996) I discuss the tonal-atonal balance in clinical music and the implications for the development of musical resources;

> The large majority of music therapy improvisation is tonally based. Paul Nordoff's teachings on musical resources (Nordoff and Robbins 1977) developed from a long history based on the romantic tradition, leaving modern classical music mostly untouched. His work heightened my urge to look more closely at atonally influenced music. I tackled this by applying the techniques of acquiring musical resources suggested by Nordoff and Robbins (1977) to present-day composers. In adapting this approach to the music of such composers as Boulez and Birtwistle, and through practice and experience in sessions, my feeling for a balance between tonality and atonality began to develop. The more confident I became, the easier it was to include these musical influences spontaneously within sessions. I never tried to enforce the style; it became instead a resource that could be drawn on when appropriate. Subsequently, my improvisational skills began to mature into a way of working that could accommodate the clinical situation while remaining true to myself as a musician and composer. (p. 21)

I go on further to say;

> Detailed musical inquiry must invite more refined listening. One way in which a music therapist might approach this is to assess where an improvisation lies along a continuum that moves from a style that is clearly tonal, through atonality with strong tonal inferences, to a tonal center with atonal connections. There are infinitesimal gradients along this scale, all of which can be treated openly with an equal emphasis of questioning. (p. 21)

These considerations on the balance between tonality and atonality in clinical improvisation continue and inspire me to look deeper into this subject.

Analyzing a passage from a clinical improvisation (see Figure 18), the balance along the tonal atonal continuum becomes evident. The lower bass's pounding figure suggests a tonal center of C, which could be seen as a rhythmic anchor rather than an attempt for a harmonic base. A stepwise motive is briefly introduced that hints at the Middle-Eastern mode–this idea being developed later in the improvisation. The therapist (r.h) balances the bass with syncopated chords (6:54–7:01) based on A flat, D flat, E, and E flat. This gives an implied harmonic center of A flat which if positioned with the therapist's overall base of C provides for many musical possibilities. At 7:01 the therapist disturbs the minimalistic bass line with fast triplet counter rhythms that challenge the stability of the music. The musical confrontation shown here was directly reflected in the therapeutic relationship. In my role as therapist there was a clear resolve to challenge the client's perseverative playing in order for him to realize the potential for other musical perspectives. His sense of being stuck pervaded every aspect of his personality and our developing relationship. The musical manifestation of implied atonality and rhythmic disbursement was a conscious and applicable clinical/musical tool.

fig. 18

Before entering music therapy, I was intrigued by posttonal music. As a composer, atonality influenced my musical growth more directly than tonality. I immersed my musical energies not only in composers such as Stockhausen, Berio, and Boulez, but also the less strident English tradition of Britten, Maw, and most notably Tippett. Through my own compositions I searched for atonal avenues while defending a sense of tonality necessary for creating a style of music that would reflect my musical growth. To highlight this balance I have chosen a passage from Paul Nordoff's flute sonata (see Figure 19). The music, although in no fixed key, is balanced with tonal chords, exuding a rapturous beauty perhaps more keenly associated with tonality. This is perfect example of music that lies midway between tonality and atonality. This pivoted expression was to influence many of Nordoff's clinical improvisations in his future work as a music therapist.

Dissonance and resolution can be paralleled between music as "art" and music as "therapy." The connections between the client's musical and psychological representations of dissonance and resolution and the therapist's role in potentially facilitating this move should be of paramount consideration in the link between musical representation and therapeutic direction. Balancing this continuum is what makes clinically appropriate impelled improvisation.

Case Material: Eddie

The following examples highlight the use of atonal music from sessions with a client living with AIDS. Eddie's use of atonality was critical to his musical and therapeutic expression, and how he lived and faced his ensuing illness and death. Eddie and I had forty-two sessions. Although Eddie had no formal musical education, he was a sophisticated and creative musician. The following examples show gradients of tonal and nontonal music-making. All the styles are contemporary in nature. The first example comes from session seventeen; Eddie: percussion, Colin: piano. This is a clear example of atonality. Eddie's playing is scattered yet controlled, every rhythm carefully placed. My music is atonal in response. Throughout this example you will hear a sense of expectancy and anticipation. Eddie's musical liberation heralds a new intimacy in our relationship. This example highlights that purity of therapeutic musical expression that comes from a refined sense of free yet defined musical structure. My improvising in this extract is influenced by Messiaen and Boulez.

fig. 19

Audio Extract Six : Session Seventeen

The next example comes from session twenty-four. If the last example was influenced by Messiaen and Boulez this example is influenced by Reich. There is no piano, both Eddie and I play a variety of tuned and untuned percussion. The instruments have been placed in a circle. Repetitive syncopated patterns emerge on two xylophones. The harmonic and melodic content is in essence tonal. The rhythmic and architectural structure, however, is fresh and unrestrained. This is a clear example of tonal atonalism. A pause in the musical direction heralds different, more percussive textures; drums and eventually cymbals appear to build the musical tension. This is a wonderful example of tuned and untuned percussion and the link between minimalist music and music therapy.

Audio Extract Seven: Session Twenty-four

THE FUTURE OF TONALITY AND ATONALITY IN FORMING A COHERENT MUSICAL LANGUAGE FOR THE 21ST CENTURY: IMPLICATIONS FOR MUSIC THERAPY

Atonality as a specific and refined clinical musical resource has yet to be formalized within the music therapy literature. The balance between tonality and atonality in clinical improvisation is an intricate and refined process. When deciding on a musical phrase, structure, and/or form in response to a client's playing we must consider the many possibilities that balance our musical and clinical intent. The continuum from tonality to atonality is one of multi-responses available from the client, therapist, and the ensuing therapeutic relationship. How we consider a harmonic base and how that fluctuates between a tonal center reflects our understanding of the process and relationship with the client. Atonality does not necessarily mean dissonance. Atonality can reflect a beauty of musical sound just in the same way as tonality. In fact, the tension and release available through a refined atonal style of improvising is perhaps more powerful than clear tonality. Atonality then can be one of the most exciting musical tools available to a music therapist.

In his investigation against tonality Scruton (1997) describes that through the precise atonal theories of Schoenberg and the philosophical ruminations of Adorno that "a change has occurred, not merely in music, and not merely in the habits of listening and performance, which has put the tonal language in question. This change involves the entire surrounding culture; it can be understood only through a theory of modernity, and if we look outside the realm of music" (p. 292). Later he balances this view with his own: "The possibility remains that tonal music is the only music that will ever really mean anything to us, and that, if atonal music sometimes gains a hearing, it is because we can elicit within it a latent tonal order" (p. 308). From this we are left with a complex question that challenges the supposed natural phenomena of tonality against the less natural experience of atonality. I would suggest that the tonal-atonal continuum makes this a more complex affair than proposed by Scruton. If we are to separate each then it could be argued that atonality is indeed less natural than tonality. If we allow each to be colored by the other, however, then what transpired is a new musical language–one that lies equidistant between the two. It is this tonal-atonal balance that is already influencing all aspects of present-day music. For music therapy to ignore these advancements is to potentially repress the future of clinical practice.

Can we dare to say that there is a "new music therapy" emerging, one that is influenced not only by medicine and pragmatic evidence, but by musicology, aesthetics, and societal change? If music therapy is to mature in the new millennium it must make decisions about its role in medicine and music. Are these polarities to become ever more separated or do we try to find a balance that allows both the artistic and empirical to positively influence one other? If our tonal language is in question and if we look outside music to try and understand how and why this might change, then music therapy could potentially have a important role to play. If we do not look outside the bounds of tonal playing then clinical music will become ever more formulaic and trite. That is not to suggest that clinical music should become totally keyless or devoid of consonant structure, but rather to make the plea that we should be more open to other nontonal influences. The rich textures of music will provide rich textures in our therapeutic relationships. Adding refined atonal colors, exploring the theories of atonality and applying them to developing musical resources, I believe could have major implications for the future of clinical improvisation.

Chapter 11

JOHN CAGE, *SONATAS AND INTERLUDES FOR PREPARED PIANO:* BEAUTY AND REVOLUTION

> And what is the purpose of writing music? . . . simply a way to wake up the very life we're living, which is so excellent once one gets one's mind and one's desires out of its way and lets it act of its own accord.
>
> –John Cage, *Silence* (1961),
> *Experimental Music* (1957)

As a young aspiring composer growing up in the late 1970's I was consumed with the trends of experimental music (Nyman, 1974). Music was being pushed to its limit. Theories were discarded, barriers were broken and conventions destroyed. This was a time of musical contention and insurrection. Notation became less precise and the distinction between music, theater, and dance less obvious. There was an air of excitement from those breaking the rules and dissatisfaction from those who felt that the essence of music was being destroyed. As a student I reveled in being in the middle of this musical revolution. The line between music and sound became less distinct. Graphic notation allowed elements of chance and improvisation and no one performance was alike. The open freshness of this movement was embraced by some and disdained by others. What made this even more exciting was that among all the exhilaration and openness there was an acute sense of distrust from the traditional bastions of music. Was this music at all? Were Cage and his followers fakes? How much farther could music be pushed before it simply did not exist? I vividly remember listening to a performance of Cardew's Paragraph I from The Great Learning. The riot that ensued demonstrated the distrust and misunderstanding for music at this time. Cornelius Cardew and John Cage became my heroes. I performed Cardew's piano pieces *Four Winter Potatoes* and *Memories of You* and studied Cage's scores. In my own compositions I began to experiment with graphic notation and elements of chance. Improvisation was a natural extension of my work as a composer and pianist. The freedom from standard notation allowed me to bridge the gap between learned and extemporaneous composition. I also became absorbed with Cage's philosophical writings, especially his book *Silence* (Cage, 1961). It seemed that the measure of his influence on music was similarly weighted through the written word. His books were as fresh and imaginative in their design as his music. Cage and the work of his contemporaries inspired me to further explore that element of unpredictability and controversy that was at the heart of experimental music.

Reflecting some twenty-five years later I realize this musical rebellion was one of the most important experiences in forging my identity as a musician and music therapist. It provided the foundation from which I now judge the validity of new developments in music and music therapy. To be contemporary is to be innovative. Music that looks backward is redundant just as music therapy that does not explore new ideas cannot advance clinical practice. The experimental movement in music was electrifying and broke all the rules hitherto established in music. What then of breaking rules in music therapy? Have we limited clinical practice by enforcing mainly extramusical theories? If an equivalent of John Cage emerged in music therapy today, what would be the response? Would the profession welcome controversial ideas or would they be rejected as against already prevailing theories? Approaching music therapy as an avant garde composer/music therapist I have tried to keep alive in my work an idealization of the contemporary, to embody in clinical improvisation music that is reflective of present-day musical trends. Is it important for music therapists to know and understand what is happening in modern music? By modern I mean not only the trends in popular music but in all aspects of classical, jazz, and world music. If we are unaware of what is happening in music today then are we not placing ourselves in a clinically disadvantaged position both for ourselves and our clients?

The influence of experimental music on my work as a therapist has been significant. Often clients are not hampered by the need for tonal boundaries and therefore music that is free from tonal center, regular rhythmic meter, and balanced melodic lines–as highlighted in Chapter fourteen–can provide the necessary freedom for discerning therapeutic growth. The clinical applications of experimental music are complex. It has taken many years of analysis, refinement, and supervision to find a balanced and coherent way of using this approach to clinical music. Defining the influence of Cage's music on my work as a music therapist has been an enigmatic yet revealing path. I remember my first experience of offering improvisation for a client who was free from formal musical structures (Lee, 1990). Stephen, a 30-year-old nonverbal client with Down's syndrome, in his 28th session improvised opening phrases on the bongos that were startlingly energized and free from formal musical organization. This was the first time he had played in such a way and my intuition was that my response needed to be similarly free. Fighting the urge to place his music within a consonant frame I meet and endorsed his emancipation of sounds. I listened intently to the nature of the music and the quality of his playing and placed myself as an instrumental/therapeutic equal. That was not to say I abandoned any sense of structure. In fact, my musical contribution was infinitely more meticulous and refined. I realized that as his rhythms and textures flew through the air I needed to catch and place them within my complex musical infrastructures. The music was a precise reflection of our therapeutic relationship and not just two wildly discharged players. As the music became more ecstatic so the sense of the experimental unfolded. The intensity of invention culminated in a twenty-minute improvisation of epic and orchestral proportions that left us both breathless and inspired. Listening back to the improvisation and indexing it in detail, I realized our relationship had strengthened through experimental music. We had become equal and therefore Stephen had found a new level of relationship and music-making.

JOHN CAGE: A CONSIDERED IMPROVISER

Much has been written about Cage's music and he has written much about his music. His influence on 20th-century music has been substantial. Keller (1994), expresses his view on Cage's lack of musicality,

> John Cage, . . . gets as near to communication-less stimulation as the unmusical can: I am not offending him with this remark, for he does not believe in musicality and does not, in fact, regard himself as a musician. (p. 122)

and Schoenberg is quoted as saying that Cage "is not a composer, but an inventor–of genius" (Yates, 1968). Like his music his words are intriguing, fresh, and contentious. It was through his interest in Eastern philosophies, especially for the nonintention of Zen Buddhism, that he turned to elements of chance and the flipping of coins to determine musical sequences. Whatever reactions Cage caused in critics and fellow musicians they were always strong, diverse, and unambiguous. To some he was the salvation of modern music and to others its destroyer. It is a sad yet cautionary tale that now some ten years after his death, there is a renaissance of his work. Cage's influence and place in history is now being understood with the magnitude it deserves.

His most controversial work, 4' 33" (1952), challenged the very foundations of Western music. The piece is in three parts and each is entitled tacet. The performer(s) sits in silence for the total duration of time specified in the title.

The music becomes the random accidental sounds of the building in which the piece is performed (Kostelanetz, 1970a). Pianist David Tudor,, gave the first performance and it is alleged that birds could be clearly heard coming from the neighboring forest (Nattiez, 1990). The responses to this work were extreme. Keller's critique catches an almost poetic essence of the work:

> . . . his silent work 4'33" (tacet) . . . sounds like nothing on earth, like something on the moon which proffers the listener-creator complete freedom (Kostelanetz, 1970, p. 243)

In 4'33" Cage challenges the listener to hear that which encompasses every nuance of present-everyday living. For Cage, are the sounds surrounding music more significant than the music itself? How does this assumption challenge clinical listening and the interpretations music therapists place on the developing therapeutic relationship? The scoring of experimental music contested the boundaries of standard Western notation. 4'33" was the first in a series of compositions where the notational realization of music became freer. Subsequent scores by Cage and his contemporaries included nonmusical delineations such as art, poetry, and movement (Nyman, 1974). Cage's collection of notations by various contemporary composers range from detailed scoring to broad strokes and diagrams resembling 20th-century art (Cage, 1969). The book itself was arranged from chance operations employed by the I-Ching.

Kostelanetz (1970b) raises three analogies that have implications for music therapy. Firstly, pure silence is physically impossible; sounds always encircle silence. Music therapists' sense of silence should be as acute as their sense of sound. When music stops, sounds enveloping silence become vital. Whether from outside (the singing of birds) or from within (physical shuffling or quiet involuntary sounds), all levels of silence should be listened to with clinical precision. Second, every performance of a work is different–this relates to the uncertainty of a music therapy session. Last accidental sounds and noises are as important as the music itself. The clinical interpretation of intentional and unintentional nonmusical sounds should be considered with equal weight. When we hear music a client offers, we must listen to the immediate and inconspicuous sounds. Each will provide us with clues for the direction of the musical and therapeutic aims. The philosophy and compositional intent of 4'33" therefore has important implications for music therapy.

Cage's writings are extensive. This fascinating literature gives us a glimpse into his thoughts and perceptions not only of music but of life, politics, and often the universe. He wrote commentaries on modern music and politics and critiqued, often harshly, the work of his colleagues. Cage was also an expert on mushrooms (1981) and mud pies (Cage & Long, 1988). His writings were often written in the form of lectures; to be read aloud within set time frames (1982).

Covering such diverse subjects as indeterminancy (1959), experimental music (1968), and *Finnegans Wake* (1983), Cage's ideas were often dictated by chance. Conversations with Barnard (1980), Retallack (1996) and his correspondence with Boulez (Nattiez, 1993) provide intriguing impressions of his life, belief in his music, and his own insecurities. Cage's influence on philosophers, musicians, and fellow artists is further captured in anthologies (Gena & Brent, 1982; Kostelanetz, 1970c) that add to our understanding of this complex yet refreshingly sincere artist.

So what of Cage the considered improviser? Much of his music has strong improvisational elements though Cage was somewhat opposed to improvisation as he believed it was based on memories and habits (Retallack, 1996). The chance elements of experimental music could be seen to be the antithesis of improvisation because they set patterns, albeit random, to which the performer must adhere. It is the chance elements of Cage and his contemporaries, however, that have established the link between the artistic and clinical in AeMT. To offer the compositional freedom inspired through experimental music is to keep the freshness and spontaneity that is the essence of Aesthetic Music Therapy.

SONATAS AND INTERLUDES: NEW SONORITIES FOR MUSIC THERAPY

The prepared piano came from a need in 1938 to provide percussion music for a dance group with limited space (Nyman, 1974). Cage studied Henry Cowell's experimentation with the inside of pianos and developed a system of placing various objects between the strings (bolts, screws, rubber bands, coins, etc.) (Revill, 1999). Cage (Kostelanetz, 1970a) explains:

> The result is a gamut of sounds moving from lower to higher octaves without the correspondences of pitch characteristic of scales and modes. These sounds are different timbres and of a decibel range comparable to that of the harpsichord. In effect, the prepared piano is a percussion ensemble under the control of a single player. (p. 76)

Cage wrote various pieces for the prepared piano including the *Concerto for Prepared Piano and Chamber Orchestra* in 1951. The *Sonatas and Interludes* were written between February 1946 and March 1948 and is Cage's most ambitious work for prepared piano. Because of the shifting pitches and tonalities imposed by the prepared piano the score is not always representative of the sounds heard. The sixteen short sonatas are interspersed with four interludes. The Eastern philosophy of categorizing white emotions as the heroic, erotic, mirthful, and wondrous balanced with the black emotions of fear, anger, distrust, and sorrow are central to the piece (Retallack, 1996). The *Sonatas and Interludes* bring together these emotions with a leaning toward tranquillity. The textures of the music are exotic; the clarity of composition creating beautiful consonant sounds. Listening to the work as a whole one is struck by a sense of time suspended, of ideas stated and repeated to produce an intense simplicity of structure.

Connections with AeMT become immediately apparent. What of the potential for using the prepared piano in music therapy sessions? How might the sumptuous sounds and the unique soundscape of the prepared piano, contribute to the musical/therapeutic relationship? The unpredictable shifting textures could provide an often needed unpredictability in the therapeutic alliance. The prepared piano has a percussive quality that is more closely linked to the percussion instruments played by clients. If taken as a basis for musical resources the *Sonatas and Interludes* could also provide specific musical components. In expanding clinical repertoire these sounds could be invaluable in broadening a music therapist's musical palette. Music therapists should always be open to creating new sounds and textures. Listening, playing, and understanding the *Sonatas and Interludes* could have a similar potential for music therapy as the impact they had on the musical world when they were originally written.

The clinical example (see Figure 20) comes from work with a young man living with AIDS, in his seventeenth session. John, an untrained musician, was heavily influenced by experimental music, especially the work of the improvising group AMM (Nyman, 1974). This group, based in London, England, began from the work of three jazz musicians, Keith Rowe, Lou Gare, and Eddie Provost. Cornelius Cardew was also involved with AMM from its inception. AMM's style of improvising was free and nonconformist. John's musical expression was heavily influenced by this musical genre. I was therefore challenged as a music therapist to find a musical forum that was similarly free and nonconformist. Because of my appreciation and knowledge of experimental music the clinical applications of this style were natural. John would insert objects between strings of the piano, creating his own prepared piano. He would place a chair on the sustaining pedal to provide a constant wash of sound. John would play percussion instruments in unorthodox ways and his piano playing sounding like soundscapes of broad climatic clusters. While essentially free, his improvising was highly selective and formal in design. He knew exactly the music he needed and would spend long periods of time experimenting until an

fig. 20

exact sound could be created. Music for John was not of Western tonality but of broad eclectic strokes allowing time and relationship to be suspended. The influence of Cage on our work was significant, from the specifics of texture and Middle-Eastern tonality to the belief that musical creativity is boundless and that clinical improvisation should reflect this.

This example I have chosen to compare with sonata No. II (see Figure 21), may at first seem disparate. Cage's musical design is simple when compared to the improvisation which is based on fast-moving appoggiaturas. Rhythmically the main part of the sonata is syncopated and accented, suddenly moving in the last two lines to freer playing. The clinical improvisation is free-flowing and devoid of rhythmic regularity. Both pieces share a sense of rhythmic freedom. Tonally, taking into account the potential pitch alteration of the prepared piano, both pieces are based on motivic series (see Figure 22). If we compare the series we get a sense of how both pieces are created and the musical basis from which they develop. Cage's series originates from Middle-Eastern modes which provides a clear tonal color for the sonata. The clinical improvisation is based around two three-note series which when considered intervalically show a close-knit musical and relational core (a-semitone, b-semitone, c-same tone).

So what of the clinical and musical connections between pieces? There is a boldness, and in terms of Cage, a simplicity of form. The textures that permeate Cage's sonata and the clinical improvisation's splashes of sounds are both examples of musical soundscapes that are free yet carefully constructed. The idea that musical freedom is devoid of consonance and shape is here contested. In both pieces there is a clarity of form that is based neither on a clear tonal base or regular rhythmic meter. There is a common musical essence that has potential therapeutic gains originating from an inventive compositional accuracy. This clarity is based on the knowledge that music, sounds, and textures have limitless possibilities. Music therapists are hindered only by their lack of experience, knowledge, and understanding of contemporary music.

My work with John was both liberating and complex. The clinical application of experimental music requires sophistication and therapeutic precision. It would be easy to allow music-making of this kind to degenerate into nonfocused and clinically inappropriate playing. The improvisations John and I shared were based on the nonconformity experimental music so refreshingly introduced.

II
16va
8va
LOCO

Cage–motivic series

Clinical improvisation–motivic series

fig. 22

CREATING A MUSIC THERAPY REBELLION?

To be clinical is to be precise and discerning. To be artistic is to be precise but also wild, free, and unfettered and still discerning. To balance these ideals is to illuminate our understanding of clinical practice. Cage as a clinical teacher shows us that theories are created to be broken and reestablished under new enlightened beliefs. Aesthetic Music Therapy is the science of musical components, relationship, and artistry. It is also a challenge to redefine that which we understand as clinical practice. In our need to quantify we should never forget that ours is a profession of artists. Artists need to challenge and be challenged. Artists need to live in the creative now. To make music therapy an entirely empirical science is to take the heart out of what brought the profession into being. I think that Cage in his challenge to Western music made a plea–a plea not to forget the spontaneity and freshness of music. A plea to show that there are many new sounds to discover. A plea that music should always grow and that what is hard to understand now will be natural in the future. Similarly, music therapy should not ignore or decry that which is new and/or controversial, for in the future these ideas could be significant. Cage offered a bigger picture for music and as a consequence was seen by many to be sensationalist and shallow. I hope music therapy doesn't make a similar mistake as new ideas and figures arise.

> After eighteen months of studying oriental and medieval Christian philosophy and mysticism, I began to read Jung on the integration of the personality. There are two principle parts of each personality: the conscious mind and the unconscious, these are split and dispersed, in most of us, in countless ways and directions. The function of music, like that of any other healthy occupation, is to help bring those separate parts back together again. Music does this by providing a moment when, awareness of time and space being lost, the multiplicity of elements which make up an individual become integrated and he is one. (Cage, 1993, p. 41)

Chapter 12

WHEN THE MUSIC STOPS

> Music reflects the depth of experience of humanity and is accessible to the uniqueness in each person. The challenge for the music therapist in terminal care lies in searching for ways to link the uniqueness of music with the uniqueness of the dying patient.
>
> –Susan Porchet Munro,
> *Music Therapy in Palliative/Hospice Care,* p. 84

It is impossible to articulate the transcendental complexities of music therapy through the written or spoken word. By rationalizing music it becomes second-hand, a concrete interpretation that opposes the nature of its essence. But we need words and the ability to articulate our practice. Music therapy is based on postulates of definition and interpretation. Our literature survives on the need to explain and articulate. We believe that if we can understand why music is therapeutic–if we use empirical methodologies, replication, and data analysis–then we will be able to understand and refine the outcome. It is undeniable that music therapy is dependent on future links with medicine and the validation of quantitative studies (Prat & Grocke, 1999). Alongside this knowledge, however, we must also celebrate the aesthetic and spiritual qualities of music. I believe that we can no more quantify the enigmas of music than we can the enigmas of dying. We may spend a lifetime trying to understand why each exists and the impact they have on living, but ultimately both are beyond rational explanation.

This may seem a curious association, but I believe the process of music and dying have qualities in common. There is an essence of incorporeality that joins yet separates both. Music is a life-giving force and while it has the potential to accurately reflect the dying process, it is by disposition of this world. Therein lies the dilemma; music can express the essence of dying but music itself mediates life. Begbie (2000) links dying with the transient cycle of a tone's birth to its decline and conclusion. There is true power in this equation. Having been immersed in music my whole life and having had the privilege of being with clients during the dying process I discovered similarities in both encounters. The beginning of a piece of music heralds the birth of a creative force that is fragile and new. As music unravels its structure so themes are stated, developed, and recapitulated. The life cycle of music is not unlike the life cycle of human existence. Music therapists can know the experience of entering musical expression but can only speculate on the experience of dying. This chapter will attempt to understand and articulate these encounters from direct clinical experiences of working with near-death clients. It is a series of meditations on this enigmatic work.

It is an extraordinary association for a musician to work with the dying. When working as a music therapist in palliative care, I often considered the personal path that had bought me to this place. How had this happened, and what skills had I acquired to aid me in finding a way of working that was creatively free, yet professionally rigorous? On one hand it seemed natural but on another there was a sense of unpreparedness on how best to use music to serve clients at the crossroads of their lives. As my musical and personal experience matured, and as time progressed, my responses became more finely graded and precise. Even now some five years after finishing my work in palliative care, I can still recall the intensity and recapture each moment of every music therapy encounter, precisely and vividly. One of the most significant lessons I learned was humility. Humility for living and dying, for thinking I had a role to play in a dying person's life, for music's power of nonverbal communication, for myself as musician, and for my fellow professionals who constantly cared and held me. Holding onto that sense of not knowing I now realize was crucial and facilitated the most dynamic of musical responses.

So what of aesthetics? How do the aesthetic qualities of music, the therapeutic relationship, and dying affect our understanding of music with near- death clients? It is strange to talk of a link between the aesthetics of music and dying, and yet when being with clients who are leaving life there is a sense that music can naturally facilitate this move. Music becomes the mediator, a purity of emotion that embraces the mystery of the process. Here music is not of this world and neither should it be. The music therapist's challenge is to discover music that may herald a move from life to death–to offer a creative response to dying. Prerecorded or precomposed music is often used at this time, either requested by the client or, if too ill or unconscious, music is chosen that was known to be important for them. It is often played quietly and/or in the background. What I am exploring here, however, is a creative musical response: music that is flexible and alive as opposed to prerecorded or precomposed music. Here, improvisation is the core. The aesthetics of relationship, music, and dying become one. Each is an extension of the other; every moment, musical phrase, tone, glance, gesture, and nuance are embraced through the essence of music.

DYING AND IMPROVISATION AS THE UNFORSEEN

Begbie (2000), in his discussion on improvisation, freedom, and time offers his view that:

> . . . improvisation, by enabling a freedom in relation to a vast array of constraints, can enable a freedom with respect to a fundamental continuous constraint which permeates them all, namely the world's temporality, . . . (p. 201).

The temporality of the world, our existence and its relation to improvisation is an enormous concept to grasp. Could improvisation in some way reflect the enormity of human existence and its passing? Improvisation as an embodiment of the unforeseen, as a window for limitless potential, may be a channel to express the bounded reality of our existence. Having been with clients who have directly faced their temporality I have found repeatedly that improvisation cuts to the core of human impermanence. I believe that our acknowledgment of the transient nature of life can be accurately reflected through improvisation. It is the balance between constraint and freedom that gives improvisation its potential to discern both artistic content and its greater place within human existence. "This is improvisation's distinctive contribution to learning to 'live peaceably with time,' and thus to a theology of human freedom" (Begbie, 2000, p. 203).

Using improvisation with clients who are unconscious is a finely balanced therapeutic enigma. In many cases my work with unconscious clients came from an extension of an already ongoing therapeutic process. I would discuss with the client beforehand the possibility of continuing with music on the ward, if they became unconscious. If they agreed I explained that I would improvise music that was a reflection of our work, relationship, and my perceptions of how they were at that time and that I would improvise in time with their breathing both on the Sounding Bowl and with my voice. This extension of the therapeutic process was always powerful and immediate. Some clients would react to the music with small physical movements, some more strongly as in the case of a client who opened her eyes to acknowledge my presence, and some would remain still. What always occurred was their breathing patterns would become more shallow and relaxed. The improvisations would oscillate between simple phrases with their breathing alongside freer more animated sections.

I would also work in a similar way with clients who had had no contact with music therapy before. Referrals came from relatives, friends, nursing staff, or the physician. The reason for referral was nearly always because the client had become agitated. My interpretations of their physical demeanor and my musical responses were always simple and more directly connected with their breathing. Again, clients' breathing patterns would nearly always relax and they would become visibly calmer.

Another use of improvisation was through relaxation. This work was initiated when a volunteer at the hospice, who conducted weekly relaxation sessions, suggested we might introduce live music to her sessions. The music was improvised to reflect the text and my sense of the group. This combination proved to be powerful and became an important part of my work at the hospice. I also gave individual relaxation sessions on the ward.

So what of the music and its aesthetic power? How is the unforseen essence of music perceived when clients are potentially not an active part of the music? Using music with near-death clients, the therapist needs to be aware of every tone and its place within the music. Every note, melodic contour, and harmonic progression becomes critical in the overall structure of the session. While the content of the music itself may become smaller the musical components should be ever more transparent and concentrated. Waiting and attending become paramount; listening to breathing as sound and music. Listening and beyond; listening at ever deeper levels that will capture that representation of the moment, the musical relationship, and that movement away from life. Music becomes an act of mediation that reflects the temporality of moving from life to death. The following case studies explore listening at its most penetrating and clinical level. They highlight the need for flexibility and clarity of musical articulation; a creative response to the essence of dying. Both examples include work with and alongside Gill, a physiotherapist. We become therapist and co-therapist, enabling both clients to find a balance for their complex musical and physical needs.

CASE STUDY–DAVID

The following is taken from a chapter on the use of music therapy in integrated cancer care (Lee, 2001):

> This case study explores work with David, a twenty-one-year-old man dying of cancer. My work as a music therapist in the Hospice was carried out in conjunction with Gill, the physiotherapist. The linking of disciplines came directly from David's physical and emotional needs. After David died Gill and I met to reflect on our work.

The session was recorded and transcribed, her comments coming directly from that meeting.

The sessions took place during the last two weeks of David's life. He was admitted to the Hospice because his tumor was developing rapidly. David also had secondary complications of spinal cord compression. When David arrived he was frightened and in great pain. David was initially referred to music therapy because he played guitar and was known to be musical. During our first meeting he was eager to discuss music and the group he had formed with his girlfriend. We discussed his favorite bands and the growing importance of music since his illness. Although not able to move freely he could sit up in bed. There was a sense of life and urgency about him. We agreed to hold our first session in his room and that I would bring a guitar.

In between this meeting and our next David was admitted to the pain clinic as his condition rapidly deteriorated. On his return to the ward, I took a guitar to the session as promised. As I entered his room, however, I realized that it would be impossible to entertain any notions of music-making. He lay on his back. The pain appeared to be so intense that he moved his head only slightly to acknowledge my presence. We sat in silence, the suspension of time holding us both. There seemed to be no words to describe the enormity of his situation. I eventually dared to speak: "It must be hard with so much time to think?" Time again was suspended as David considered my words: "Yes, it certainly is." I felt foolish at my words. After a lifetime of silence I stood up to leave. At this moment Gill entered the room. She too saw the desperate physical and emotional pain of David's presence. Gill immediately and insightfully suggested that we might try relaxation work with touch and music. David nodded in agreement.

I began the reflective meeting with Gill after David's death by trying to describe the awkwardness I felt during the first session. The suggestion of our working together was liberating for me. Up until now I was sitting in silence with David. At first the silence was comfortable, but after a time I thought "What can I say?" "What should I say?" "How can I begin to acknowledge the death and dying of such a young man?" When I finally spoke I knew the enormity of my words would be awkward. I trusted the silence between us, but on another level it seemed so strong as to be crushing me. Gill replied, "David was a frightened young man. He was on his back constantly. He couldn't sit up and face his situation." She paused as if considering the depth of our work, "We enabled him to let go."

The format of sessions consisted of relaxation and touch along with improvised music on a sounding bowl (a stringed instrument of contemporary origin). The music balanced the movements of Gill's hands, as well as trying to capture David's disposition and the ensuing tripartite relationship. The physical and musical responses were clinically graded to provide David with the opportunity to relax and release tension, as well as being able to enter a non-verbal relationship that was hopefully representative of his fears and emotions.

Gill commented on the therapeutic process, "When the music started, and after I touched him, you could feel the tension coming out. The three of us became one. It was like following the dream lines." We offered David two sessions each day; one in the morning and the other in the late afternoon. The intensity of our relationships deepened at every meeting. There were few words spoken. During our third session however David opened his eyes and spoke in spite of himself, "It's all so avant-garde. So enlightened." We can offer no explanation for these words. We accepted them as statement deep from inside. Gill spoke at length about our quickening relationship and these moments of opening, "There were many occasions when he moved his lips, as if he were trying to say things. It seemed as if from this time each session continued as one. There were no preliminaries. His face became remarkably beautiful. He lost all his lines of tension and pain. It was almost as if he decided to move away, but then came back. After he spoke these words he was, I'm sure, ready to let go completely."

Gill further articulates the efficacy of our work from her perspective, "What we did with David was clear and not in any way a vague and undefined process. We had clear aims; we knew what we were doing and why we were doing it. I was aware that when the music started my approach to touching him changed. In the early sessions he would come back, more vigorous, and then ease away. I was fascinated how your music matched that experience. The music seemed related to his strength. Spiritually the music was aware. It was like being in a beautiful bubble. Yet we still had to remain in control, to be in the present. During these moments we glimpsed a union. We were terribly privileged. It wasn't uncomfortable, it was magical." I respond, "To reach out and touch the layer between life and death?" Gill acknowledged my thoughts, "A communion that produced a whole that was greater than the parts. We were able to allow our intellect and emotions to come together. It was something more than communication, it was a joining, a oneness of minds. It's you being allowed into someone else's space, but allowing other people into your space as well. I felt that our work was something he needed. It was a release for him. He could move away from his bed. David was tied to the pain and his bed. This experience allowed him to move away and fly. For me this was one of the most profound experiences I have had in my work at the Hospice. It was a tremendous honour to be there. It was giving and taking. The satisfaction that you were able to make a difference, a totally generous giving and giving. It became a special bubble and he would always say, 'I've been waiting for you.' We both knew at the final session that we wouldn't see him again. We didn't want him to die. We wanted the experience to continue."

These insightful and reflective comments by Gill helped us both to place the immensity of the experience. As the sessions progressed so David's physical and spiritual presence became evermore distant. Perhaps we may never know the impact of our work with David. However we do know the influence David left on both our lives. His gift to us was that he allowed us into his life at this time of transition. The intensity of our relationship has not diminished with the passing of time. I remember our beautiful bubble with continued clarity; it enriches my living and keeps David's spirit alive in me professionally and personally (p. 149–151).

CASE STUDY–LISA

I too clearly remember Lisa's indomitable essence. That purity of need that demanded respect and clarity of professional and personal response. Lisa was a young woman in her mid-thirties diagnosed with breast cancer. For her the potency of music was intoxicating. Lisa allowed music to illuminate her spirit as if it were the most spiritual yet practical of encounters. The three times we met before her death were some of the most challenging yet revealing experiences of my career and the strength of her presence remains with me to this day.

Lisa was referred from the ward, my first day after returning from Christmas holidays. The day had been full with ongoing clients and it was my intent to meet Lisa later and arrange a session the following day. As I entered her room that afternoon to introduce myself, Lisa turned her head, staring directly toward me, at me, and through me. She sat up in bed with such a startling disposition that I froze. Lisa was obviously very ill and yet her face was alive and radiant. I was at a loss as to what to say or do. She broke the silence and beckoned me to sit on the chair next to her bed. Lisa immediately began talking at a very intense and personal level; sharing her feelings of loss and hopelessness at her impending death. Throughout the dialogue Lisa would pause briefly to concentrate on her searing pain. The reality of her anguish made one catch one's breath in response. Lisa was clearly in both physical and mental distress. I listened and interjected occasionally to acknowledge her words. After what felt like an age of listening, I steered our conversation to the possibility of engaging in music if we were to meet again. We decided it would be impractical to have a session in the music therapy room even though it was near the ward, and that we would look to ways of creating a musical experience in her room. Lisa showed an interest in combining music and art and showed me art materials and paper that she had bought with her to the hospice. We decided to explore a combination of improvised music and art the following day. As I stood to leave Lisa again looked directly into my eyes and asked for my home telephone number in case she needed to speak with me before our next meeting. This was the first time a client had so clearly and knowingly attempted to break the boundaries of the client/therapist relationship. It was a clear challenge and my response was one of both panic and resentment. I knew I could not concede to her demand; the therapeutic relationship we had been developing so carefully during the last hour began to disintegrate. I took a deep breath, remembering how my parents had taught me to speak slowly and clearly when speaking in public, and stated simply that I could not comply with her request. Lisa's eyes flared as if in some way I had betrayed her. She said our conversation had been crucial and this being so, it was my duty to continue our alliance at this the most difficult time of her life. I answered that if such was the case we could not continue our relationship. My exterior was calm but inside I was dissolving. As I stood to leave Lisa reluctantly agreed not to pursue this and we arranged to keep the time of our session the following day. We ended our first meeting in an unresolved and uncertain manner.

Leaving her room I immediately went to seek advice from my clinical nurse manager. Trish had become my mentor at such acute times; her experience radiated to all those who needed her wisdom. I knew it was important to make sense of this encounter before leaving the Hospice. Trish listened deeply as I explored my uncertainties as to my role of music therapist with such a needy and volatile client. On one hand I had felt a connection with Lisa but on another I was confused that she was colluding me into a role that was out of my bounds as therapist. Even though we had not made music I felt confident that it could be a medium for us to explore. Trish listened carefully to my concerns and told me that other nursing staff were also finding Lisa needy. It was clear I would have to honor our session the following day even though I could think of many reasons why I might not be able to see her. As we concluded our meeting Trish helped me to acknowledge that my feelings of uncertainty were a natural part of the process with such a demanding client. She also assured me that she would be available the following day if I needed her.

I did indeed enter Lisa's room the following day with feelings of uncertainty. I had with me a portable keyboard and a small range of percussion instruments. I resumed my position next to Lisa's bed. She held my hand tightly and continued her dialogue as if no time had elapsed. The intensity of her words grew ever more profound. She spoke of visions and dreams, of people that she had known, and of a feeling of being pulled to a new and different level of consciousness. These words held an authenticity I dared not break. After a while there came a pause when I suggested we might link music and art, but her pain suddenly returned. Chaos entered the room and she asked me to call a nurse; the moment had gone. Lisa's agony caused her to cry out spontaneously and there seemed little point in continuing our session. The nurses decided to change her dressing and asked if I could come back later. I now felt that introducing music would be impossible.

Speaking later with Gill, the physiotherapist, we discussed Lisa and my dismay at our work. Gill said she too had seen her the previous day and felt it would be of benefit to try and get Lisa out of bed. Gill suggested that we go and see her together and that if we could get her moved then potentially we could have a session in the music therapy room. I was relieved at this suggestion though nervous at what might transpire from this change in direction. As we walked toward the ward her cries could be heard coming from the room. Lisa's sound had an ethereal quality that was acutely distressing. The dressing had been completed but she was obviously still suffering. Gill entered and asked if Lisa was willing to get her out of bed and that potentially we would move to the music therapy room. I was secretly hoping Lisa would say "no", but she nodded in agreement. The next half-hour was an agonizing series of events as Gill attempted to help Lisa out of bed and into a wheelchair. I stood by helplessly, wondering what on earth we would do if we did get to the music therapy room. Once in her wheelchair Gill slowly pushed Lisa from the ward, down the corridor, and into the music therapy room. In the room the pain seemed even greater and Lisa continued to cry out. Gill moved Lisa next to the piano, knelt by her side, and held her hand. It was my turn to intercede.

At this moment I realized I must do something or admit failure. Certainly Lisa had expended too much agony and pain for me to quit. There was a connection between us but certainly not a musical one. I knew I had to do something. What musical experience could I introduce that would in any way help or be vaguely therapeutic? Improvising for Lisa was my only option. I explained that I would like to play for her, that I would try and improvise on the piano and with my voice, my sense of her despair. I sat at the piano, paused, and looked down at the keys. I tried to gain some sense of calm and then started playing. From the moment I placed my hands on the piano the most extraordinary thing happened. Lisa threw back her whole body, stopped crying and began quietly to inwardly sob. The sound was now not of a person in physical distress but of someone feeling great sadness. I remember listening intently to her sounds, the quality of her voice, the measure of her phrases, and the musicality of our connection. I tried to step back from my own purpose, to allow Lisa to affect the flow and architecture of the music. This technique of intuitive improvising became fundamental in my future work with acutely ill clients. Lisa's sounds became ever more musical. The music naturally evolved from and around the key of B minor. Perhaps my own subconscious reactions to Lisa and the spiritual intensity of Bach's B Minor Mass (see Chapter 2) affected such a musical connection:

The first improvisation lasted approximately twenty minutes (see Figure 23.) The music developed from the opening theme, became more animated as Lisa's singing/crying grew, and finally recapitulated to form a structure that was musically complete. At the end Lisa's head dropped and we all held a long inward silence. All sounds had ceased; the music had stopped. The power of this silence was indomitable. Eventually Lisa raised her head and simply said "play more." The second movement, as it were, was different. It felt less intense and more resigned. Musically it was no less sophisticated but emotionally it was more radiant. For this I was greatly relieved. The key of this second intuitive improvisation was balanced between D minor and D major. As the second improvisation finished and as we prepared to take Lisa back to her room I knelt down to thank her for allowing the music. She looked directly into my eyes and said: "I don't know what to say other than I loved your music." I walked back with her and Gill to her room and left quietly. Lisa died the following day.

Reflecting after Lisa died, I somehow felt incomplete. After much reflection I decided to allow myself time to improvise a personal response of my relationship with Lisa (see figure 24.) This reflective improvisation was crucial even though she had died. It was my way of "letting go", an opportunity to internally reflect on the intensity of our brief yet powerful meeting. Musically I needed to add a personal coda to our work. Reflective improvisation became a fundamental part of my work after clients had died, a time to individually contemplate the many intense relationships that are a part of the ongoing work in palliative care.

MUSIC AND DYING

My eight years' work as a music therapist in palliative care was based on the following overriding principles:

- that music reflects both living and dying
- that nonverbal communication can be critical when facing a life-threatening illness
- that creativity portrays the essence of life
- that music is spiritual and as such can transcend the realities of living and dying
- that music in palliative care should be nonthreatening and flexible
- that improvisation can reflect the passing nature of living and dying

During this time my philosophy of music therapy dramatically changed and had a profound influence on the development of AeMT. Acceptance and respect are two crucial components that affected my work in palliative care and AeMT. The questions raised were: "When should the therapist intervene with a therapeutic challenge?" "When should the therapist stay alongside the client and wait?" "What right does the music therapist have to decide upon a course of therapeutic action for the client?" Theories of therapy, are for the most part, based on aims, objectives, and potential for growth. Within the dying process there is always the potential for growth, but then the question becomes: "Should the music therapist in palliative care expect quantifiable change?" I believe that if the therapist waits and reflects, the client will allow their unique signposts to emerge for challenge and growth. If these signposts are either disregarded or imposed the immediate needs of the client may be overlooked.

So what of a philosophy of AeMT in palliative care? Is it possible to create an approach that could link the seemingly disparate archetypes of living and dying? Using music with the dying is in and of itself perhaps the most acute use of music in therapy. Every note, every phrase, every musical utterance must have the greatest significance. The expectation of succeeding sessions is often unrealistic, so the therapist must make every experience and musical encounter

Example 1

fig. 23

count. Living in the musical moment becomes a reality tinged with that which is known and that which is not. Keeping a clear sense of personhood is enigmatic and overidentification a reality, especially when using an overtly emotional medium such as music. The nature of the work also demands that the therapist be vulnerable and in doing so there is a danger that both client and therapist become immersed in a process that in itself may not be therapeutic.

Music and dying has filled my professional life on many levels–coming to music therapy in palliative care was like facing a reflection of my values on life. My experiences were often ones of insecurity and doubt and yet above these feelings was the granite knowledge that music could have a role to play for people facing the end of their lives. Even now if I were to try and articulate exactly the emotions music contains in these encounters it would be difficult to ascertain and articulate. I believe that the mysterious and incorporeal nature of music and dying remains a testament to the work. What am I left with at the end of this work? What did I give and what did I receive in return? How did I balance my (perceived) failures alongside the clarity and intent of the therapeutic instant? What does it mean to succeed as a music therapist in palliative care? How do we measure emotional success?

It is crucial that all therapists in palliative care remember the clients they have worked with. When a client dies, the therapist can be affected deeply and experience intense feelings of bereavement. Because music therapy is built on expression and imagination, the intensity of relationship can belie the reality of time the client and therapist have spent together. I would often find myself knowing and understanding a client deeply after only a few meetings. My sense of loss was always marked and passionate. Using World AIDS Day (December 1st) as a catalyst for remembering the clients I worked with who have died, I find that the accuracy of memory heightens as time elapses. The clarity of each presence has become a part of my life and a constant reminder of the compelling nature of humanity and relationship.

Example 2

fig. 24

Chapter 13

MOVING INTO THE AGE OF AQUARIUS: AESTHETIC MUSIC THERAPY WITH A STRING QUARTET

> When a performance is in progress, all four of us together enter a zone of magic somewhere between our music stands and become conduit, messenger, and missionary. In playing, say, the cavatina of Opus 130, we join hands to enter Beethoven's world, vividly aware of each other and our objective performance responsibilities, and yet, almost like sleepwalkers, we allow ourselves to slip into the music's spiritual realm. It is an experience too personal to talk about and yet it colors every aspect of our relationship, . . .
>
> –Arnold Steinhardt,
> *Indivisible by Four:*
> *A String Quartet in Pursuit of Harmony* (1998)

I have explored, through the writing of this book, the aesthetic qualities of music therapy; to bring together the strands of clinical practice from a music-centered perspective. The work described in this chapter, perhaps more strongly than any other, illuminates this striving for cohesion between clinical and musical form. To be innovative is to contest that which we consider fact and allow it to become an enigma. Music therapy over the last fifty years has acquired a broad range of theories and knowledge. Future inquiry will determine how these outcomes influence contemporary questions raised in the next millennium. The challenge is not whether we should be focusing on empirical evidence or qualitative and humanistic thought, but rather how we refine the quality and nature of these discussions for our understanding and the substantiation of practice for others. While being only one part of this growth, I believe a music-centered perspective as advocated in AeMT is, nevertheless, a fundamental one. It is our inner self-analysis and openness that will establish the credibility of music therapy with affiliated professionals in the future. If we are to gain respect from the field of music we must be prepared to demonstrate the quality of our musical interventions. Working with musicians is a natural and liberating evolution in this process. Even though potentially daunting, this work can provide an opening for future practice that is informed from music itself. To face the challenge of this work is to expand our musical and therapeutic horizons and in doing so discover new ground-breaking models of music therapy.

Music therapy with musicians has gained little recognition in the evolution of clinical practice or in the literature. Rachel Verney's (Ansdell, 1995) description of her work with Jane, a flute teacher, provides a powerful testament to the potential of this work. In speaking of her music therapy encounters Jane expresses that:

> I experienced that all the possibilities in music–if they are used creatively and sent into the center of us–are like a self-regulating system. My singing, my making music has really changed, and also the way I listen has changed (p. 185).

Jane came to music therapy because of a presenting problem with her wrist. Once becoming immersed in music, however, her physical condition disappeared and her involvement in improvising, particularly singing, became the therapy. Her words are a clear indication of the strength of this work, but it is the audio extracts that speak most clearly to the vitality of music making. Listening to the first audio example (note: please refer to accompanying CD, *Music for Life*, Ansdell, 1995, track 21), one is struck by the strength and unity of the musical relationship. The section of improvisation included is an aesthetic experience embedded in the developing relationship. Rachel's exact clinical listening as therapist, the simple yet directed piano accompaniment, and the interpretations of Jane's vocal phrases allows a musical and therapeutic creative duet of epic proportions. This work shows that clinical improvisation with musicians depends, even more explicitly than in other areas of clinical practice, on the immediacy of the musical moment. Exterior interpretations serve to inform the process but it is the music itself that is unquestionably the therapy.

In the final chapter of *Music at the Edge* (Lee, 1996), in the section On Being a Musician as Client in Music Therapy, I wrote:

> Musicians often lose spontaneity in their trained renderings of other people's music: improvisation permits the intuitive expression of a musician's authentic sense of music self. For the therapist there is often real testing of musical ability. The therapist must . . . be assured of his or her improvisational skills when working with musicians. This does not mean that the music therapist has to be up to a virtuoso standard. It is possible to work with musicians who have superior musical skills; what is important is to listen carefully to their musical contribution. It is not enough to think in terms of an overall musical

> structure. The therapist must consider the smallest intricacies of expression within the music relationship. (p. 153)

This challenge to the therapist is to provide musical commitment. I remember vividly my reaction to meeting Francis; that when learning he was a musician I wanted to run and escape. It can seem a daunting task to improvise with a musician. That the musical demands of this work are great there is no doubt. If we are prepared to risk the challenge, however, and strive for ever more higher musical standards, than the rewards of this work may be even greater.

Louise Montello developed work culminating in the Music Therapy for Musicians (MTM) method (Montello, 2000, 2001). She initially used breathing techniques to consider the stress facing professional musicians (Montello, 1995). Techniques have been further explored, considering the underlying problems of performance stress and repetitive strain injuries, using breathing, guided meditation, and clinical improvisation (Montello, 1996, 1997). Improvisation is used as a specific tool to "express the energy of a bodily symptom musically, in order to give voice to feelings that may have been suppressed or dissociated" Montello, 1996, p. 5). Through research of the MTM method she has discovered that specific music therapy techniques not only reduce performance anxiety but also increased musicality.

BACKGROUND

The summer of 2000 was spent in England visiting family and friends, and contemplating my fifteen years of work as a music therapist. Having made the critical decision to stay in Canada, I found myself reviewing past achievements and planning future ones. What new avenues of work would I now explore and how could I further combine my roles as musician, composer, and therapist? I had a feeling of being at a musical and personal crossroads. Having worked within a music faculty for two years I had become immersed not only in the running and teaching of the music therapy program, but also in interdisciplinary connections with composition, performance, and musicology. These professional affiliations had a significant effect not only on my developing musicianship, but on my insights in understanding the strands of clinical improvisation.

The string quartet is a medium that has always fascinated me. Intermusically and interpersonally I am intrigued and in awe of this, the most personal of musical associations. Wilfrid Laurier University is privileged to have as quartet-in-residence the Penderecki String Quartet. Listening regularly to their concerts I began to hear and see patterns in their playing that fascinated me and gave rise to questions. What where the intricate musical and physical gestures they used and how did these relay the subtle communication needed to perform the often intimate works of the string quartet repertoire? What personal dynamics, if any, were occurring between players and could these in any way be related to the dynamics of clients in music therapy? Could a music therapist work with a string quartet in the same way as a group in music therapy?

The more I pondered these questions the more absorbed I became by the potential of working with the Penderecki String Quartet. On one hand it seemed a natural evolution of clinical practice but on another I wondered if this would be classed as music therapy at all. On returning to Wilfrid Laurier I decided to approach the quartet to see if they would be interested in working with me on a pilot project. I explained little other than this was an idea that had come to me during the summer, and wondered if they would be interested in professional contact between us. They agreed, acknowledging that it might be difficult to arrange a series of concurrent sessions due to their busy teaching and concert schedule. The work described here is based on the two sessions we have held to date.

THE SESSIONS

Listening Guide

Read the text describing session one, listen to extract. . . . Read the text describing session two, listen to extract. . . . Read the transcription of the interview and listen again to both improvisations.

Session One

I had many apprehensions preparing for this, our first session. How would I explain clearly my ideas? How would I take the role of therapist? What would their expectations be of me and the session? Was I musically competent to meet the potential of their playing? Where they feeling as nervous as I was? I prepared the room in the same way as I would for a group session though I decided not to have available percussion instruments (note: these first two sessions have been held solely on their string instruments. We have, however, discussed the idea of introducing percussion instruments in future sessions). Entering the clinic the quartet quietly prepared and tuned their instruments. My opening words were (nervously) concise. I explained these were ideas in formation based on the hypothesis of musicians improvising together within a music therapy framework. I further went on to explain that it would be my role as music therapist to contain and reflect their playing. I explained that it was important that they start the improvisation, that the direction of the music should come from them.

The silence that ensued was broken by a opening violin phrase; the rest of the quartet soon joined in. I listened intently to the quality of their playing and tried to discover some kind of tonal center. Taking a deep breath I entered their musical arena beginning with the suitably ambiguous interval of a major 7th (G and F#). The music immediately took on a life of its own. Structurally the improvisation was not dissimilar to the long improvisations I had become accustomed to in my developing work with clients living with HIV and AIDS. The seven sections were divided with short resting plateaus. As each was introduced the more inventive they became. I was caught in an experience of musical liberation that left me breathless. As the improvisation came to a close there was a long extended silence.

It seemed that the quartet were as intrigued as I at what had taken place and were eager to talk about the experience. The opportunity to play both free from a score and have no musical expectations placed on them were dynamics not often available. We talked about what would happen if we continued the work; what would be the focus and how would working in music therapy help them as a quartet? After much discussion two main questions appeared: Could clinical improvisation affect the quartet's concert playing outside sessions? How might the interpersonal relationships of the quartet be explored through the musical dialogue? We decided to arrange another session later in the term.

On reflection I knew something extraordinary had happened. Listening back to the tape I tried to uncover why this musical experience had been so powerful. It seemed that the aesthetic perception of music and the human connections made were more precise than I had ever encountered in other areas of clinical work. What impact could this work have, if any, for music therapy? I felt a sense of looking into a huge canyon. If this was music therapy then perhaps it was the purest form of music, communication, and the human condition I have ever been privileged to be a part of. What were the boundaries of the therapeutic relationships and process in this context? How was the music balanced as pure expression and relationship? I decided that what had happened in this session was either highly significant or highly irrelevant. What of my roles as composer, pianist, and therapist? To musically hold, contain, mirror, and reflect with such remarkable musicians seemed a daunting task. Should I musically intervene and challenge? These questions and others continued to penetrate my thoughts until the following session.

Session Two

The second session was different from the first on various counts. First, we decided to change the venue to the Maureen Forrester Hall so a better quality recording could be obtained. Second, I had been approached by Hele Montague, a producer for CBC radio, to include our work in an upcoming program on music therapy. We agreed that Hele would interview us directly after the session. There were two improvisations included in this session. The quartet asked for the first improvisation that the violins (Jeremy and Jerzy) and viola (Christine) could be free to move around the platform, while the cellist (Paul) sat immediately in middle stage to my right. The piano lid of the piano was opened and at various times during the improvisation members would play into the sounding board which I would allow to sound by keeping the sustaining pedal down. The opening of the improvisation was exploratory in nature.

Audio Extract Eight: Session Two, Improvisation One

- The cello plays a descending glissando heralding a slow, defined, and romantic legato theme.
- The music becomes tango-like with clear phrases and open textured playing. Rhythms are established and thrown from player to player.
- A short bridge passage allows the music to find a new direction.
- A fast-moving and syncopated section develops. The music builds in dynamic and emotional intensity. Fast repetitive phrases lead into the following section.
- Romantic tonal music builds slowly. Stunning, intense listening and an exquisite sense of chamber music playing evolves.
- The music reaches a climax ending with a high ascending phrase on the violin.
- Bridge passage.
- The final section is syncopated and rhythmic.
- The music moves toward a coda and the rhythms become less intense.
- End of improvisation.

For the second improvisation the quartet again requested a change in their positions. This time they asked to sit equally around the piano. The sense of being enveloped was a powerful one that had a great impact on my playing. The music was developed from the opening violin D. It is this note that contains the overall musical invention and floats over the improvisation as the architectural tonic. The intensity of relations and the theatrical/emotional quiet of this improvisation is a testament to the power of musical and emotional form. This, I believe, is a clear example of music therapy with musicians.

Audio Extract Nine:
Session Two, Improvisation Two

- An intense silence is broken by D on the violin. Small transparent textures are intertwined with small motifs. Sounds come and go. There is a sense of acute listening.
- The music gains more direction and strength.
- A climax ensues.
- The music becomes lighter and more open in texture.
- A second huge climax takes the music to its highest emotional peak.
- The music dissolves and the viola leads a new melodic invention.
- The music continues to be small and transparent.
- A third fleeting climax leads again to quiet inner music.
- The music becomes smaller and smaller.
- The improvisation ends with a held silence.

After the improvisation we sat in silence for a time, before moving to the room for the radio interview.

THE INTERVIEW

HM: Hele Montague (interviewer), CL Colin Lee (music therapist), JK Jerzy Kaplanek (violin), JB Jeremy Bell (violin), CV Christine Vlajk (viola), PP Paul Pulford (cello)

HM When you were first approaching the members of the Penderecki String Quartet, what is it that you told them?

CL The idea of working with the quartet came quite spontaneously. I had worked before as a music therapist with musicians so in some ways this was a natural extension. I remember hearing the Penderecki and thinking about the way they made music. How they interacted together musically and interpersonally. I thought it might be exciting if I could give the quartet the chance to play and freely explore with me as music therapist. It seemed a simple idea though at the same time I was aware that it was potentially loaded.

HM What did you say by way of explanation?

CL I kept it open. That this was just an idea. I hadn't theoretically or clinically made any assumptions beyond the idea itself. I think even now after two sessions we are at the beginning, so I'm starting to have questions and to think what it really is that we are doing. Is it music therapy? Is it simply us improvising together? What are we actually doing? In our first session we all discussed this at length. What should be the aims of our work? I think that's still being formulated. As a qualitative researcher I wanted to be open so that the work would find its own level and direction.

HM (To PP) Why did you think this would be an interesting project?

PP I think the concept of improvising for a group such as ours, which puts such a high premium on exactness and getting it right and consistency, at least for me, was kind of frightening. You're basically losing control of those elements. You never know what's going to happen. You have to be responding constantly rather than having any kind of plan, although even in improvisation presumably there is some kind of plan. We all have the same training in Western music. For me personally, it was a challenge. I was curious to see what would happen and I was curious to see whether the quartet could do it.

CV I was interested in working with Colin; he's a fine person aside from being a very well-known music therapist, but just the energy I felt from him as a musician and person. I thought as a group we could benefit from working with him. I too felt open-minded about what might come up. The idea of participating in something with the quartet that is not so exacting–it's really in the moment and it's fresh and it's being created by us–and then it's gone. I like that.

JB For me it feels immediately therapeutic, that we can let our guards down. You can't even begin an improvisation if you're feeling defensive or competitive–that premise cannot be in the room. It's a more pure way of communicating with music among the four of us. It feels like doing scales as a group in terms of being cleansing emotionally.

You can let your personality come out. You try to engage other people in the flow of the music. It reminds me of a comment from Anner Bylsma, an amazing European baroque cellist, who in a master class made a point of saying the first thing you should do in the morning is to improvise for twenty minutes so that you cultivate your own voice––cultivate what you want to feel, get in touch with your emotional response to music. I think this is a wonderful idea; it's a very basic exercise and I think it's terrific.

JK Being able to explore different angles of music is very important as a musician and improvising has always been a big part of that. Even though I don't improvise very much on the violin I improvise quite a bit on the piano and when I was younger I played the organ and improvised. Improvising always freed me up and after working for so many years with my colleagues in a very scheduled and profound way, I realized that I had never really got to know them as creative improvising musicians. I was really curious to explore that. After spending so much time trying to get everything done perfectly and in a certain way with stylistic differences and intonation perfection, one can get away from that when one is improvising. It was really interesting to see the different responses and emotional contents of responding to each other's phrases and sounds. We've worked so much together. With new music, where we sometimes get asked to improvise, you can sometimes hear our direct emotional response. You know, I'm not really able to completely let go. There were times during the improvisation that I would feel like–well, I would like to follow this person, or follow this person and even if I don't think about it my instincts would push me there. That would really not happen when I did it myself. So not having a particular plan like you would have for our other improvisations–it keeps this angle completely open–yet all the time coming back to those habits from rehearsals, and from the music that you've been learning, and then having Colin around that. I was interested to hear how he would read our responses and I was interested to talk to him about it afterward.

HM What happens in a session? Is it structured in any way?

CL I always wait for the quartet to start so that the musical direction is open to them. In the first session we played and then we talked for quite a long time. This morning we played two improvisations and this is the first time we have talked about the experience.

HM How do you know when it's time to begin?

JK When we started the second improvisation everyone was quiet. In the first improvisation we experimented walking around with our instruments and so the leadership was almost shared by that too. When we started the second improvisation we said, let's sit down and see how different that would feel. When the tape started nobody made a gesture, nobody made a sound. I was sitting more like a first violin–I should explain that Jeremy and I switch violin positions in the quartet– and I suddenly felt like, wow, somebody needs to give a cue, so I did that. I played one note and everybody started to join me. The first sound is the piece, so this beginning was interesting.

CL There can be tension at the beginning of an improvisation. Who will start? If nobody takes the initiative there can be a sense of tense suspension–this of course is a part of the therapeutic process. Sometimes the opening silence can get to the point where no one dares play and then tension begins. The amazing thing is that there are many levels of silence. For me that opening silence was very cleansing.

JK Absolutely. I felt as if whatever I do this will initiate the whole first part of the improvisation and the direction that it is going to take. That is a real responsibility.

JB Part of the tension was because our first improvisation included a fair bit of activity. There was much energy initially and then in the second improvisation I think we all thought, How can we make this different? Where can we explore this time? I think we had to back way off and that's exactly how the second improvisation felt: calm.

CV In the first improvisation we walked around except for Paul and Colin. They were stuck to the ground. In the second improvisation not only did we all sit down, we sat around the piano. I felt in a sense we were all facing each other–there was a certain vulnerability in that. We all closed our eyes, but still you could feel the presence of people right there.

PP This silence reminds me of what the first performances of John Cage's 4'32" must have been like, where someone comes and sits at the piano and prepares to play and doesn't. The piece becomes the silence and the response of the audience to the silence. It's a brilliant concept. Would that be therapeutic for an audience?

CL I think it potentially could be.

PP Silence is as much a part of improvising as playing is.

HM Stravinsky said music is a series of tensions looking for a resolution. Do you agree with that?

JB Obviously tension and release–the scope of that–can be very different depending on the context-how things are going along. I think in improvisation there is that basic narrative and it's generally in play, especially the first improvisation of today. There was very much a sense of well, if we're going to go this far, then somehow we have to balance that with something else. I'm not sure if it's because we are accustomed to that as a narrative with Western classical music; that we feel that's polite. I thought the second improvisation had more sense of spatial–more Feldmanesque, less goal oriented. (note: explain that the quartet have played music by Morton Feldman and who he is)

PP That's a guy I wouldn't want to improvise with–Morton Feldman!

HM A more fundamental question: everybody is classically trained and you do have that classical sense of music, but what is that sense of music? What is your sense of what music is? And the second follow-up question would be, How does this work with Colin alter that, change that, move that, reaffirm that? This is a big question–a historical thing, a learned thing. How is coming together to improvise a therapy? Does this experience reevaluate your sense of music, what music can be?

PP One of the things that fascinates me about Western music is the concept that the music of different composers represents the world in which they lived. The music of Bach in many ways is an aural representation of the world in which he lived, just as the music of Stravinsky is an aural representation of the world in which he lived. As we move into the 21st century and we start to see the impact of technology on the music that's being created. Being trained to play music from other centuries–it's kind of curious. You end up playing music which is not represented in the world we live in on a daily basis. We kind of time travel. When we play Mozart we are in a time when there were no machines. Probably the loudest noises you would hear would be a blacksmith, or a horse going down cobble- stones, or thunder. The sounds of nature very much would have been the dominant sounds. When you are improvising there is no way to leave your world behind even when you're using harmonies or gestures from Mozart or Beethoven or Brahms. There's no way you can leave your world behind and the things that impact on you every day. What Jeremy was saying about how it feels therapeutic–for me that's one of the things–the dirt of your everyday life comes out a bit. You soothe yourself with these gestures which might take you to another time, another place, which in many ways was much gentler than walking down the street today in Toronto.

JB Being in a professional string quartet you are asked to play a certain piece and the concert date is set, and you wake up that morning and you don't have a choice; the show must go on no matter what's happening. You wake up that day and you may not really feel like playing Shostakovich. What's good about improvising is that you can have complete control–well, not complete control. You encourage your colleagues to put the improvisation in a certain direction by coaxing them politely. What I found in the first improvisation–I wanted there to be a kind of energetic, motoric section. I felt like I needed to do that, I needed to just go there for a while. I really wanted my colleagues to go there and we did it and it was exciting. For me that is what music is about–you want to feel the kinetic energy, you want to feel the vibration in the way which most immediately grabs you, that you're always very, very connected. The most exciting thing about music is when you are feeling that. When you're in a string quartet you may get glimpses of that but there are times when you have to focus on something else. You have to focus on ensemble-those feelings can be fleeting-that's another wonderful thing about improvisation.

HM (To CV) Have you led in the improvisations?

CV I led the first improvisation of the session–that feels a little odd for me as a violist. That may sound strange but sometimes I lead and I certainly I have my stubborn side. I can be vehement about things at times but during the improvisations many times I felt like I wanted to stay stage left–if you're looking at the audience this is were I sit. I kept feeling pulled to Paul. I'm finally getting this off my chest–just something about that. I almost had to force myself to not be there–but yes I lead. I want to say one thing about what music was if I could just take a moment. When I think about music I think about universality, the universality of it and how it exists in all cultures. The primitive, primal nature that we all need to express ourselves, that every culture has. There is some quality about improvising that reminds me of when I was a child, when I was engrossed in the sound and experience of it. It's a feeling that oftentimes as a professional I long to feel. In improvising I feel free and childlike.

JK A few words on your question about the broader view of music–I feel that music in a big sense is for me a tool of communication, like a language. Being in the role of communicating between myself and the audience, that's what I usually do. We try and bring the interpretation of the piece to the audience that they will understand what the composer wanted to say. Being able to improvise, it felt almost as if I was able to write my own journal. We often think of therapy sessions as being a place where you can speak and be listened to by someone. I felt having Colin there was for me maybe this moment–being very personal and having him there, not necessarily as an interactive person, but as the one that lets me be vulnerable, be open to say what sits inside of me. (To CL) I would be curious to hear a little of how you see that as certainly for me there was a moment of letting go and being able to talk from my own vocabulary.

CL It's not my job to overidentify with whom I'm working with. I need in some way to remain apart and reflect. Having said that I think things change and in the second improvisation I felt a surge of intimacy between us and I was very moved. I felt as if the five of us were totally together and at that point I did let my guard down. This changes how I perceive music therapy. It can't be like other work that I've done. I didn't want to come into our work full of assumptions. I felt strongly the need to be open and I think your question about music and how we as human beings–if in any way us working together could change the quartet's perceptions of how they relate to music then these experiences will have been a success. I know that it's going to change my perceptions too. I want to go back just briefly to the universality of music as it makes me consider why I am a music therapist and why I'm so passionate about the music in music therapy. I think music therapy is and has been in danger of eliminating the aesthetic qualities of music. I feel so strongly that we mustn't allow that to happen. Working with the quartet is the finest example of doing that. Working with the quartet is both therapeutic and aesthetic and therefore this has been one of the most exciting experiences for me as a music therapist. You can work with a severely disabled client that can't speak, that is profoundly physically disabled and yet in music we can be equal. That's why I'm also passionate about what music therapy can achieve–that I can be with somebody no matter how ill or disabled and we can experience music equally. In the second improvisation I feel we were equal. For this reason alone I feel this makes what we did together clearly music therapy.

JK Yes, we don't look for particular musical effect from the tape–we just . . . we did what we did, felt what we felt, and that more or less is where that stops. When you're always performing music, even improvising in different circumstances–in jazz–you would look for a particular music effect and artistic statement. I don't think this was like that. It was just for us.

HM How is what you're doing different from a jazz improvisation group?

JB To elaborate on an earlier comment, Jerzy was saying that we have a vocabulary that we draw from, in fact there were moments where it sounded like one of the Schafer quartets. Tone moments, like Webern and there were other moments like Debussy. That struck me as something that's enriching that, our own repertoire in that sense, that we're extrapolating the repertoire which we're doing professionally.

HM (To CL) You talked about the aesthetics falling out of music therapy. Can you talk about that and why you feel aesthetics are important in music therapy?

CL I am trained in the Nordoff and Robbins approach to music therapy which was started by Paul Nordoff, an American composer, and his colleague Clive Robbins. Being a composer for me is a fundamental part of my thinking as a music therapist. I want to wave the flag of the musical interpersonal relationship. What happens when we improvise together musically? What are the qualities of the music itself that makes it so powerful? We can talk about this until the cows come home but I don't think you can ever articulate accurately the experience through words. You might indeed be able to quantify the musical experience and turn creativity into numbers, but what does that mean? What does it tell us other than, yes it works? How it works–well, that is altogether another and more challenging question.

HM You have had two sessions. What's the progression for the quartet as a group? Is there something that's beginning to change, or evolve, or alter in some way? Or is it too early to say?

PP I can only speak for myself. The key for me is not to have any expectations–not to expect change, not to expect growth or stasis–simply to have no expectations, and that includes an expectation of whether it's going to be good or bad or indifferent, but rather to try as much as possible to be in the moment and let that moment lead you. If at a particular time you don't feel you've got anything to say, not to manufacture something-just to stop playing until you feel you do have something to say. To that end the answer to your question is "no." I don't see it going anywhere other than it is fascinating and I think I feel I'm learning about people, but not in a way I could put into words. The music resides in a place that is not a verbal place. It's something else.

CL I'm not sure I want there to be in-depth verbal psychotherapeutic meaning to what we are doing. I think what we've done must mean something, but it's enough to be as it is at this time. I'm not burning to make it any more that what it is now.

CV I think it would be interesting for our process as a group, to have some summary of what our roles are. I think we're expressing various aspects of our process, not musically but interpersonally. I'd be curious to know what a music psychotherapist would have to say–perhaps we would then say "no" and we would argue with her just like groups can do.

PP Your such a typical violist!

CV No, I'm not, I'm just curious to see the summary of our dynamics.

JB If I were to assess what is taking place and what has happened in an interpersonal way, I always sense a desire when we are improvising that the four of us want to be equal. No one is looking to be the hero, or be passive–there may be moments where someone is leading, or someone is bowing out for a bit. What strikes me is that as a collective, we're trying to come together and create something as one in a very nonhierarchical way, and there are times when we don't always get the opportunity in our work to do that–so that's wonderful.

JK Having an opportunity to improvise together, it means to me that I was able to be there with my colleagues and they know that I was able to express something very personal. I was trying to be very personal in the music and I think you all were too. Just having this around us–that we actually have done it, and that we are not afraid to go into this room and do that and just be who we are–it might help somehow down the road. In a very different way, on the stage, we do have to use this feeling of improvising–I shouldn't use the word improvisation– rather, being spontaneous. I think that's maybe just another step to achieve a little more of that on stage. We all were able to have this experience without any expectations and without judgments. I think it's a very valuable experience.

HM The question of composition being an act of therapy. Paul, you mentioned that every composer writes from their era and time, but are your improvisations, are they compositions, and if so is what Schubert was doing, or Duke Ellington, a kind of therapy?

JB I think it's very different when you write something down and you publish and sell it. That's a very different sort of gift, than having people who know each other and it's not leaving the room.

CV I might call it a piece and not a composition. Somehow composition implies notation and writing down. A jazz tune has the tune, or the head, and then one improvises off that, off the chord progression. So it's not a piece in that sense. I've done spontaneous improvisation in jazz class and it was similar to what we're doing now, but there are a few more jazzy riffs and licks in it. I think what we did today was a piece. It was sound, music, and expression and it happened. We even have a tape to prove it!

PP What we were doing had an element of performance. When a composition is created, I think there is a sense or at least a hope, if not an expectation, that somebody will play it and other people will listen and hear it. One of the fundamental elements of what we are doing–at least up to this point–is that we haven't been doing it for anyone else, we've been doing it for ourselves, and since it's not performance, it's not anything other than interaction. It just happens that we're using our own instruments to interact. It's defined by *how* we're communicating, not that we're communicating.

JB Nothing is done for posterity's sake.

CL If by composition you mean "form," then it was a composition. But it's not a composition in terms of something that's completed and written down. I think the important thing about any improvisation is that it has form, that there is a sense of shape and architecture about the whole experience.

PP Your imposition of a very human and intellectual concept of structure which could have been random. One could record the sound of the wind or the ocean and with our human attitude find a structure and say it's a composition therefore we're imposing an external structure, but in fact it doesn't need to have structure. I agree that what we did has structure, but one need not necessarily see it in those terms.

CL I think the music therapist's job musically is to provide a sense of shape and structure, so going back to what Jerzy said when he played the opening D of the second improvisation–I always see a note suspended over the whole piece–and in this instance it was Jerzy's opening D. I think I played an A in response. The D potentially gave the music shape and continuity. So even though it's spontaneous and of the moment, I'm thinking intellectually as well.

PP Yes, I understand.

This interview is interesting on many levels. There is a sense of work in transition. After two sessions the quartet is committed to future work. That none of us are fixed in our ideas means all possibilities remain open. The musical examples speak to the potential of music therapy with musicians, not only for the quartet, but for music therapy as a whole. Reflecting on Christine's (viola) question, how a psychotherapist might view their work, I decided to invite a group music psychotherapist to give her impressions on the evolving process. The following interpretations give a psychotherapeutic viewpoint and adds further richness to the discourse.

PERSPECTIVES FROM HEIDI AHONEN-EERIKAINEN: A GROUP MUSIC PSYCHOTHERAPIST

As a group analyst and music psychotherapist I have experienced that non-referential improvisation can be a powerful technique and that different musical images can be used as a pathway to the unconscious. It is music itself that is the therapy. And still there can be many things that happen in the player's minds. Individual group members sound different and together they make music. Each instrument is needed to make the unique sound of the group. But–as typical for the musical expression–it is often more than words can articulate. It goes beyond words.

I was interested to read the interview from a group analytic perspective and to investigate whether any elements that are common to group analytic music therapy (Ahonen-Eerikaninen, 1999) occurred during the two sessions with the string quartet. Group analytic music therapy offers a view into the individual's internal world and psychodynamics–he interactive field between members of a group and the group matrix, i.e., the group as a whole. Music also has its own role when moving on different levels of the group matrix: on the level of social interactions, on the level of transference, on the projective level, and on the level of collective unconsciousness (Foulkes 1964; Kreeger, 1991; Salminen, 1997). These levels of the group matrix which can be identified in the music therapy process, can also be found in this work with the Penderecki String Quartet.

The Level of Social Interactions

The interaction between group members can be achieved by the nonverbal language of music. The role of music includes a means of communication–telling a story about oneself and to others. In music it is possible to send messages and receive them without talking. At the same time, one can experience being understood and accepted on an emotional level. The level of social interactions is presented in group music therapy, this idea being aroused in the interview after the two improvisations:

- "I feel that music in a big sense is for me a tool of communication, like a language."
- "Being able to improvise it felt almost as if I was able to write my own journal."
- "It was interesting to see the different responses and emotional contents of responding to each other's phrases and sounds."
- "You try and engage other people in the flow of the music."
- "Have to respond constantly rather than having any kind of plan."

The Transference Level

Music may take the player to his/her past and represent life situations or portray people with a similar mood that was reflected through the music. For example, music may remind us of a situation or person we have known. Music can also "feel" similar to previous life situations. The group member at the level of everyday defenses acts according to the same operational strategies and emotional patterns as in his/her everyday life. The stage of the group and the transference of emotions allows these strategies to move and allow protective measures. The improvisation of the quartet was a pure expression of the players relationship; "I always sense a desire when we are improvising that the four of us want to be equal. No one is looking to be the hero, or be passive . . . " During free improvisation the sound may create various transference figures in which a group can place his/her emotions and thoughts: "There's no way to leave your world behind even when you're using harmonies or gestures from Mozart, Beethoven, or Brahms. There's no way you can leave behind the things that impact on your everyday life."

The Projective Level

The group member may feel that the music represents "me." "This is how I am." "This music sounds like me." We can transfer our own primitive fantasies and internal world, for example: hopes, fears, different kinds of internal figures and partial objects, to music, other group members, and to features of the entire group (Foulkes, 1964; Salimnen, 1997). Projective identification also comes in musical images:

- "You can let your personality come out."
- "You soothe yourself with these gestures which might take you to another time, another place, which in many ways was much gentler than walking down the street today in Toronto."
- "In improvising I feel free and child like."
- "You want to feel the vibration in the way which most immediately grabs you."
- "You are always very connected."

The Level of the Collective Unconscious

As a music therapist working in a group analytic model, I believe that the imageries and symbols aroused through music are personal objects which carry meanings that are potentially charged. They are like dreams that one can reflect upon the following morning: "Why did I have that dream last night?" Everyone has a certain mental picture of himself/herself and their internal and external world. The task of improvisation is to expand the internal imagery map of oneself, find new alternatives, activate problem solving, new points of view and possibilities. The goal can also be to bring out subconscious material, confront new feelings and mental integration.

It would have been interesting to share the feelings and images of the string quartet during the improvisations because often the level of collective unconscious becomes obvious in the musical images of the group members. The collective symbols derive from dreams, fantasies, and fears of the early days of humankind (Salminen, 1997). It is common during improvisations that there will be group associations around similar themes.

When Colin asked me to write some psychotherapeutic views of this work I decided to start by first listening to the music. I closed my office door, turned off the brightest light, took a relaxed posture in my chair, closed my eyes, and prepared myself to step into the world of music. I had a beautiful "trip" and many different feelings and images. Some of these images, such as the ones referring to nature, were archetypal:

Silence
Peace on the earth
Calm surface of the deep waters
But I am not alone.
And we all wait.
Waiting fulfills the landscape.
Is it already coming?
I am ready.
The surface of the waters is bright like a glass.
Or is this only a reflection?

Sorrow?
Slow sorrow that slows everything down?

Now it begins
The surface of the water is moving.
There is something there.
It waits for THE moment . . .
YES!
That's it!
It's there! The fire works. The Northern lights. The volcano. The top of the universe!
It is full! And it ripples! And it is SO full. It is free!

I listen.
I meet you.
I share.
We are together.
We are alone.
We are equal.

After listening to the music and writing my images and feelings I read the interview. It was astonishing to find that they had similar feelings about their playing. My feelings of being equal was also expressed by one member of the quartet. We all experienced some level of catharsis in the tension resolutions and freedom. For example the quartet described the process as: "Losing control" and by saying: "You never know what's going to happen," and "can let our guards down," and "being cleansing emotionally." Stravinsky's idea that "music is a series of tensions looking for resolution" was highlighted in my music images also.

The Role of the Therapist

The role of the therapist in the group was crucial. The therapist's improvising was full of therapeutic interventions. He supported the group members (harmony, themes, dynamics), reflecting the different musical ideas as they occurred. He also respected the musical pauses of the group, one member of the group noting that: "Silence is as much a part of improvising as playing is." It was important that the therapist did not try to lead the group but rather let them choose the direction of their improvisation. The therapist's music was both holding and containing. With his musical interventions he reflected the feelings of the individual group members and the music of the group as a whole. He was supportive and gave group members permission to express themselves freely. I think the therapist created the protective conditions to allow the therapeutic climate to develop. "I felt Colin was there . . . being very personal and having him there, not necessarily as an interactive person, but as the one that lets me be vulnerable, be open to say what sits inside of me."

CLOSING THOUGHTS

Chamber music is one of the most intimate forms of musical relationship. Groups often work together closely for many years, there being a sense of "marriage" in their commitment to music and fellow members. Just as with an ongoing group in music therapy, struggles and tensions appear that must be resolved if the group is to flourish and survive. What makes one group's playing great and another's sedentary? It is more than the combination of notes that result in mystical playing. Outstanding chamber music is a combination of musical sensitivity and understanding of each player's idiosyncratic responses. While musicians may not always acknowledge the importance of interpersonal relations, there is not doubt they play an equally important role. The same issues arise for music therapy. How does a group facilitate a way of playing that is therapeutic? The connections between group members and their relationship with the client, the ensuing musical dialogue, the musical input of each group member, and the expertise of the therapist in reflecting and challenging this results in the potency of the process. To play in a sensitive and open manner with a group of fellow musicians, either artistically or therapeutically, means each member must listen deeply and on many levels. I believe that the Penderecki's sense of chamber music in improvisation became ever more acute because they were able to listen and respond on a level that is not possible through precomposed music. They were able to traverse the rigors of musical precision and enter into music that was a true reflection of their relationships. This highlights that the process of chamber music and group music therapy have many elements in common.

The evolution of AeMT is based on the assumption that musical and clinical form have rudiments in common. Music therapy with musicians is the quintessential essence of combining music and therapy, an example of AeMT in its purest and truest form. Throughout my years as an active music therapist I attempted to find that balance between being a composer and music therapist, to embrace a way of working that could be respected in both therapeutic and musical circles; a link that would result in a truly music-centered approach. The symphonic reaction of AeMT to the emphasis on empirical and scientific evidence comes from a deep-seated belief in the human contact of music. That to be artistic and creative is to be free and whole. That music therapy with a string quartet could provide new approaches to clinical practice bears testament to the potential of other sapient ideas. To be open to new developments, such as these, is to rejoice in the limitless possibilities of our work. The questions and approaches raised in this chapter are not infallible but they are unashamedly and intensely musical. I believe that this work with the Penderecki String Quartet opens many doors; what lies beyond I am not sure.

Chapter Fourteen

FROM A COMPOSER'S POINT OF VIEW

> Part of the poet's, the painter's or the musician's job is just that of renewing our sense of the comely and beautiful. If, in the music I write, I can create a sound wherein some, at least, of my generation can find refreshment in their inner life, then I am doing my work properly.
>
> –Michael Tippett,
> *Moving into Aquarius* (1959)

Very much like the music therapy process, composing lives through the unforeseen. This is both the dilemma and the potential spark for creativity. Allowing the presence of, and being affected by, the moment to moment passage of tones, contains the spirit of musical reality. To compose is to be open to all possibilities. The blank page provides limitless potential to explore and conceive individual expression; this is the challenge to all artists. Being musical should not be limited by knowledge and composing should not be confined by rules. Our clients face ambiguity; that of balancing their lives between order and chaos, illness and life. Music can redress this discrepancy and provide human strength. What can composers bring to music therapy? Are there similarities between the compositional process and the therapeutic process? What does it mean to think of clients as composers and artists? The client as composer is the blank page of the therapeutic process; it allows equality. This is the essence of AeMT. As together the therapist and client uncover the design and direction of the relationship, so this is reflected through musical potential. Just as my path as composer is driven by both exhilaration and apprehension, so in my growth as a music therapist I must balance that which is known against that which can never be. If we can balance freedom and structure, then maybe our understanding of the bridge between the clinical and the artistic may become clearer.

During my early years as a composer I was consumed with finding my musical voice. Being influenced by a myriad of styles and artists, and growing up in a white middle-class environment, I aspired to write music that expressed my personal struggles. I was aware, albeit naïvely, that music embraced both sound and human potential. The music that moved me also affected how I perceived the world. It inspired me to look beyond contemporary thought and embrace new musical parameters. I was influenced by the experimental music of John Cage and Cornelius Cardew and the romantic English tradition of Gerald Finzi, Benjamin Britten, and most notably Michael Tippett. Alongside this are the avant-garde rock music developments of Frank Zappa and King Crimson, which balanced with my love for the pop songs of Kate Bush and Harry Chapin. The process of composing felt like a creative surge alongside the uncertainty that my musical expression was unique. These multiplicity of influences both inspired and bewildered my growth as a composer. I searched to speak and find music that was mine, an articulation of my music of the spheres. I wanted to attain that sense of rapture that as a music therapist I try to provide now for my clients, of being caught in a musical whirlwind, a conglomeration of impassioned forces that are discomfiting yet illuminating–the temporal polarities that combine to affect a lasting impression on those who dare to invest in the creative process. I sought to be impassioned in my music and sought those composers and musicians who could provide me with a sense of heightened ephemeral expression. I think that to this day, I continue searching for ever deeper levels of musical nirvana for both my clients and myself.

Unwittingly, my maturation as a composer led naturally into becoming a music therapist. For many musicians there is a void in providing music for a highbrow audience–that music should be available to more than just those who can afford to pay. My path was energized by the need to find a more personal and direct form of musical communication. Western classical music is elitist and does not, for the most part, advocate for those who do not have informed knowledge. That people with disabilities can gain as much enjoyment from an orchestral concert or opera as everyone else I do not believe is considered a priority. Where do we see in publicity or advertising that people with disabilities are actively encouraged to attend concerts? The Western concert tradition is bound by strict unwritten rules. There is the concern that if people are unable to conform to these rules, the phenomenon itself may be in danger of disintegrating. Is this not be a bad thing? In grappling with these issues I turned to music therapy. What I found to my amazement was that music therapy was about precise and defined musical communication. Disability and illness were only a part of the process. It was the music itself that provided the inspiration and source for growth. I entered music therapy with a sense of expectation and exhilaration that has not diminished over time. After fifteen years of continued questioning, through AeMT I have found a balance, a truth of musical humanness that unites the musical and clinical in my work.

What does it mean to be a composer/music therapist? How can the compositional process inform the therapeutic process? Every musical statement and response to a client should be framed within the structure of the whole, to watch and listen for intricacies of musical and human response. The minutiae of the musical moment is a delicately balanced procedure. The smallest movement, gesture, or musical reaction can change the direction of the music, the sessions itself, and the overriding aims. The inner interval of a chord, the subtlest rhythmic pattern, or delicate change in melodic inflection can acutely affect the therapeutic direction. The seemingly most inconsequential of musical components become significant. The splitting of musical consciousness, while remaining poised over the complete architecture of the session, is frighteningly exact in terms of the therapist's expertise but miraculously liberating for the client.

During my formative years as a music therapist I tried consciously to separate my compositional self from my clinical self. "Music-therapy speak" alienated me from my colleagues. The talk was always related to psychological, medical, or psychotherapeutic theories but never musical ones. There seemed to be a professional club that I could not join because my interests lay in another direction. For many years I tried to deny the composer in my work. I felt that in some way being clinical was not to be freely compositional or artistic. Why was this? What did it say about my developing work and music therapy in England at this time? As highlighted in the previous chapter, I believe the relationship between music and music therapy is changing in this, the new millennium. Therapists are poised to herald new directions in awareness, relationships, and our inner connections with music. AeMT advocates a new way of perceiving music and clinical practice. It challenges the profession to reevaluate the role of music in music therapy. To be a composer/music therapist or a performer/music therapist is more than a conceptual way of existing. It is a theory that can inform both clinical practice and artistry.

As a composer before becoming a music therapist, I wrote a song for baritone voice and piano, based on the poem "The Final Mystery" by D. H. Lawrence. Looking back, I see compositional approaches that have influenced my growth as a clinical improviser. The music is developed from four thematic ideas: 1) a skeleton harmony, 2) fast-moving treble counterpoint, 3) two-part invention, and 4) octaves. Ideas are stated, developed, and interlinked to form a structure that is dependent on the individual parts and the whole. Themes are evolved and moved into different positions. As the song evolves so the complexity between themes becomes more intricate. This can be clearly linked to the process of clinical improvisation. The therapist must compose a theme that can be repeated, defined, and remembered. Counterthemes are created that combine to form a sophisticated piece of open musical invention. Not withstanding the fact that musical development in clinical improvisation is dependent on two co-creative people and composing is the refined product of one, the philosophy of themes, development, and recapitulation are the same. As was discussed in Chapter 9 there are clear links here between musical form and clinical form.

The harmonic progression (see Figure 25), provides stability for the extended final section of the song. The chords are intended to survive as isolated experiences but also to form a musical cohesion that is dependent on the interrelationships. I wanted to give a sense of being grounded (Chords 3 & 6) yet suspended (Chords 5 & 9). I avoided giving a clear tonal center and the song ends with a chord based on two overlaying 7ths (Chord 13). The chords themselves are not predictable in their makeup and yet give a clear sense of tonality. In clinical improvisation the unfolding of harmonic progressions speaks to our understanding of the therapeutic process. Overly simplistic harmonies can nullify creativity. Chords and their relationships are not dissimilar to human relationships. The richer and more sophisticated they become the deeper they develop. It is important to give the client a sense of being musically grounded but also the opportunity to be free and move away from any inferred tonal center. Harmonic progressions should be open to all possibilities and should avoid the banal or predictable.

A clear example of being a composer/music therapist is the contrapuntal invention of Theme 2 (see Figure 26). This was used as a direct intervention in a music therapy session with a client living with HIV. The client was improvising, at the time, in the treble register of the xylophone. The playing was fast, yet disembodied. There was an agitated ethereal quality that I wanted to meet and develop. The florid music with trills and the fast-moving counterpoint of this theme felt the right music to meet this situation. I used the thematic material as a means to elevate the therapeutic and musical intensity. The form developed into a four-part invention, three parts on the piano and one on the xylophone. As the emotional quality grew so the intricacy of the music heightened. This music proved to be the right choice and facilitated an experience of musical and emotional freedom. The client gives his impression of the experience:

> The music feels like I did at that time . . . frustrated. I didn't care. I felt hostile and angry. I wanted to express this by making splodges of sound and lose any sense of trying to get things right. The high quality of the music was matched with the trills. We both explored treble motives. From an aesthetic viewpoint questions are raised for me in terms of this style of musical expression that is so free and yet in formal terms is textured and formed. The tense feeling of the music is balanced within an overall structure of intense beauty.

As I reflected on the session through detailed assessment and the client's evaluations, different meanings were raised. The client described how the music expressed his feelings of hostility, not having "to get things right," and the overriding aesthetic content of the music. AeMT is a direct response to this understanding. That music can confront feelings of anger that are therapeutic,

Harmonic Outline

fig. 25

fig. 26

while being caught within an artistic framework speaks to the essence of AeMT. My recollections of this musical meeting are vivid because this was the first time I had directly taken a theme from a composition and brought it into a session. It was the building of a bridge that I have researched and that has evolved over the years.

Two-part inventions (see Figure 27) can be a dynamic means of providing musical equality between therapist and client. Interweaving melodic lines as a clinical technique is complex. The register, sophistication of thematic material, instrumental timbre, and interrelations between parts all impact the process. It is important as a therapist to find a musical line that is responsive and reflective and one that has the ability to challenge the therapeutic direction. Octaves (see Figure 28) are also a specific musical resource that, if chosen with care, can produce clear clinical results. In this instance similar to the previous theme the octaves of the piano part are based on a two-part invention. The rise and fall of the octave lines as pitched against the voice and the association of intervals are intended to provide a musical whole that is bare yet supported. Often clients will sing or play freely phrased musical ideas. The therapist's responsibility is to find an open, reasoned response. Octaves can provide grounding and support. They do not necessarily infer tonality and have the ability to be therapeutically poised. Octaves, if precisely chosen, can allow a freedom of musical response that is open for the ongoing possibilities of the moment and continued direction of the session.

BALANCE AND GENESIS

Being a composer and a music therapist is a unique combination of imagination and focus. The revelation joining disciplines provides a union of thought, idea, and creativity. Clinical improvisation allows client and therapist to rediscover a sense of the world and their place within it. As a composer I aim to provide for the listener a deeper sense of their inner world. In this sense composing and music therapy are the same. Music is a source of inspiration and it is through musical innovation that true therapy begins. The opportunity and ability to be a musician is a gift and to be a music therapist is an even greater gift. To share the unique revelation of music directly with people is to be given the experience of wholeness. As an artist I spend time reflecting and thinking. As a music therapist I often find myself in deep contemplation before, after, or during a session, reflecting on the client, the music and the compositional mechanisms

Tempo III (♪=150)
Voice
Piano
freely
mf
And then I knew I had ta - ken_ my
mouth from her throat
And I raise
tr

fig. 27

Tempo IV (♩=46)
Voice
Yet looking again at the
night Still I could not

fig. 28

that I must ever refine. Through inner introspection I am able to assess and reassess the coordination that makes my role as composer and music therapist ever more compelling.

While working at Sir Michael Sobell House Hospice, Oxford, I was referred a young composer with AIDS. Our one meeting was to dramatically change my thinking as a music therapist and composer. As I entered his room I was surprised to see manuscripts scattered all over the bed and side cabinets. This statement of his creativity caused an immediate emotional response within me. I was caught between my role as a therapist to formally assess the situation and my personal stronger desire to see his scores and speak with him about composing. My sense of being a composer overtook my role as music therapist, for there is an adrenaline rush in seeing a fellow composer's scores. As we began talking and as he shared his music with me my roles as composer and music therapist merged. I pondered the fact that if he had not been admitted to the hospital then we would have probably never met. Our time together was extraordinarily rich and inspiring. We intimately explored his compositions and in doing so shared his inner life. We talked of the doubts of composing and the struggles of creativity, the solitary existence, and the joy and pain of being an artist. Through this conversation we knew each other instantly and completely. As I scanned his orchestral scores and chamber music, I remember contemplating that I could be in the presence of a gifted composer and how many talented musicians had died from AIDS. The music jumped off the page. I could see and hear his colorful sense of orchestration, his complex use of counterpoint, and his avant-garde form of notation. His music seemed new and fresh. As he spoke and explained each piece our understanding of this inner creative process deepened. I innately understood his music and was able to identify with him both as a fellow composer and human being. The compositions acted as the therapeutic catalyst–they gave a focus and provided the union for our brief developing relationship. I left our session full of questions, but in eager anticipation that this was the beginning of a new developing music therapy relationship. That he died shortly after our session came as shock. Due to the intensity of our musical connection I had not noticed his acute illness. I was left with many unanswered questions but also a sense that our session had been somehow crucial for both of us. After much intense self-analysis I realized that my roles as composer and music therapist here were one. I realized I could not–and should not–have actively separated them. Even though consciously I knew this had not happened, at a subconscious level there was a split that infiltrated all levels of my ongoing work. This was due in part, I believe, to my fears of being misunderstood as a music therapist who championed music. The many criticisms of my evolving music-centered approach to music therapy had left me vulnerable and scarred. This session and our work was therefore a revelation and gave me a new inner sense of strength that culminated some years later in the writing of *Music at the Edge* (Lee, 1996).

More recently, becoming a full-time educator has afforded me the opportunity to reestablish links with composing. This return has further clarified my role as a composer/music therapist. Developments have included:

- concerts of solo piano improvisations based on clinical themes (see Chapter 15 for a detailed description of this work)
- music therapy with a professional string quartet (see Chapter 13)
- arranging notated clinical improvisations for orchestra and chamber ensembles (Chapter 15: "Sketches for a Clinical Symphony") and
- a personal return to composing.

These developments, along with the preparation and writing of this book, are dependent on and encapsulate the true meaning and nuance of AeMT.

> Haydn embraced trees and birds and chords in this inspiration. Liszt depicted mountain and stream and the benediction of God. Berlioz showed us the musician in the hallucination of the creative moment. Wagner strove to depict the whole reality and human emotion in a single work of art. Debussy gave us an entire gallery of seascapes, landscapes, woodscapes and portraits, Ravel gave us a menagerie. Janacek studied the rhythm of nature and the law of life. Copland revealed the multiplicity of approach out of time into eternity. Xenakis has welcomed the age of the computer. All of this and heaven too is now our heritage, and if reason could not cope with resonance today, then all is allowed. Our unified sensibility may cavort amidst a wider range of awareness which makes ours one of the richest ages of music, poetry, sculpture, painting and architecture alike.
>
> –Colin Lee,
> "Coda: On the Creative" from *Music at the Edge*
> (1996, p. 160)

Chapter Fifteen

REFLECTIONS AND NEW DIRECTIONS

> Music is the one incorporeal entrance into the higher world of knowledge which comprehends mankind but which mankind cannot comprehend.
>
> –Ludwig van Beethoven,
> quoted by Bettina von Arnim,
> *Letter to Goethe* (1810)

Music and therapy are intrinsically linked. To be musical is to be therapeutic, and to understand the nature of musical communication one must be prepared to consider how and why music is such a passionate force. Music cannot exist in a vacuum and must have human reactions to survive. Listening to music can cause extreme emotions, creative music-making stimulating this reaction to be ever greater heights. Understanding the complex strands of clinical improvisation has been the focus of AeMT and the evolving arguments in this book. As music therapy endeavors to understand and quantify the constructs of clinical outcome, it should never forget that its creative nucleus is, and will always remain, an enigma. It is this enigma that makes the power of the music therapy relationship so affiliated with the human condition. Music and emotions are one and it is this cohesion that influences the clients in making sense of their world. In music there can only be consonance and normality. In music the client is free and empowered to be healthy and it is through creativity that healing occurs.

This chapter is subjective. It offers opinions on differing aspects of music therapy and makes suggestions for the profession in the new millennium. AeMT came from a personal need to identify an approach that would begin to understand the processes of music therapy from a composer's point of view. For many years I fought conceptualizing AeMT because I considered it an extension of Nordoff and Robbins. It was through my work in palliative care, however, that I began to realize music therapy could be directly related to the compositional process. Through analyses of precomposed music, I further came to understand that there was a potential link of learning from the major works of the classical Western repertoire. It was as if the field was missing a whole spectrum of musicological and music analytic thought. I felt on the edge of a precipice and only now, as I look to drawing the strands of this work together, do I realize that informing clinical practice from musical theories is an aspect of work that has been sadly neglected.

Conceptualizing this book has been a revelation. Considering the creative writing process similar to that of composing, I was able to free my thoughts, associations, and beliefs. The many questions that have been posed are intended not as puzzles to be solved, but rather as broad statements and challenges. Why are aesthetics important and how can medicine/empirical evidence and the artistry of music connect more closely? What links lie between psychotherapeutic and musical interpretation? As a profession the knowledge of music therapy is still young. The field must look beyond the impermanency of its individual members to realize that the affiliation between music and therapy, within our life spans, will remain a mystery. It is for others to fully understand the building blocks of clinical outcome and musical process. A balance, however, must be found if music therapy is to begin articulating, quantifying, and understanding why music is intrinsically healing.

This final chapter then returns to the core of AeMT, that of considering music as the basis and crux of therapy:

- Music as tone
- Music as listening
- Music as relationship
- Music as learning
- Music as outcome
- Music as process
- Music as inspiration
- Music as creativity
- Music as spirituality
- Music as precision
- Music as freedom
- Music for the client
- Music with the client

THE AESTHETICS OF RESEARCH

Research is an attempt to understand the enigmatic qualities of music and relationship. What critical questions should contemporary music therapy be asking and what methodologies are available to help forge an identity within the medical, psychotherapeutic, and artistic communities that will strengthen our position in the new millennium? Music therapy research faces many challenges. Are there specific questions the profession should be addressing and what of the balance between quantitative, qualitative, outcome, and process? Comparing research to an aesthetic experience is to demystify its status. Research by its nature denotes impartiality. The terms data, methodology, hypotheses, and analysis are all objective and serve to alienate the reality of process. By extracting that which can be interpreted and/or counted adds credibility to the field but does not communicate the true emotional essence of music and relationship. Considering research as creative and aesthetic is liberating because it opens the doors of questioning and knowing.

As a struggling researcher, many questions have emerged with respect to my ongoing speculations into clinical practice. How can an intrinsically artistic focus to research help in our understanding of the process? Entering research unwillingly I found myself within a mire of theorems and methodologies, none of which seemed relevant to the questions I was formulating. Research appeared remote from my day-to-day practical work and I wondered how nonmusical methodologies could have implications for the music-centered approach that was becoming fundamental in my work. Now, some ten years later and after numerous experiments to find an authoritative musicological path relevant for the analysis of clinical improvisation, I have found a sense of balance. It is my belief that research should:

- be generated from clinical practice and not introduced as exterior thought
- be creative and not bound by theories of methodology
- be an attempt to answer the most intimate of questions and as such not constrained or reductionist
- be available to all music therapists who dare to challenge and question
- serve both the needs of the profession and the questions of the individual researcher
- be accessible and clear.

Articulating research takes determination and foresight. Once published, the researcher lays oneself open for both accolade and criticism. Research and therapy can often seem at odds as academics criticize and speculate their own results at the expense of others. Findings then have the potential to illuminate and also intimidate. The passionate researcher is essential if music therapy is to continue pushing the relevant bounds of its knowledge. Someone who can contribute authentically and honestly, without bias, the questions needed for the profession integrated with the burning speculations of the individual. Research should not be elitist or deemed for those with superior intellect. Its essence is to answer passionate, articulate questions through methodologies that are sympathetic and clearly defined. Research, like therapy itself, demands honesty and integrity. All questions are valid and all music therapists have the right to be involved in research.

MUSICAL GENIUS AND PATHOLOGY

The idea that a client could also be a musical genius is intriguing. The savant caught in pathology or illness, begs the questions:

- Where does genius originate?
- Does the purity of music allow it to be affected by disability?
- Is there such a thing as disabled music?

AeMT is based on the belief that all clients have limitless potential. How the therapist is able to open this portal is the "art" of clinical experience and learning. That every client has the capacity to be a genius means that every therapeutic encounter has the capacity to produce great and influential music.

The term "composer" denotes a role that is learned, a profession based on a balance between scholarship and creativity. A composer has a respected role to play in society and adds to the richness of contemporary culture. What then of clients as composers and how does this potential change the therapist's perception of their role? To consider clinical improvisation with the same intent as a work by a present-day composer is to give music therapy the artistic status it deserves. There are clients whom I have worked with that I believe, had it not been for their pathology, could have been proficient composers or performers. That there is the possibility for all clients to be outstanding musicians means the therapists must strive, at all costs, to facilitate each potential. Every client therefore has the capacity to be a great composer or performer.

Does Western music protect its rights of normality and learnedness by creating titles such as composer and performer? Music therapists must believe that music is an innate medium open to all. But to what level of musicianship can clients attain? We couldn't possible equate a profoundly disabled client with a great composer. Or could we? I have experienced improvisations with clients with profound intellectual disability that could be compared in stature and content with seminal pieces of music. These moments of musical greatness were caught because of the musical and therapeutic needs of the client and the therapist's sensitive musical/clinical responses. All clients have the potential to create great music and all music therapists should be aware and be ready to respond to this potential with clarity and insight.

Most therapists would agree that the music clients create in music therapy is valid, but to suggest that it could be artistically magnificent may be stretching the bounds of what is understood as clinical practice. But why? Greatness can come from the most unexpected of encounters. As described in Chapter Four (see: "Musical Equality", (p.76), the finely graded response of a physically disabled client can hold a sense of distinction that far belies the actuality of the response itself. When Beethoven wrote his symphonies, where did his genius come from? I liken brilliance to a subliminal tap being turned–something that is greater than the reality of the moment. Is there a possibility then, that there could be the essence of Beethoven's creativity in all clients? Taking the proviso that when one sense is diminished another is heightened, could it be proposed that a client with a disability may have an increased and developed sense of musical creativity? If this is nurtured and developed, then is there further the possibility that it that could evolve into genius? Music can reflect and translate emotions but I believe music itself cannot be afflicted. Music is inherently healthy and so if a client's physical presence is affected this may in turn pronounce the healthy musical side of their persona. This argument concludes that it is logical to think of a client with a pathology or disability as a conceivable musical genius.

How is greatness defined and what makes a piece of music celebrated ? I would suggest that a great piece of music is one that:

- is crafted beyond the norm
- can cause physical reactions
- endures time
- reflects intense human emotions
- reflects humanity
- has an essence of mystery

All of the above considerations can be related to music therapy. Taking this into account, is there a danger in elevating too high, the spontaneous nature of a client's spontaneous creativity? It is important not to elevate musical outcome to a level that may detract from the essence of the clinical process. Allowing the possibility, however, that clients could be equal in stature to Beethoven could possibly change the nucleus of what music therapy essentially means.

THOUGHTS ON BEGINNING A SESSION

Entering a music therapy session takes courage, foresight, and tenacity. Music therapists believe that music has the capacity to heal, find emotional liberation, and affect aims. The varying balance between artistic inspiration and clinical appraisal is the foundation of every philosophical and theoretical approach. Psychotherapeutic, medical, educational, humanistic, and behavioral perspectives all have one thing in common–that of an intervention based on creativity and spontaneity. Music radiates through all of these and it is music that determines the exact nature of therapeutic fortitude necessary for the client's maturation.

What does the therapist experience as an improvised AeMT session evolves? What sensations and thoughts conspire to produce work that is balanced and coherent? Developing the musical and therapeutic architecture of a session is fraught with challenges. How does the moment-to-moment revelation of creating relate to the specificity of aims and assessment? When does the therapist take control and when do they relinquish in favor of the unhierarchical nature of spontaneous music-making? The balance and continuous shift in improvising means the therapist must be aware on many levels. Creating structure, leading to activities, and then relinquishing musical conformity toward the potential for freedom and nonstructured playing is a complex continuum that needs constant reevaluation in the moment of creation and through assessment. The demands for the clinical improvisor can at times seem insurmountable. To acknowledge, understand, and collate a myriad of musical and nonmusical exemplars and then accommodate them into the musical/therapeutic dialogue is indeed complex. To fully understand the multi-complex strands of clinical improvisation in AeMT is to understand the nature of human existence, music, and the relation between the two. This lifetime's commitment to the use of music in therapy is what makes the raw yet precise originality of the work.

The possibilities and uncertainties of entering an improvised music therapy session are not unlike that of a composer viewing blank manuscript paper before a work is begun. Endless potential can seem liberating and daunting. Just as the composer waits and attends for the inspiration of musical beginnings so the therapist must wait for a dialogue that is communicative and motivating. By beginning, the composer sets boundaries for the material that is to developed. Similarly the therapist must find themes that reveal the client's needs and that can be used as a basis for the developing dialogue. As client and therapist step into the unknown, the world of music and relationship is revealed. Waiting for a client to enter the music therapy room one's thoughts are filled with musical and human expectancy. How will the session begin? How will the client present themselves when they enter the room? Will the client find the strength to play and enter the beginning relationship? Where might the music develop and will I, the therapist, be able to adequately amplify the client's inventiveness? It is that sense of expectancy that allows the client to establish their intention and for the therapist the inspiration that is at the cornerstone of AeMT. Waiting for a session is like unlatching a spiritual window, a sense that all is possible and available. Making accessible the entire breadth of music and relationship is, I believe, why the artistic endeavor is such a powerful force in society. Music when translated to the therapeutic context defines and redefines the nature of art itself.

THE FUTURE OF MUSIC IN MUSIC THERAPY: A THEORY FROM WITHIN

The inception and development of AeMT was a response to being at a musical and therapeutic crossroads. Knowing significant events had occurred musically in a session, and not having a foundation from which to assess them, I became more and more frustrated. Finding a balance between music as "art" and music as human connection became a constantly shifting concern. By defining an aesthetic approach to music therapy I initiated a path that acknowledged musical structure as critical to the process. Redefining the roles of performer and composer, rather than eliminating their intent as nonclinical, provided new possibilities for balancing the "art" and "science" of practice.

This leads naturally to the idea of performing concerts based on themes taken from music therapy sessions. The linking of art and clinical improvisation developed from a need to return to my artistic roots as a music therapist. These concerts have now become integrated into my professional life as a musician and music therapist. Specific themes are balanced with general feelings and impressions of therapeutic encounters. As improvisations develop, artistic and clinical influences transform to produce music that is led from clients' impressions on my subconscious. Once I have transcribed the themes and know them intimately I allow them to intermingle as the improvisation evolves. While performing I try to step back from the actuality of the experience and allow the clients and their impressions on me to dictate the direction of the music. I will either base improvisations around a group of clients or focus on one individual. The length of improvisations span from ten to fifty minutes.

The following extract is taken from a series of improvisations that were recorded one evening in the Maureen Forrester Hall at Wilfrid Laurier University.

These were my first attempts at "art" improvisations based on clinical themes. The improvisation is a reflection of my work with Lisa (see Chapter 12). The central D minor theme portrays the intensity of our relationship and the deep effect her presence had on my life. The movement between keys and tonality further illustrates the complex balance in our short relationship. It is an outpouring of my emotions as I reflect on loss.

Audio Extract Ten: Solo Improvisation

Dr. Michele Forinash's reaction to hearing the above recording during a presentation raises specific questions with regard to how clients potentially receive music therapy:

> I had the strangest experiences on hearing the improvisation. It was as if I didn't know how to speak and that somehow I was mute. I was having so many sensations and feelings simultaneously. They were very intense, complex, and contradictory, yet it was good to be experiencing them. It was as if there were multiple levels of experience happening at once. All the sensations and feelings were swirling around me as if in a whirlpool of air. I had no desire or ability to reach out and touch these feelings and sensations –no desire to pinpoint or hold onto the feelings, they were just swirling around me. It was very intense, but it was OK to be experiencing this.
>
> When the music was over, there was silence. A young man began talking. It was jarring. It was as if his words were strident and harsh and I couldn't get my mind to hear their meaning. It was if he was speaking in another language. I stopped trying to understand him and just listened to the sounds he made, the sound as such that I heard in his talking. It hurt and was disorienting. It took me another fifteen minutes before I could reconnect to the people talking.

Entering into intense experiences of improvisation can be emotionally and physically disorienting. Logical thought is often abandoned, with true therapy often occurring through this experience. The therapist's responsibility at these times, is to stay in the conscious logic of the here-and-now. Dr. Forinash's response shows that music can have the affect of abandoning coherent thought and allow a person to feel disoriented after music has finished. Her comments highlight the need for the therapist to be sensitive to the intense processes of music and the time allowed for clients to disengage from music and the session itself.

What new directions can contemporary music therapy take? What new avenues are available? Are there contentious ideas that dare to challenge the established norms of clinical practice? The future of music therapy must be held in the belief that the field knows little and has much to understand. Whether using scientific, humanistic, musicological, or psychotherapeutic models, the field has only begun to unearth the complexities of its process. Has the time come to consider a music therapy theory from within, one that is not reliant on exterior thought but that comes from an understanding of music, creativity, and a therapeutic focus idiosyncratic of music therapy? How might such a theory develop and where might it originate? AeMT is an attempt to balance an understanding of music in the therapeutic framework. It speaks to my struggles and challenges as a composer/music therapist. Its answers are primarily addressed to therapists who are deeply concerned about the nature of music in clinical improvisation. A music-centered theory of music therapy may be considered antagonistic because it takes its primary lead from the structures of music, placing them into a clinical context directly from the musical dialogue. To achieve a theory of music therapy the profession must first consider music-centered approaches with equal weight to medicine and psychotherapy. Until this occurs studies will be imbalanced–if music therapy can't understand the nature of the process, how valid in and of itself is the outcome? Celebrating music celebrates communication, relationship, and artistic endeavor. Music therapy has the ability to transcend conscious logic and enter areas of emotion that profoundly affect the human condition. Let us hope that music therapists are also able to transcend and open their senses to the potential of a theory from within.

Coda: Sketches For A Clinical Symphony (see Figure 29)

During this book I thought of writing as composing–discovering themes, counterthemes, and balancing consonance against dissonance. The result that has emerged hopefully provides a view of music therapy that is unfettered and free. As a composer, clinician, therapist, and teacher, formulating AeMT has been an inspiration. As the writing developed and as I began to define my approach I was constantly amazed at the possibilities available for new and controversial thought.

I would like to end this book with the opening phrases of a clinical improvisation arranged for symphony orchestra. These beginnings are to be developed into a three-movement clinical symphony taken from three separate improvisations from the work with one client. Each was transcribed via computer thus ensuring accuracy of notation. It is my hope that by taking clinical music into the arena of classical music that music therapy may begin to be respected as an influential part of contemporary trends. That clients have the potential to be great musicians, as discussed earlier in this chapter, is at the cornerstone of this conviction. Combining the roles of composer and music therapist are never more present than in arranging this clinical symphony. How the final work will look and sound remains to be seen. What is evident in this example, however, is the inspirational bridge between the artistic and clinical. This bridge continues to consume my thoughts, actions, and research.

As I try to find a balance that will allow a true sense of the therapeutic qualities of music I continually turn to my knowledge of music. Music identifies music therapy and it is as a musician foremost that I enter every session. If I trust music then I can trust the therapeutic process. If I understand music then I can understand the therapeutic relationship. Finally, if I know music then I can know the possible outcomes that music will have for the client and the developing work. Music is my life, my inspiration. It is the reason I continue to realize my teaching, clinical practice, and research. If in some small way this book will have added to the contribution of music-centered music therapy then it will have achieved its purpose.

fig. 29

(fig. 29)

References

Addis, L. (1999). *Of Mind and Music*. Ithaca, NY, and London: Cornell University Press.

Adorno, L. (1973). *Philosophy of Modern Music*. Tr. S. Weber & S. Weber. Cambridge, MA: Seabury Press.

Adorno, T. W. (1998). *Beethoven. The Philosophy of Music*. Cambridge, MA: Polity Press.

Agawu, K. (1991). *Playing with Signs: A Semiotic Interpretation of Classical Music*. Princeton, NJ: Princeton University Press.

Ahonen-Eerikäinen, H. (1997). Itsereflektiota omasta musiikkiterapiatyöskentelystä. *Musiikkiterapia*, 1, 36-43.

Ahonen-Eerikäinen, H. (1999). Ryhmäanalyyttinen musiikkiterapia. (engl. "Group Analytic Music Therapy"). *Musiikkiterapia*, 2/99, 5, 23.

Aigen, K. (1995a). An aesthetic foundation of clinical theory: an underlying basis of creative music therapy. In C. Kenny (Ed.), *Listening, Playing, Creating: Essays on the Power of Sound* (pp. 233–257). Albany: State University of New York.

Aigen, K. (1995b). Philosophical inquiry. In B. Wheeler (Ed.), *Music Therapy Research: Quantitative and Qualitative Perspectives* (pp. 447–484). Gilsum, NH: Barcelona Publishers.

Aigen, K. (1998). *Paths of Development in Nordoff and Robbins Music Therapy*. Gilsum NH: Barcelona Publishers.

Aigen, K. (1999). Revisiting Edward: An exemplar of tacit knowledge. *Nordic Journal of Music Therapy,* 8(1), 89–95.

Aldridge, D. (1996) *Music Therapy Research and Practice in Medicine*. London, and Bristol, PA: Jessica Kingsley Publishers.

Aldridge, G. (1996) A walk through Paris. The development of melodic expression in music therapy with a breast-cancer patient. *The Arts in Psychotherapy* 23(3), 207–223.

Aldridge, G. (1999) The implications of melodic expression for music therapy with a breast cancer patient. In Aldridge (Ed.), *Music Therapy in Palliative Care. New Voices*. London, and Philadelphia: Jessica Kingsley Publishers.

Aldridge, G. (2000). Improvisation as an assessment of potential early Alzheimer's disease. In Aldridge (Ed.), *Music Therapy in Dementia Care*. London: Jessica Kingsley.

Ansdell, G. (1995). *Music for Life: Aspects of Creative Music Therapy with Adult Clients*. London: Jessica Kingsley Publishers.

Ansdell, G. (1997). Musical elaborations. what has the New Musicology to say to music therapy? *British Journal of Music Therapy*. 11(2), (pp. 36–44).

Ansdell, G. (1999). Keynote presentation. 5th European Music Therapy Congress, Naples.

Ansdell, G. (2000). Will the real Edward kindly stand up? *Nordic Journal of Music Therapy*, 9(1), 90–96.

Ansdell, G. (2001). Musicology: Misunderstood guest at the music therapy feast. The 5th European Music Therapy Congress, Naples.

Arnason, C. (2002). An eclectic approach to the analysis of improvisation in music therapy sessions. *Music Therapy Perspectives*, 20(1), 4-12.

Austin, D. (2001). Peer Supervision in Music Therapy. Forinash (Ed.), *Music Therapy Supervision*. Gilsum, NH: Barcelona Publishers.

Bailey, D. (1992). Improvisation: its nature and practice in music. The British Library National Sound Archive.

Bateson, G. (1980). *Mind and Nature*. London: Fontana.

Begbie, J. (2000). *Theology, Music and Time*. Cambridge, U.K.: Cambridge University Press.

Bergstrom-Nielsen, C. (1999). The music of Edward, session one, as graphic notation. *Nordic Journal of Music Therapy*, 8(1), 96–99.

Bergstrom-Nielsen, C. (1999). Intuitive Music Therapy and Graphic Notation. Music Therapy Monologues. Aalborg University.

Bergstrom-Nielsen, C. (2001). Monologue published from Aalbrourg University, Denmark.

Berliner, P. F. (1994). *Thinking in Jazz. The Infinite Art of Improvisation.* Chicago and London: The University of Chicago Press.

Blacking, J. (1973). *How Musical Is Man?* Seattle and London: University of Washington Press.

Bonny, H. (1978). Facilitating GIM sessions (GIM monograph 1). Salina, KS: The Bonny Foundation.

Borczon, R. M. (1997). *Music Therapy: Group Vignettes*. Gilsum NH: Barcelona Publishers.

Bradt, J. (1997). Ethical issues in multicultural counselling: Implications for the field of music therapy. *The Arts in Psychotherapy*, 24(2), 137–143.

Bruscia, K. (1998). *Defining Music Therapy*. (2nd ed). Gilsum, NH: Barcelona Publishers.

Bruscia, K. (Ed.) (1998). *The Dynamics of Music Psychotherapy*. Gilsum, NH: Barcelona Publishers.

Bruscia, K. (2001) A qualitative approach to analyzing client improvisations. *Music Therapy Perspectives*, 19(1), pp. 7–21.

Butt, J. (1991). *Bach: Mass in B Minor*. Cambridge, U.K.: Cambridge University Press.

Cage, J. (1959). Lecture: In: *die Reihe*. Vol. 5. Reports. Universal Edition.

Cage, J. (1961). *Silence. Lectures and writings by John Cage*. Middleton, CT: Wesleyan University Press.

Cage, J. (1969). *Notations.* West Glover, VT: Something Else Press, Inc.
Cage, J. (1981). *For the Birds. John Cage in conversation with Daniel Charles.* Boston, and London: Marion Boyars.
Cage, J. (1982). *Themes and Variations.* Barry Town, NY: Station Hill Press.
Cage, J. (1983). *X Writings '79-'82.* Middletown, CT: Wesleyan University Press.
Cage, J. (1983). *John Cage Writer. Previously Uncollected Pieces.* New York: Limelight Editions.
Cage, J. (1988). *Mud Book. How to Make Pies and Cakes.* New York: Harry N. Abrams, INC.
Cage, J. & Barnard, G. (1980). *Conversation without Feldman. A Talk Between John Cage & Geoffrey Barnard.* Darlinghurst, NSW, Australia: Black Ram Books.
Carr, I. (1992). Keith Jarrett. The Man and his Music. London: Harper Collins Publishers.
Carter, A. (1990). *The Role of the Leitmotif in Music Therapy.* Unpublished Master's thesis. The City University, London.
Chailly, J. (1963). *Tristan et Isolde de Richard Wagner.* Paris: Centre de documentation universitaire.
Cook, N. (1990). *Music, Culture & Imagination.* Oxford, U.K.: Oxford University Press.
Cooper, B. (1990). *Beethoven and the Creative Process.* Oxford, U.K.: Clarendon Press.
Dalhaus, C. (1994). *Ludwig van Beethoven. Approaches to his Music.* Oxford, U.K.: Clarendon Press.
Davies, S. (1994). *Musical Meaning and Expression.* Ithaca, NY, and London: Cornell University Press.
Davis, M., & Troupe, Q. (1991). *Miles: The Autobiography.* New York: Simon and Schuster.
Davis, B., Gfeller, K, & Thaut, M. (1999). *An Introduction to Music Therapy* (2nd ed). Boston: McGraw Hill College.
De Nora, T. (2000). *Music in Everyday Life.* Cambridge, U.K.: Cambridge University Press.
Dewey, J. (1934). *Art as Experience.* New York: Wideview/Perigee.
Dewey, J. (1958). *Experience and Nature.* New York: Dover.
Ericsson, K.A., & Charness, N. (1994). Expert performance: Its structure and acquisition. *American Psychologist* 49:725–747.
Estrella, K. (2001). Multicultural approaches to music therapy supervision. In Forainash (Ed.), *Music Therapy Supervision.* Gilsum, NH: Barcelona Publishers.
Ferrara, L. (1984). Phenomenology as a tool for music analysis. *The Musical Quartley*, 70(1), 355–373.

Ferrara, L. (1991). *Philosophy and the Analysis of Music: Bridges to Musical Sound, Form, and Reference*. New York: Excelsior Music Publishing Co.

Firth, S. (1990). *Performing Rites - on the Value of Popular Music*. Oxford, U.K.: Oxford University Press.

Forinash, M. (2000). Dialogues on the study of Edward. *Nordic Journal of Music Therapy*, 9(1) 83–89.

Forte, A. (1973). *The Structure of Atonal Music*. New Haven, CT: Yale University Press.

Forte, A. (1988). Pitch class set genre and the origin of modern harmonic species. *Journal of Music Theory*. 31:2.

Foulkes, S. (1964). *Therapeutic Group Analysis*. London: George Allen & Unwin, ltd.

Foulkes, S & Anthony, E.J. (1990). *Group Psychotherapy*. London: Karnac.

Foulkse, S.H. (1984). *Introduction to Group-Analytic Psychotherapy*. London: Mansfield. Reprints.

Gaston, E. (1968). Man and music. In E. Gaston (Ed.), *Music in Therapy* (pp. 7–29). New York: MacMillan.

Gena, P., & Brent, J. (1982). *A John Cage Reader in celebration of his 70th birthday*. New York, London, Frankfurt: C.F. Peters Corporation.

Gilroy, A. & Lee, C.A. (1995). Juxtapositions in art and music therapy research. In Gilroy & Lee (Eds.), *Art and Music: Therapy and Research*. Londonand New York: Routledge.

Goertzen, V. (1998). Setting the stage. Clara Schumann's preludes. In Nettl (Ed), *In the Course of Performance* (pp. 237–260). Chicago and London: The University of Chicago Press.

Hagberg, G.L. (1995). *Art as Language*. Ithaca and London: Cornell University Press.

Hartley, N. (1999). Music therapist's personal reflections on working with those who are living with HIV/AIDS. In Aldridge (Ed.), *Music Therapy in Palliative Care. New Voices*. London and Philadelphia: Jessica Kingsley Publishers.

Hartley, N. (1999). Mary and Steve. Creativity and terminal illness. In Pavlicevic (Ed.), *Music Therapy. Intimate Notes*. London and Philadelphia: Jessica Kingsley Publishers.

Herrick, R. (1891). *The Works of Robert Herrick, Vol. I*. Alfred Pollard (Ed.), London: Lawrence & Bullen.

Higgins, M.H. (1997). Musical idiosyncrasy and perspectival listening. In Robinson (Ed.), *Music and Meaning*. Ithaca and London: Cornell University Press.

Heble, A. (2000). *Landing on the Wrong Note*. New York and London: Routledge.

Hintz, M. (2000). Geriatric music therapy clinical assessment: Assessment of musical skills and related behaviours. *Music Therapy Perspectives*. 18(1), 31–40.

Imeson, S. (1996). *"The time gives it proofe." Paradox in the Late Music of Beethoven*. New York: Peter Lang.

Kartomi, M. (1991). Musical improvisations by children at play. *The World of Music*, 33(3), 53–65.

Keller, H. (1994). *Essays on Music*. Cambridge: Cambridge University Press.

Kendall, W. (1997). Listening with imagination: Is music representational? In Robinson (Ed.), *Music and Meaning*. Ithaca and London: Cornell University Press.

Kenny, C. (1989). *The Field of Play: A Guide for the Theory and Practice of Music Therapy*. Atascadero, CA: Ridgeview Publishing.

Kenny, C. (1996). The story of the field of play. In Langenberg, Aigen & Frommer (Eds.), *Qualitative Music Therapy research*. Gilsum NH: Barcelona Publishers.

Kivy, P. (1990). *Music Alone*. Ithaca and London: Cornell University Press.

Kivy, P. (1991). Is music an art? *Journal of Philosophy*, 88, 553-554.

Kivy, P. (1995). *Authenticities. Philosophical Reflections on Musical Performance*. Ithaca and London: Cornell University Press.

Kostelanetz, R. (1970a). John Cage: some random remarks. In *John Cage. An Anthology*. New York: Da Capo Press.

Kostelanetz, R. (1970b). Influential art. In: *John Cage. An Anthology*. New York: Da Capo Press.

Kostelanetz, R. (Ed.) (1970c) *John Cage. An Anthology*. New York: Da Capo Press.

Kramer, L. (1995). *Classical Music & Postmodern Knowledge*. Berkely, CA: University of California Press.

Kreeger (1991). The twice weekly group. In Pines, M. (Ed.), *The Practice of Group Analysis*. London: Routledge.

Lecourt, E. (1998). The role of aesthetics in countertransference: A comparison of active versus receptive music therapy. In Bruscia (Ed.), *The Dynamics of Music Psychotherapy*. (pp. 137–159). Gilsum NH: Barcelona Publishers.

Lee, C. A. (1989). Structural analysis of therapeutic improvisatory music. *Journal of British Music Therapy* 3(2), 11-19.

Lee, C. A. (1990). Structural analysis of post-tonal therapeutic improvisatory music. *Journal of British Music Therapy* 4(1), 6-20.

Lee, C. A. (1992). *The analysis of therapeutic improvisatory music with people living with the virus HIV and AIDS*. Unpublished Ph.D. thesis. City University, London.

Lee, C. A. (1995). The Analysis of therapeutic improvisatory music. In Gilroy & Lee (Eds.), *Art and Music: Therapy and Research*. London and New York: Routledge.

Lee, C. A. (1996). *Music at the Edge*. New York: Routledge.

Lee, C. A. (2000). A method of analyzing improvisations in music therapy. *Journal of Music Therapy* 37(2), 147–167.

Lee, C. A. (2001). Music Therapy. In Barraclough (Ed.), *Integrated Cancer Care*. Oxford U.K.: Oxford University Press.

Lee, C. A. & Khare, K. (2001). The supervision of clinical improvisation in aesthetic music therapy: A music-centred approach. In Forinash (Ed.), *Music Therapy Supervision*. Gilsum, NH: Barcelona Publishers.

Lerdahl, F. & Jackendoff, R. (1983). *A Generative Theory of Tonal Music*. Cambridge, MA: M.I.T. Press.

Levinson, J. (1990). *Music, Art & Metaphysics*. Ithaca, NY: Cornell University Press.

Levinson, J. (1997). *Music in the Moment*. Ithaca and London: Cornell University Press.

Lockwood, L. (1992). *Beethoven. Studies in the Creative Process*. Cambridge, MA, and London: Harvard University Press.

McClary (2000).

McMaster, N. (1995). Listening: A sacred act. In Kenny (Ed.), *Listening, Playing, Creating*. Albany: State University of New York Press.

Magrini. T. (1998). Improvisation and group interaction in Italian lyrical singing. In Nettl (Ed.), *In The Course of Performance* (pp.169–198). Chicago and London: The University of Chicago Press.

Manuel, P. (1998). Improvisation in Latin American dance music. History and style. In Nettl (Ed.), *In the Course of Performance* (pp. 127–147). Chicago and London: The University of Chicago Press.

Marissen, M. (1995). *The Social and religious designs of J.S. Bach's Brandenburg Concertos*. Princeton, NJ: Princeton University Press.

Meyer, L. (1956). *Emotion and Meaning in Music*. Chicago and London: The University of Chicago Press.

Monson, I. (1998) Oh freedom. George Russell, John Coltrane, and modal jazz. In Nettl (Ed.), *In the Course of Performance* (pp. 149–168). Chicago and London: The University of Chicago Press.

Montello, L. (1995). The 5th Annual Meeting of the International Association for Dance, Medicine & Science, Tel Aviv, Israel.

Montello, L. (1996). Artist-in-Residence Program at Berklee College of Music, Boston, MA.

Montello, L. (1997). Health and the Musician International Conference, University of York, England.

Montello, L. (2000). The Second Annual AMTA Conference, St. Louis, MO.

Montello, L. (2002). *Essential Musical Intelligence: Using Music as Your Path to Healing, Creativity, and Radiant Wholeness*. Wheaton, IL: Quest Books.

Moreno, J. (1988). Multicultural music therapy: The world music connection. *Journal of Music Therapy*, 25(1), 17–27.

Moreno, J. (1995). Ethnomusic therapy: An interdisciplinary approach to music and healing. *The Arts in Psychotherapy*, 22(4), 329-338.

Moreno, J., Brotons, M., Hairston, M., Hawley, T., Kiel, H., Michel, D., and Rohrbacher, M., (1990). International music therapy: A global perspective. *Music Therapy Perspectives*, 8, 41–46.

Munro, SO. (1984). *Music Therapy in Palliative / Hospice Care*. St. Louis, MO: Magna Music, Baton Inc.

Nattiez, J-J. (1990). *Music and Discourse: Toward a Semiology of Music*. Princeton, NJ: Princeton University Press.

Nattiez, J-J. (1990). Can one speak of narrativity in music? *Journal of the Royal Musical Association* 115, 240–57.

Nattiez, J-J. (Ed.) (1993). *The Boulez-Cage Correspondence*. Cambridge, U.K.: Cambridge University Press.

Nettl, B. (1974). Thoughts on improvisation, a comparative approach. *Musical Quarterly* 60, 1–19.

Nettl, B. (Ed.) (1998). *In the Course of Performnace*. Chicago and London: The University of Chicago Press.

Nettl, B. (1998). An art neglected in scholarship. In Nettl (Ed.), *In the Course of Performance*. (pp. 1–23) Chicago and London: The University of Chicago Press.

Nettl, B., & Riddle, R. (1998). Taqsim Nahawand revisited. The musicianship of Jihad Racy. In Nettle (Ed), *In the Course of Performance* (pp. 369–393). Chicago and London: The University of Chicago Press.

Neugebauer, L. (1999). Meeting Edward - thoughts on case study material at different stages of a professional life. *Nordic Journal of Music Therapy*, 8(2), 200–203.

Nordoff, P., & Robbins, C. (1965). *Music in Therapy for Handicapped Children*. Blauvelt, NY: Ruldoph Steiner Publications.

Nordoff, P., & Robbins, C. (1971). *Music in Therapy for Handicapped Children*. London: Gollancz.

Nordoff, P., & Robbins, C. (1977). *Creative Music Therapy*. New York: Harper & Row.

Nordoff, P., & Robbins, C. (in press). *Creative Music Therapy*. Gilsum NH: Barcelona Publishers.

Nyman, M. (1974). *Experimental Music: Cage and Beyond*. Cambridge U.K.: Cambridge University Press.

O'Shea, J. (1990). *Music and Medicine. Medical Profiles of Great Composers.* London: J.M. Dent.
Overduin, J. (1998). *Improvisation for Organists.* New York, Oxford: Oxford University Press.
Parker, E. (1999). Drawn Inward - Sound and Improvisation. Liner notes from Evan Parker, Electro-Acoustic Ensemble Drawn Inward ECM 1693 547 209-2.
Pavlicevic, M. (1997). *Music Therapy in Context.* London and Philadelphia: Jessica Kingsley Publishers.
Pavlicevic, M. (2000). Improvisation in music therapy: Human communication in sound. *Journal of Music Therapy*. 37(4), 269–285.
Prat & Grocke. (Ed.) (1999). Music Medicine 3. Music Medicine and Music Therapy: Expanding Horizons 1999. Parkville, Victoria, Australia: University of Melbourne.
Pressing, J. (1978). Towards an understanding of scales in jazz. *Jazzforschung/Jazz Research* 9:25–35.
Pressing, J. (1984). Cognitive processes in improvisation. In Crozier & Chapman (Eds.), *Cognitive Processes in the Perception of Art*, 345–363. Amsterdam: North Holland.
Pressing, J. (1987). The micro- and macrostructural design of improvised music. *Music Perception* 5:133–72.
Pressing, J. (1988). Improvisation methods and models. In Sloboda (Ed.), *Generative Processes in Music*, (pp. 129–78). Oxford: Clarendon Press.
Pressing, J. (1992). *Synthesizer Performance and Real-Time Techniques.* Madison, WI.: A-R Editions; London: Oxford University Press.
Pressing, J. (1997). Some perspectives on performed sound and music in virtual environments. *Presence* 6:1–22.
Pressing, J. (1998). Psychological constraints on improvisational expertise and communication. In Nettl (Ed.), *In the Course of Performance* (pp. 47–67) Chicago and London: The University of Chicago Press.
Priestly, M. (1994). *Analytical Music Therapy.* Gilsum NH: Barcelona Publsihers.
Racy, A. (1998). Improvisation, ecstasy, and performance dynamics in Arabic music. In Nettl (Ed.), *In the Course of Performance* (pp. 95–112). Chicago and London: The University of Chicago Press.
Retallack, J. (Ed.) (1996). *Musicage. Cage Muses on Words Art Music.* Middletown, CT: Wesleyan University Press.
Revill, D. (1999). Liner notes. *John Cage: Sonatas and Interludes for Prepared Piano*. Naxos 8.559042.
Robarts, J. (1999). Clinical and theoretical perspectives on poetic process in music therapy, with reference to Nordoff and Robbins' case study of Edward. *Nordic Journal of Music Therapy*, 8(2), 192–199.

Robbins, C., and Robbins, C. (1998). *Healing Heritage. Paul Nordoff Exploring the Tonal Langauge of Music*. Gilsum NH: Barcelona Publishers.

Rolvsjord, Randi (1998). Another story about Edward. *Nordic Journal of Music Therapy*, 7(2), 113–120.

Ruud, E. (1998). *Music Therapy: Improvisation, Communication and Culture*. Gilsum NH: Barcelona Publishers.

Said, E. (1991). *Musical Elaborations*. London: Vintage.

Salas, J. (1990). Aesthetic experience in music therapy. *Music Therapy: Journal of the American Association for Music Therapy* 9 (1), 1–15.

Salminen, H. (1997). *Ryhmäanalyysin perusteet*. Helsinki: SM-julkaisut.

Scalenghe, R & Murphy, K. (2000). Music therapy assessment in the managed care environment. *Music Therapy Perspectives* 18(1), 23–30.

Schenker, H. (1979). *Free Composition (Der Freie Satz)*. (E. Oster, Ed. and trans). New York: Longman (original work published 1935).

Schoenberg, A. (1966). *Harmonielehre*. Vienna: Universal Edition.

Schoenberg, A. (1954). *Structural Functions of Harmony*. New York: Norton.

Schoenberg, A. (1967). *The Fundamentals of Musical Composition*, Gerald Strang, Ed. London: Faber and Faber.

Schoenberg, A. (1984). *Style and Idea*, Leonard Stein, Ed., and Leo Black, Trans. Berkely, CA: University of California Press.

Scientific Commission's Rational. (2001). 5th European Music Therapy Congress, Naples.

Scruton, R. (1997). *The Aesthetics of Music*. Oxford U.K.: Clarendon Press.

Sharpe, R.A. (2000). *Music and Humanism. An Essay in the Aesthetics of Music*. Oxford, U.K.: Oxford University Press.

Slawek, S. (1998). Keeping it going. Terms, practice, and processes of improvisation in Hindustani instrumental music. In Nettl (Ed.), *In the Course of Performance*. (pp. 335–368) Chicago and London: The University of Chicago Press.

Sloboda, J.A. (1985). The musical mind: the cognitive psychology of music. Oxford U.K.: Oxford University Press.

Smith, C. (1998). A sense of the Possible. Miles Davis and the semiotics of improvised performance. In Nettl (Ed.), *In the Course of Performance*. (pp. 261–289).

Smeijsters, H. (1997). *Multiple Perspectives: A Guide to Qualitative Research in Music Therapy*. Gilsum NH: Barcelona Publishers.

Smith, G. (1991). In quest of a new perspective on improvised jazz: A view from the Balkans. *The World of Music* 33:29-52.

Spence, C. (1996). *On Watch. Views from the Lighthouse*. London, and New York: Cassell.

Standley, J. (1986). *Music research in medical/dental treatment: Meta-analysis and clinical applications*. Journal of Music Therapy, 23(2), 56–122.

Stauffer, G. (1997). *The Mass in B Minor*. Schirmer Books.

Steele, P. (1988). 'Foreword'. *Journal of British Music Therapy* Vol. 2, p. 3.

Stern, D. (1985). *The interpersonal world of the infant*. London: Academic Press.

Stige, B. (1998). Hypertexts in music therapy. Paper at the 9th World Congress of Music Therapy, Washington, DC.

Sutton, R. (1998). Do Javanese gamelan musicians really improvise? In Nettl (Ed.), *In The Course of Performance* (pp. 69–92) Chicago and London: The University of Chicago Press.

Suzuki, Surnryu (1973). *Zen Mind, Beginner's Mind*. New York: Weather-Hill.

Swain, J. (1997). *Musical Languages*. New York, and London: W.W. Norton & Company.

Tippett, M. (1959). *Moving Into Aquarius*. London: Routledge.

Titon, J. (1992). *Worlds of Music: An Introduction to the Music of World's Peoples*. 2nd ed. New York: McGraw-Hill.

Tovey, D.F. (1935). Essay in musical analysis. *Vocal Music, vol. 5*. London: Oxford University Press.

Trans-Global Underground (2001). *Yes Boss Food Corner*. Ark 21 Records.

Treitler, L. (1997). Language and the interpretation of music. In Robinson (Ed.), *Music and Meaning*. Ithaca, NY: Cornell University Press.

Turry, A. (1998). Transference and countertransference in Nordoff and Robbins music therapy. In Bruscia (Ed.), *The Dynamics of Music Psychotherapy*. (pp. 161–212). Gilsum NH: Barcelona Publishers.

Viswanathan, T., & Cormack, J. (1998). Melodic improvisation in Karnatak music. The manifestation of Raga. In Nettl (Ed), *In the Course of Performance*. Chicago and London: The University of Chicago Press.

Waller, D. (1993). *Group Interactive Art Therapy*. London: Routledge.

Walton, K. (1997). Listening with imagination: Is music representation? In Robinson (Ed), *Music and Meaning*. Ithaca and London: Cornell University Press.

Watson, D. (1994). *The Wordsworth Dictionary of Musical Quotations*, Hertfordshire, Denmark: Wordsworth Reference.

Wheeler, B. (Ed.) (1995). *Music Therapy Research: Quantitative and Qualitative Perspectives*. Gilsum NH: Barcelona Publishers.

Wolpert, R.S.. (1990). Recognition of melody, harmonic accompaniment, and instrumental: Musicians vs. nonmusicians. *Music Perception* 8(1):95–106.

Yates (1968). *Twentieth Century Music*.

Zuckerkandl, V. (1956). *Sound and symbol. Music and the external world*. Princeton, NJ: Princeton University Press.